Telephone : 01 - 340 3343

HIGHGATE LITERARY & SCIENTIFIC INSTITUTION

920
WIG

11, SOUTH GROVE, N.6   13029

Time allowed FOURTEEN Days

The Memoirs of a Maverick

MAVERICK. 1872 (f. the name of Samuel A. *Maverick*, a civil engineer, who accidentally owned unbranded cattle in Texas). 1. *U.S.* In the cattle-breeding districts, a calf or yearling found without an owner's brand. 2. *transf.* A masterless person.

SHORTER OXFORD ENGLISH DICTIONARY

*I should not talk so much
about myself, if there was
anyone else I knew so well.*
Thoreau, WALDEN

By the same author

My Court Casebook
The Passionate Angler
Fishing For Beginners
Teach Yourself Fly Fishing
In Spite of the Price of Hay
Troubled Waters
My Life On Wheels
Life With Badger
The Angler's Bedside Book (editor)

MAURICE WIGGIN

The Memoirs of a Maverick

NELSON

THOMAS NELSON AND SONS LTD

36 Park Street London W1
P.O. Box 336 Apapa Lagos
P.O. Box 25012 Nairobi
P.O. Box 21149 Dar es Salaam
P.O. Box 2187 Accra
77 Coffee Street San Fernando Trinidad

THOMAS NELSON (AUSTRALIA) LTD
597 Little Collins Street Melbourne C1

THOMAS NELSON AND SONS (SOUTH AFRICA) (PROPRIETARY)
LTD
51 Commissioner Street Johannesburg

THOMAS NELSON AND SONS (CANADA) LTD
81 Curlew Drive Don Mills Ontario

THOMAS NELSON AND SONS
Copewood and Davis Streets Camden New Jersey 08103

17 142005 5

PRINTED IN GREAT BRITAIN BY
WESTERN PRINTING SERVICES LTD, BRISTOL

TO
DENIS HAMILTON

All I never was

Author's Note

I am the sort of writer who needs a guru, midwife, editor and impresario. Composing with words is both my trade and my vocation and few activities give me more pleasure, yet without initial and continuing encouragement I doubt if I should even begin, much less conclude, any literary work whatever. When I have dreamed a page or paragraph, composed it in my mind, I am quite happy to leave it at that, being culpably diffident about the value of communication. It follows that an impresario who sets me a deadline, and keeps me up to scratch, is as necessary to me as oxygen. I am a compulsive writer but not a compulsive publisher. I enjoy talking to myself, and you know what that's a sign of.

Naturally, then, I am grateful, and must express my gratitude, to all who have got me into print. Of these the most pertinacious, and I like to think the most perceptive, is Leonard Russell, who has persuaded me to commit to print more than one book—I can think of at least three—which would otherwise have remained at worst daydream, at best conversation; or perhaps I mean monologue. It was he who conceived the idea of this book, and saw it through. Reluctant to see a book talked-away, and unwilling to accept the situation that two previous autobiographical books, *In Spite of the Price of Hay* and *Troubled Waters*, were long out of print, Leonard urged me to set down my recollections of fifty-odd years of chequered experience, and incidentally to resuscitate some material that was buried in those two early books. He is not to blame for anything which the reader may find blameworthy within; what some may consider bizarre opinions and eccentric stances are all my own. On the other hand, he is entirely to blame for the fact that it appears at all.

Chapter One

'Please, Miss, Sam Wiggin's got 'is 'ead stuck in the railin's.'

'It's 'is ears, Miss. They'm folded over.'

'Miss, *Miss*, it was Gilbert Terry as rommed 'is 'ead in the railin's. They was 'ommering each other.'

It was rustling and bosomy Miss Stokes who dragged me out backwards from the railings, ears and all. Miss Stokes was Headmistress of the Infants school. It was a lie about Gilbert Terry. The little girl who put it about was actuated by jealousy. She was in love with Gilbert but her affection was not returned. It was true we had been hammering each other. We hammered each other every day, out of pure affection. But the sparring session had nothing to do with my head being rammed in the railings. I ran to the railings to watch a tram go past on the single track, rocking over the cobbles. Some crafty little perisher gave me a shove from behind and there I was, fixed. My head stuck out at the back in a way we all took to be a sign of poetic sensibility or something—the bump of idealism, Old Man Tibbits called it—but what with that and my ears, it wasn't a very safe head near railings. Ramming lads' heads in the railings was a popular sport, a diversion which never failed to please. I should have known better.

We set great store on bumps. Old Man Tibbits was an amateur phrenologist and he was always in demand at Sunday suppers, running his great hairy hands over people's heads and pronouncing, 'You must be very careful in money matters, dear. Your bump of calculation is not very well developed.' He enjoyed running his great hairy hands over young ladies' heads best. Somehow I never took him quite so seriously as some people did. He might look like Moses half-way down the mountain, but something about him struck me as phoney. I was a far better judge of the phoney when I was a totally uneducated nipper than after I'd been force-fed with education till it was running out of my ears. Something about the way Old Man Tibbits had a sermon ready for every occasion, but never actually gave anything away, got across to my untrained receptive faculty like a slight but persistent bad smell. Now that I'm pretty well as old as Old Man Tibbits was then, I'm right back on form, a first-class Grade A smeller-out of the bogus. I rarely have the scent out of my nostrils, worse luck. But in between there was an awful great long tract of educated gullibility, which was just getting under way when Miss Stokes pulled me backwards out of the railings.

Actually the sterilising process had begun a year earlier, about 1916 or possibly 1917, when I was sent to a dame's school to get a head start on the poor. We were not only respectable, we were getting on in the world, and it is a well-known fact that though the best things in life are free, some of the second-best things are well worth buying. These included education, on which we were all red-hot. My father and his brothers didn't have much of it, but since they were gifted with great natural vitality and lively intelligences, well, some of them, they managed very nicely with what little education they had. However, one of the funny things about education is that when you've done very nicely without any, you get this idea fixed in your head that your children simply must have lashings of what you missed. Whether they like it or not and quite irrespective of whether they can take it. I could take it, to a certain extent, or leave it alone. On the whole I preferred to leave it alone.

I hated the dame's school right away, just for being a school, i.e., prison; and also, or perhaps mainly, because it took me away from the farm. We had just got this little farm and it would have suited me to spend the days on it. When we left the factory I was going to have a broken heart any time, but when it dawned on me that I was trading a factory for a farm I thought that might be all right, after all. As of today, more than half a century later, I am still unable to make up my mind which I like best, factory or farm. And I've got neither. My father, who made a far better job of his life, despite having no education to speak of, managed to have both. At the same time.

I must tell you something about my mother that has always pleased me more than most things. If I don't get it down now I shall forget. When she was young she was known as Pretty Lucy. This was the first great gift from the gods, and by a long chalk the most valuable. Not that I realised it at the time. Pretty Lucy gave to her children, unequally, certain gifts of character, or perhaps I should say of temperament, which were of debatable value. We did not debate them, for we admired and loved her; but apart from a tendency towards insouciance and wilful irrationality when the heart seemed much wiser than the head, I doubt if they did us a great deal of good. But the gift of comeliness, which we under-valued, which our upbringing practically forced us to under-value, was, I realise, the most valuable she could bestow. One can enjoy life with very limited mental equipment and a scant minimum of ethical ballast, but without a certain aptness of the flesh there can be no joy in this life, which is nothing if not founded in a grateful animality.

I do not wish to suggest that we were raving beauties, not by a long chalk. One of my sisters, at least, had that radiance of the flesh which is even more attractive and desirable than absolute beauty, whatever that may be. The rest of us were at any rate reasonably comely, not actually ugly. I was a pretty baby who grew into a pretty boy. It is not a type that matures well. There is no such thing as a pretty old man. The eyes, indeterminate in colour but vaguely classified as grey, are set a shade too close together to inspire instant trust, though I can look pretty innocent if I try. The nose, especially since being broken, is quite an event; if it were a shade less fleshy it wouldn't look too bad on a Red Indian. The chin is a let-down. The brow is far from noble. A better phrenologist than Old Man Tibbits would have seen immediately that that combination of modest brow and modest chin augured ill for the outstanding scholarly career which my parents deeply desired for the lad. But we put all our store on that remarkably distended back-of-the-head, and hoped for the best.

Naturally I attached myself eagerly, gave my adoration, to boys with strong square chins, wide candid eyes, and no backs to their heads. All my best friends are round-headed men. This did no harm; but far from harmless, productive of much embarrassment and disappointment, was the associated tendency to imagine myself the solid, square-cut type which I admired in reaction against the mirror. I cast myself continually in roles for which Nature had not designed me. What she *had* designed me for, I never found out.

Pretty Lucy, the merry young milliner, married Sam, fourth son and fifth child of James and Harriet. The Wiggins of my father's generation were named as follows: James Enoch, William, Mary, Joseph, Samuel, Hiram, Noah. One of many questions I reproach myself for not having asked, while there was time to get an answer, is how did William get into that roll call of names taken straight from the Family Bible, which, huge, ponderous, brass-clasped and forbidding, used to stand on top of the harmonium. Is there a William in Holy Writ? I don't think so. I wouldn't put it past somebody to discover one, of course—the Bible is full of surprises, and so are the gaps in my knowledge; but I don't think so. In which case it was an aberration into which they who fancy signs

3

and portents may care to read a certain significance, for William, though born second, became indisputably first. Uncle Enoch, a most lovable man, a great romantic who lived the daydream with alluring panache, lost his leadership of the hierarchy when at the height of his histrionic powers, and Uncle Will, equally I think a romantic, but a romantic who never quite confused the dream with the reality, became head of the family and remained unchallengeably responsible, senior, and wise until his death.

But these events were unguessable, shrouded in the impenetrable obscurity of the future (which we spent a lot of our time trying to penetrate, though) when I got my head stuck in the railings. I must get the chronology sorted out. Is there anything in literature or the drama more teasing, tantalising and finally unbearable than that trick of dodging back and forth, with flashbacks, etc.?

I was born, Pretty Lucy's second surviving child but seven years younger than the first, in a tall, dark, double-fronted house in Church Street, of which I have no memories save the occasional nightmare. My Church Street début was my closest connection with religious orthodoxy. Religious unorthodoxy, or unorthodox religiosity, comes into the story a good bit, in fact it provides much of the humour which lights this ramshackle tale; but although I was born within spitting distance of the church, I never entered it until I attended Uncle Will's funeral nearly half a century later. We were chapel, at the time, and later we became decidedly queer, flirting with several oriental fads and making quite a career of spiritualism. This was the Black Country, home of doughty nonconformists. You didn't catch people who had seen the light of freedom going in for all those 'rigid creeds and dogmas' of orthodoxy. No fear. We made up our own as we went along.

When I say 'we' I mean Sam and Lucy's little brood. I mustn't involve the rest of the clan in our particular eccentricities. There are any number of responsible and commonsensical Wiggins who have both feet firmly on the ground and I do not wish to contaminate their reputations.

While I was still nobbut a babby ('nothing but a baby'—I can still speak Bloxwich pure and undefiled, and indeed I once in Normandy saved myself from being shot on the spot as a disguised German parachute infiltrator by doing so) we moved to another double-fronted house, an even older one, possibly dating back to the great building dream of the Industrial Revolution. It fronted the cobbled hill and the tramlines; immediately behind it, separated from it only by a dirt

4

yard—and even that was partly roofed over, to make the contact unequivocal—rose the factory.

This is really where my life began, my conscious life and also that thread of dream which is interwoven in the same cloth; some managing with less, some demanding and contriving more. This was the milieu in which the triple retinae of eye and mind and spirit, the ineffable trinity—'all things are trine'—received those early images, the pristine key pictures, which, Camus says, a man spends all his life thereafter in trying 'through all the circuitous ways of art' to identify, recapture or rediscover. I do not know if he is right, but for what it may be worth, I am a child of the Black Country at its most attenuated and peripheral, the Black Country petering out into the green countryside of Cannock Chase; and also a child of the Industrial Revolution, which, when I was an infant living literally in the factory, was still in flow, saved from petering out, revivified and re-licensed, by the Great War of 1914–1918, which broke out when I was scarcely two. Tiny but vital organisms struggling ceaselessly in the undertow, we were cast up by its last receding waves on the shelving shore of affluence.

Affluence, authority, power.... How relative these things are. Were we really rich, or really poor? In the kingdom of the blind, the one-eyed man is king. We were better-off than many of our neighbours, among whom we passed for rich. There were people still better-off, and by far; we did not envy them, but they received the respect due to age, the respect which new money pays to older money. We had our anxieties, but we had a surplus over immediate basic needs, and that surely is what is meant by being rich. To me, at any rate. Though one of nature's spendthrifts, I have always fancied the simple life; a paradox which fails to worry me. When I was very young I was unaware of snobbery or the rancours of class distinction. Perhaps they existed; undoubtedly there were social stresses, envies and aspirations; but I don't think they really poisoned life. They certainly didn't poison mine. This fresh and equal air probably owed something to the strength of Methodism in the area. The Anglican church, historically the propagator of divisive class legends, was relatively weak, and the Roman Catholic church, which is now strong and prosperous and influential in the district, was then a humble cell which cherished its own and nourished its own strange version of elective democracy. There were other equalitarian influences, purely secular. The dominance of heavy manual labour in an area does tend to foster a sort of breezy indifference to social graces and gradations, and a popular contempt, almost irresistible, for the separatism of social ambitions. I do not know how it is now: I am speaking of the time I best remember, say between 1916 and the end of the Twenties. Then, at any rate, nobody in our village was ostentatiously rich, most people managed though the stresses were often severe; the poor were buoyed up by neighbourliness—they had to be—there was a good deal of actual charity, and the chapels proclaimed and asserted though they did not quite assure the democracy of Jesus.

Our village, Bloxwich, was as big as many towns. The population was several thousand. It lay on the very edge of the Black Country; some people are not even sure that it belongs to the Black Country, but I've walked to Willenhall many a time. However, while on the south and south-west Bloxwich was firmly tied to the Black Country, on the north and east it lay open to farming land. It was a borderline case: full of countrymen who could spend all day in the factory and the evening in the fields. Naturally it bred borderline cases, people like me, who don't really know if they are town or country. (But the pursuits of our leisure hours were almost wholly country pursuits.) Bloxwich is really a district or parish of the Borough of Walsall, two and a half miles distant but tenuously connected by single-track tram and very nearly connected then (now, of course, quite) by ribbon development. But this connection was theoretical; an abstraction existing only in the tidy minds of bureaucrats. Bloxwich men and women always had a reputation for sturdy individualism and an extreme form of local patriotism. The road from Walsall climbed all the way: it was a proud boast that the tip of the spire of St Matthew's, parish church of Walsall, was only just level with the foundations of All Saints, parish church of Bloxwich. In every sense we looked down on them. We lived on a bracing high plateau, 600 feet above sea level; an island entirely surrounded by water, even if it was only the porter-coloured water of the canals. It was not exactly a place of falcons, but the air was keen, and whichever way you took out of Bloxwich, you went down.

On this windy height, ringed by pits, men worked iron. The craft seemed almost immemorial. Long before the factories rose, swart men worked on their own account in the backyards or courts of little houses, grimed with smoke. They turned out awls, edge tools, all sorts of small metal wares. A trade grew up of lock manufacture. Bloxwich helped to supply the considerable leather trade of Walsall with what it needed in the way of fabricated metal parts. So began my paternal grandfather, James, in the third third of the nineteenth century. He began by forging horse furniture, as it was pleasantly known—bits and stirrups and bridle parts—in the brewhouse in the backyard. Halcyon days of freedom when a man could put his backyard to whatever use he chose. My grandfather was a great man in a small way. I remember him well, though he died when I was a little boy. He was tall, erect, trimly bearded, with piercing pale eyes and a manner that somehow combined autocracy with the benign aloofness of the contemplative man. He was a notable local preacher, much respected for practising what he preached, and, with all his idealism, a practical man. In some of his descendants the one factor or faculty has been known to outgrow the other. His hobby was carpentry, the trade of Jesus. He gave me my first lessons, in both mysteries, and bestowed on me some of his tools. Alas, I made little headway in either.

Long before my day, grandfather's enterprise had far outgrown the backyard workshop. Fortune favoured the brave, and the firm of J. & J. Wiggin Limited was strongly established, employing hundreds of men and many women, and an influential factor in local life. I am happy to say it survives and prospers, directed by my capable cousins. Grandfather bought land and built workshops, and as a crowning stroke, wonderfully symbolical, he took over the Old Hallelujah Mission Hall, in Revival Street, when its following fell off for reasons, I fancy, of increasing sobriety in a population which traditionally sought relief from the horrors of life in drink or religion, sometimes both. There are still dozens of pubs in Bloxwich and the beer of Bloxwich Brewery used to be noted. My father was frequently converted by visiting missionaries in the Old Hall. True, he stood in no need of conversion, or perhaps I should say no particular need. But he was highly emotional and prone to theatricality, and over and above he had a happy talent for telling people what he thought they would like to hear. This is an exquisite form of courtesy, common among Celts. Of course, it leads to trouble, inevitably. But it springs from a fund of natural good manners and good humour, and I cannot bring myself to despise it though I have seen, time and again, how troublesome it can be. In myself, it battles continually and on the whole successfully with the opposite tendency, to respect reason and truth and to deprecate emotional display. Sometimes one aspect is in the ascendant, sometimes another. One is known for inconsistency.

My father, as I say, was in the forefront of the converted. It came natural to him to leap up from the bench and accept Jesus just before the cocoa came round. Less volatile characters might think that to accept Him once was enough; once and for all; but that is to ignore the rich satisfaction (to some natures) of public confession. We are all autobiographers in our different ways, save the naturally secretive, who write their negative confession stealthily and even unwittingly, on a palimpsest of events which can be interpreted only by their victims. Since I know exactly how my father felt at the moment of confession and acceptance, I know that he was utterly sincere. Sincere as a second-rate actor is sincere; a sincere reading of the lines. His very sincerity made him a second-rate actor: first-rate actors know better than to get emotionally involved, they are the masters of technique. Since the whole process was emotional and irrational, naturally the feeling wore off. But it was sincere at the time. For people of this temper, all life is an utterly sincere balls-up. I am of this temper myself, and though for the last twenty years at least I have tried to reason myself into a more rational attitude, it is quite useless to fight against your nature. Like my father, I am converted once a week, though not, indeed, necessarily to Jesus. People like us do not lead their own lives at all: liable to be reduced to tears—literal warm salt tears—by a face in a crowd, a dog or cat, a bird with a broken wing, a snatch of song or verse, a kind word or a sad story—how can we claim to lead our own lives? Between the tears and the equally poignant stabs of pure irrational joy, and anger, lie timeless tracts of beige-coloured rationality when we pass for normal. No-one would ever suspect us.

Where the converts and the cocoa had flowed, then, rose the Old Hall Works. I believe there were several like it in the Black Country, converted chapels with Gothic windows, ministering to other appetites. The old place was burned down in the late Twenties, making a splendid blaze, but the name remained. They now make Old Hall tableware there, of stainless steel, of which I hope you have a sufficient supply. However, this was not the factory in which I lived my early childhood. 'We' had bought the business of V. J. Broadhurst & Co., a little way down the road towards Walsall, and it was here, at what was always known as Bro'duss's, that I came to consciousness.

Our house was also the office: in those days the ratio between paper work and real work was reasonable, bumf was despised and 'administration' was virtually non-existent. A boss was his own welfare officer; personnel relations were personal relations. My father was manager of Bro'duss's jointly with Uncle Joe: they ran it on the lines of a family, strongly flavoured with a mission. Everyone knew everyone and everyone's entire family history. Though authority was unquestioned, there was but little scope for socially divisive practices. My father and his brothers wore fawn twill overall coats and leather leggings: these working accoutrements alone were the badges of office. They could do anything they asked the men to do, and they took the same risks. One of my earliest dramatic memories is of seeing my father supported from the factory by two men, tottering, blood streaming from a gash around his eye. A flying splinter of white-hot metal had caught him. He lay on the kitchen sofa—horsehair-stuffed, covered with American cloth—deathly pale, blood oozing and seeping through a pad of gauze. For a few long moments I gazed at my hero, fascinated and full of awe, before they discovered me and bustled me away. So . . . the mighty could be reached, the impregnable wounded. First intimations of vulnerability and blind chance. Nothing ever quite the same again. I did not know then that other little boys' daddies were being killed and maimed, in France and elsewhere on the tortured earth, at a rate undreamed of before. That knowledge came a little later. I knew, though, that my daddy, so tall and jolly and buoyant, could be struck down.

However, he was soon up again. That one momentary glimpse of him lying, perhaps unconscious, on the sofa, was all I had of the drama. Next time I saw him he was on his feet and going about his business, with some stitches in his cut. The stitches left an interesting scar on the temple shaped like a shepherd's crook, the handle curling around the brow. One valued a good scar. The factory was reasonably dangerous, one always knew that; danger gave it some of its glamour, and the ethos of the area was pre-eminently stoical. Colliers and iron workers need to be stoical. A man was lucky to come through his working life without being crippled. Little bumps and knocks were of no account; indeed they were valued as badges of manhood.

This being 1915–16, and not the effete yet tyrannous world of make-believe we inhabit now, I was permitted to move freely within the factory, even as a toddler, and here I picked up my images, and acquired the framework or rather the foundations of my social attitudes. What we learn unconsciously we learn best. I dare say it was a sort of hell, or would appear so to some sensitive souls, but to me it was, literally, home. A dark and cavernous place, shot through with flaring light: I have few early memories of daylight. The great drop forges elemental as a forest: huge blocks of steel rising and falling between tall steel slides, as high, it seemed, as a house: these were the giants and the men who served them were the gods. From each stamping block a fabric belt went up and over a turning pulley, one of many on a shaft, coming down again to end in a tail of rope. To operate the stamp, a man had to jump high in the air and grip the rope end. A human clutch, he bore down on it with all his weight, so that the pulley gripped the belt and the block rose between its slides. Down he went, down he bent, heaving with all his strength, ending in an oriental crouch on the dirt floor.

9

When he let go of his rope tail, the block swished down, crashing on to the ingot of white-hot metal which another man held on the base, crumpling it into the shape of the die. A good man would get in several leaps and bashes before the metal cooled from white to cherry red.

Almost as thrilling as the forge was the foundry, in another part of the forest. It was great to mount the ladder and hurl pieces of scrap iron into the flaring furnace of the cupola: is there anything more satisfying than to minister to a fire? Then the great moment when it was tapped, so casually, so primitive-looking an operation, by a skilled man with a sort of poker who knocked out the cement with which the furnace had been sealed, and a long line of men gripping clay pots in enormous iron pincers received the full weight of the stream of liquid metal, hurrying away to pour it into the moulds. I am glad that I knew the foundry when it was still in the age of Stephenson.

Forge and foundry were the dramatic nodes of the factory, but everywhere in serried ranks were mustered the machines, lathes and millers, grinders and drills, on which the forged or cast products were finished; among them, at this time, innumerable shell cases for the armies in Flanders. Though I did not understand their purpose then. I can still smell the slurry that ran ceaselessly to cool the metal as the cutters shaved it off; a faintly acrid smell, not unpleasant. But the heart of the entire drama was the battery of great primitive gas engines which supplied our power. Heaven knows how old they were; perhaps they replaced original steam power; soon they were to be replaced by silent, dull electric motors. They were indescribably thrilling, vast horizontal cylinders, really rather like steam, with great spoked flywheels about eight feet in diameter, and all the lovely machinery exposed to view. To start them, in the morning, a man would leap up and cling to one of the spokes of the flywheel. Gradually the weight of his body would pull it round, over compression. I don't know if it was the capricious nature of the ignition, or the quality of town gas, but they ran with an irregular chug-chish-bang, maddening if you tried, as I so often did, to anticipate the beat. Many a morning I hurried out to watch them started; taking a nap after dinner with my mother, in a darkened room, I listened with my heart to their mad toccata. The great bass boom of the drop hammers, the whish and slur and tinkle and yelp of the lesser machines, the rhythm of the engines, the clank of metal being moved, and occasionally a voice crying hoarsely in warning or command. ... These were the noises with which we lived, a gross and vibrant orchestra of purposive and vital sounds. Between the house and the factory was that little dirt-surfaced yard, partly roofed. I trotted in and out on my spindly little legs, getting in the way. 'Lucy, that lad of yours will do himself a mischief yet,' one would say, leading me home after some unusually feckless or desperate misdemeanour. But mother only laughed. She was happy-go-lucky Lucy. She let me share breakfast with men who fried bits of bacon on coke shovels. She never tried to keep me away from the scene I valued most, when the gas engines were started up. The slowly turning flywheel, the *hiss* and *suck* of the monstrous piston, the slyly moving, oily crank. . . . These, and the flaring fires, the cavernous chiaroscuro, the scent of hot metal and slurry and sweat, the gruff voices of muscular, kindly men, the boom of the great hammers, the flash and glint of sparks . . . these were my native images, the geography of the known world. Almost the whole of my life has been spent in very different pastures, but this was the native and creating clay.

Had we done less well, had the war not propped us up, I might have attained my life's desire, to become a small factory manager in the Black Country. I might actually have been at Bro'duss's now, wearing the fawn twill smock. I do not say that it is highly likely, but it is possible. It is a role I should have fitted like a glove. I am no craftsman, alas—I wish I were—but at any rate I can tell good work from bad. I could have supervised craftsmen quite effectively—indeed I did so, later, in the Royal Air Force—and how I would have loved to run a little place where things were made. But it was not to be. Modest affluence and its concomitant, modest education, plus a family factor of some insignificance, put my feet on a different path.

Chapter Two

Until quite recently, I always used to wish that I had been born a few years earlier. Now, of course, I would give quite a sum to have been born a lot of years later. But I always regretted not having personal knowledge of that period before the First World War when life was so very different; more personal, it always seems, more primitive of course, and somehow more flavourful. Doubtless this is an illusion, but the horse-drawn world was so obviously different from the motorised world that I wish I had actually smelled it.

Still, I smelled the last whiff of it, for the changeover was gradual, and when I was a lad, although motors were definitely coming in and life was already mechanised to some degree, horses still had a place and the general poverty was such that motors only came in in penny numbers. In our lives horse and motor co-existed, side by side. Walking in the evenings one smelled stables. We were very early motorists, but we were also, in a small way, farmers. This was a factor of significance, in shaping my life, out of all proportion to the magnitude of the agricultural operation.

Living on the working premises, like proper tradespeople, was very sensible, but it also carried some sort of slight social stigma and people were getting away from the factory as fast as they could. Our lot were the last to make it. The rest of my father's brothers had already qualified for nice houses in residential roads—the roads themselves being brand-new—and I dare say my mother put some pressure on dad to follow suit. But he was not a man who pushed himself forward. However, in due course, it would be late 1916 or just possibly very early 1917, our turn came to make the social grade. Stafford Road was grandest, but Lichfield Road was grand enough. These were the modern residential roads, strung out on the perimeter of the village. We moved to Lichfield Road and drew a real bonus—a few fields and some stabling and piggeries and cowsheds which (I don't know why) went with this quite newish, utterly 'residential' house, built of smooth red brick—high class!—and a bit of roughcast. Indeed, it was only a semi-detached: with a touch of the family's nice mingling of astuteness and togetherness, we bought or possibly built the lot, both houses, and in the other one were installed grandfather and grandmother, later joined by Aunt Mary and Uncle Charlie to look after them. So it was a pretty solid family fortress; but not at all a farmhouse, that you would notice. However, looks aren't everything, and the farm was administered therefrom. Too late again to ask, but I imagine that my parents had rented the fields from a local farmer. The stabling and piggeries looked old, to me. The cowshed was the old pavilion of the Bloxwich Cricket Club, made over for the duration.

Here, then, in this curiously ambivalent situation, we settled down to make the grade. Every morning dad set off for the factory, with that brisk gait the Wiggins cultivated, or inherited; and mother set off for the cowsheds. I didn't know which way to turn, and still don't. Sometimes I would toddle the mile or more to the works; more often I hurried out to the farmery with mother. If grandfather felt up to it, he would keep me out of mischief in his workshop, where it was his pleasure to make chairs. I 'helped' him to make a little wooden armchair, all for me: I remember that the seat was a sheet of three-ply drilled with quarter-inch holes, in imitation of the old cane-bottomed chair. We stained it a reddish-brown. It would doubtless have held an honoured place in the nursery, had we boasted such a thing.

Propinquity is the great matchmaker, and gradually the farm won out over the factory; which became, in any case, forbidden territory. And now began that long love-affair with the natural creation, that half-mystical and wistful attachment to the 'integrated' and 'organic' life of field and byre. It is all expressed in the feel of grass under your feet. To this day I feel liberated, brought nearer to the truth of life, when I get my feet off the hard road or pavement and on to grass. I have the strongest feeling that when the living surface of the earth is covered, sealed off, by tarmac or paving stones, life is sterilised and made unreal. The sight of concrete affects me almost physically, it is anti-life, part of the process of segregating us from the pulse of the living world. A village is tolerable for a time, and even a small town, but big cities are absolutely inimical to life; I suffocate in them.

This all began down Lichfield Road. We kept half a dozen cows, a pony which nominally belonged to me, a breeding boar, sows and their families, fowl, rabbits, a loft of homing pigeons and tumblers. We made hay and grew swedes, mangolds, turnips, potatoes, and doubtless other crops which I have forgotten. It is difficult for me, now, to estimate even vaguely the viability of this little farmstead: accountancy was not the all-pervasive disease it is today, people did things because they liked doing them and because they put a proper value on a way of living. It was war time. We produced milk, and things to eat. That was of paramount importance, I fancy. And my mother loved the life. She had a lovely uninhibited feeling for animal life, and animal life responded to her. True, a touchy cow once kicked her off the milking stool; we thought it a great joke, and teased her unkindly. But by and large, she was happiest pottering about with breeding beasts. There is a certain rich pullulating squalor of fecundity which some people simply cannot take, which others respond to immediately as the essence of living. My mother gloried in litters. She was not in any sense a coarse person: indeed, she very much wanted us to become a refined family, all the upbringing tended in that direction. She was thoroughly imbued with the notion of respectability. But this was something that had been grafted on to her natural warmth and generosity, her instinctive response to animal life, to the richness of the swarming creation. There was no tragic dichotomy: she managed, on the whole, to combine the diverse impulses, and why not? But although her taste in civilised trappings may have been uncertain, her instinct for the animal reality never wavered: she responded instantly, unerringly, and I am sure rightly, to the appeal of breeding beasts. Her own maternal instinct was strong, and she was firmly, instinctively and warmly on the side of motherhood. So far as animals went, that is. Human pregnancy was another matter, often regrettable: at an early age I became familiar with the spectacle of tearful mums sitting in the kitchen with a cup of tea and a drop of whisky in it, explaining to our mother how their daughters—our maids —had gone off the straight and narrow. But that was a bit later on.

I was already being pulled in two directions, torn between farm and factory, between natural life and machinery, and now a third factor entered my life: education. I have never understood education, or the hopelessly mixed and mangled motives associated with it. I grow more and more confused about it as I grow older, though I have never stopped acquiring it. The confusion all began with my first taste of it, at a dame's school a little way down Lichfield Road, a solitary house set in the fields, and opposite our hay meadow. There was nothing wrong with it, and nothing wrong with my parents' motives for sending me there, at the great age of four, almost five. But I was in no mood to have my liberty curtailed, and imprisonment in Mrs Baldwin's parlour was no sort of substitute for the perfect freedom of the farm. I reacted viciously.

Down at Bro'duss's I had moved among men preoccupied with

physically stressful tasks: their attitude was tolerant and jolly, but their language was rough. I had also played with the little children of the rows of grimy old terrace houses nearby: their language was worse still. Mad Chink the cripple had taught me some strange words. Avidly but naturally I had acquired a vocabulary, free it is true from actual obscenity, but larded with swear words chief among which was bugger. For many years I thought of it as bugar, as in sugar. It was a word you could apply to virtually everything: much depended on the tone of voice in which it was spoken, it could be a term of affectionate abuse or something a little more decisively disapprobatory. It was a verb and a noun. 'Yo' daft bugger' . . . 'Well, Oi'll be buggered' . . . "e's a funny old bugger' . . . 'Well, bugger me'. Not until many years later did I learn, with a touch of stupefaction, that it had a sexual connotation. Homosexuality was literally unheard-of: I mean literally: I was a grown man before I got a hint of its existence. I grew up in a healthy society, you see: very sexy, as they all are, but straight, not bent.

My precocious command of language stood me in good stead when I was left at the dame's school that first dreadful morning. I let them have it. The effect was appalling. Little girls were rushed into another room, little boys bundled out of the way while dear Mrs Baldwin, the soul of rectitude, strove to staunch the flow. But it was staunchless. I wasn't having any. This was my very first contact with social servitude and the response was purer than it has ever been since. Being caged up with people indoors, and damn-all to do but sums—it struck me then, and I may say it strikes me now, as total waste of life. I offered everybody out, as a matter of routine—'Oi'll foight the bloody lot on yer' was the traditional form the challenge took—and then, evading restraint, got the door open and hared away. Of course it was a foredoomed and hopeless gesture, but I'm somehow glad that it was made.

I knew better, even then, than to run screaming home. If They had sent me to school, They wouldn't be very well pleased that I rejected their decision. This was the very first moment in life, I think, when consciously I had to accept that there was a division between authority's wishes and my own, and that authority, though huge and powerful, was somehow, most strangely, inexplicably, wrong. For that I chose right when I chose freedom, I had and have no doubt at all. Had that happened which was always being foretold, had 'the gipsies' run away with me, thus making true the threat that was hung over us, then I might well have had a life infinitely more suited to my nature than the one I have had. I have had much happiness in my life, but I'm perfectly sure that I should have had even more, should have grown up straighter and more supple, calmer and healthier, had the gipsies really run away with me and brought me up their way, untaught except in some practical matters, completely outside 'society' but cosy within the cocoon of the private, secret, familial society: an outdoor animal, a savage tribesman, living the day and the night as they came.

Subsequent truancies, and they were many, were directed towards this end: I always ran outwards, away from the chimneys and the streets. But on this occasion I was really too little to face the great unknown countryside alone. I ran for the haven that I knew, the community in which I felt at home, the factory. It was a long trot, more than a mile, perhaps a mile and a half, but at length I turned in again at Bro'duss's, inhaling the acrid fumes of coke and slurry and hot metal, drinking in the heavenly raw sounds. I wandered around happily among old friends, until dad discovered me. He let me stay until the hooter went, and took me home with him, shocked to the core, though not exactly angry, perhaps. There's a big difference. There was a scene, of course, but I don't recall any feeling of special wickedness or of being out of favour. After midday dinner mother took me with her for a nap, as usual, and told fairy tales until I dropped off. Next day I was escorted to Mrs Baldwin's and settled in at once, bored but acquiescent, lying low. I could read already.

I don't suppose anyone remembers exactly how or when he learned to read. But I was an assiduous reader while we lived in Lichfield Road, and we left there when I was six. I read the newspapers—the *Daily Express* and the *Daily Chronicle*, a balanced diet—and the *Children's Newspaper*. But most of all I read the *Children's Encyclopaedia*, edited by Arthur Mee: that wonderful eight volumes of basic book was, for me, the foundation of all knowledge, the rock on which is built the whole edifice of scrappy information that I possess, fragments of precarious information about so many things. The only thing I have ever become an expert on is angling; though I certainly learned a lot of poetry, and how to produce newspapers. But there are relatively few subjects, from typography to clairvoyance, from the internal combustion engine to the metaphysical poets, from geology to Chinese cooking, on which I haven't picked up a smattering, at one time or another. And the foundation of this vast vague rickety edifice of general knowledge was the *Children's Encyclopaedia*, which I read right through, sitting at a mahogany dining-table covered with a dark lustrous red chenille cloth, with tassels, in the front room of the house in Lichfield Road.

You see we were devoted to it. We really believed in it. You could not possibly *know* too much. We respected learning, much as the peasants of the Middle Ages goggled admiringly at the Latin-loving clerisy. The Forster Education Act of 1870 was bearing fruit. My father's generation, though it got no farther than the elementary school, had got a whiff of the stuff, and the stuff was heady. It was not only an absolute good in its own right, it was the passport to almost undreamed-of heights of respectable forging ahead. And we were distinctly in favour of respectable forging ahead.

The progressiveness, the modernity of the Wiggins, seems a bit laughable now, from some angles, but it was very real in its day. I remember once showing my assembled uncles (we were an intensely gregarious family) certain working drawings in the *Children's Encyclopaedia* which purported to explain the internal combustion engine and indeed the whole motor car. I suppose ours was a pre-war edition. The sectional drawings showed a cutaway car of considerable naïvety, which must have been well out-of-date even then. It had a single-cylinder engine and the drive to the rear wheels was by chain. I remember the uncles passing the book from hand to hand and laughing heartily. For by this time they all possessed cars with four-cylinder engines and a final drive by propeller shaft and differential. Since I had only just got the working of a motor car off pat, from these same drawings, I was a little shaken by their scorn. It was the first occasion on which I came up against obsolescence, which is a very sad thing. Within a few years I was myself intensely with-it in matters mechanical: that is the nasty thing about machines, they keep on getting better, or at least different, and there is simply no point in anachronism, it's a contradiction in terms to be both mechanically minded and nostalgic. (Not that that stops a great many people from being precisely that: look at the old steam engine fans.) However, I did learn how the wretched things worked. It was knowledge I could well have done without. Since I was not destined to become a motor mechanic, designer or engineer, it was a private luxury, and it was to cost me dear. But I enjoyed acquiring it.

I enjoyed a good many things. By many a standard of comparison, mine was a happy childhood. I could quite easily knock up a dandelion-days dream about it. I often have. And this happy side is true. A tremendous sense of family unity; loving and indulgent parents who nevertheless had high principles; a modest affluence, a comfortable home; a precocious love of the word allied with a lively feeling for the physical, great gregariousness allied with a strong self-sufficiency and a taste for solitude and adventure—these were the ingredients of a happy childhood. I have no complaints about my luck: it has always held. But the third eye threw it out of focus, all too often: the seeing eye of compassion. Though we saw the rightness of forging ahead, we also saw the rightness of pity for the less well-equipped. The poor, we knew, were always with us. They were indeed. The dark shadows of my childhood were inhabited by other people's troubles, not my own. From very early days, I have always been suffused by a sense of wonder that my own life should be so lucky, a sense of the irremediable unfairness of life in that it should treat other people, who deserved far better, so badly. Most of my sorrows have been vicarious.

It follows that I could never have made a farmer. I could never have separated the weeping calf from the sorrowing cow.

Yet I could kill. I learned to kill quite early, and killed without remorse. It all depends what you are destroying. We went ratting around the byre and piggeries and the haystacks. Sometimes we killed by terrier and club, sometimes a man would bring his ferrets. Bigger boys had catapults, and one, an airgun. There is no pity for the rat. I never associated the rat with my pet white mice. When a rat was bitten in two by a dog, one squealed with excitement. One had the word from on high—rats were vermin, enemies of ourselves and of every living thing. So there was nothing but ardour, resolution, a sense of adventure, in the remorseless chase. Something about the secrecy and furtiveness of the rat confirmed or excused these rational objections to it. It moved without revealing its method of locomotion. It slid along on its belly. That, I am sure, the weird inexplicability of its progress, was what really made it hateful. At any rate, I was a member of the expedition at every opportunity. The girls squealed when they saw a mouse, leaping on to kitchen chairs. I think I might almost follow suit, now, so deeply ingrained has become my loathing of the rodent's furtive locomotion. But when I was a little boy, it was a matter of pride and actually of joy to tackle the intruder. And out in the fields, lurking in the dusk around the wooden buildings and the fragrant rick of hay which I had 'helped' to build, riding home on top of the wain's load, vertiginous and triumphant, this was man's work, this was elemental and incomparable. Now I heard for the first time of men who would bite a live rat's head off for half a pint of beer. But that was in the pub, which was unknown territory. The pub came later. It was many a year before I first slipped in and ordered half a pint of mild. Meanwhile, one lingered and loitered in passing the open door, whence came a faint and puzzling, rather nasty yet somehow intriguing, waft of beer-smell, a scent of sin.

For we were teetotallers all. Some of the menfolk smoked, but I dare say that was frowned on too. Indeed, I know it was—time and again I have heard Grandma Wiggin sneer at smokers. 'You couldn't have been properly weaned,' she would say; and perhaps she was on to something there. However, my father smoked Gold Flake, which meant that I smoked Gold Flake too, though not until I was seven or eight. There were pipe smokers around, too, and occasionally, at Christmas, the rich, exotic aroma of a cigar. But most people who smoked, smoked Woodbines.

On strong drink, though, we were utterly solid. We were against it. Every child at the appropriate age was signed in as a member of the Band of Hope: the treasured certificate hung in every decent house, evidence that the innocent child named thereon (at the age of about one year, if I remember rightly) would be protected from the demon drink by parents and godparents, and encouraged in the paths of abstinence. It had been a pretty boozy area for a long time, and drink, doubtless, had caused almost as much pain as it had alleviated. We were perhaps the first, or possibly the second, tea-drinking generation. It was our panacea. We drank it about six times a day, hot and strong. Typhoo Tips tea, Pear's Soap, and Daddies Sauce; those are the brand names I recall from 1917. Wright's Coal Tar and H.P. Sauce came a little later, and lasted longer. But what a paucity of brand names it is, compared with a contemporary child's mythology of advertised legends. Almost everything was still home-made.

At this time the baking of bread was just going out. My wife's mother, who lived in the same village at the same time, was one of those who still had a baking day, once a week: but the baker's cart was winning. Lack of fuel and shortage of time to bake, during the stresses of the war: these were probably the final reasons for the decline in home baking of bread. Home-made cake was still obligatory, though if you wanted a madeira for special occasions, for *company*, you could get it from Arch's Dairy up The Street. The baker's roundsman and the milk roundsman still used horses, of course. The milkman drove a float, an open little cart with a couple of churns of milk standing in it. He ladled out your pint or half pint in a galvanised scoop with a handle soldered on to it—so unhygienic it would make you shudder now. All the milk open to the air, unpasteurised, untreated: just milk, straight from the cow that day.

I accompanied the milkman on his rounds many a time, and served, rather sloppily I suppose, many a gallon of the rich, undoctored stuff. There was an elemental pleasure in dipping it out of the churn and pouring it into the housewife's jug. I suppose my milk-round days were in the holidays. We also at one time sold milk ourselves, in the dark days of the war. I remember the queue at the back door; always in memory it seems to have been the evening, after dark. I don't know that we were doing anything illicit, though: that would be quite unlikely. Perhaps mother, who was prone to impetuous decisions, had suddenly decided that she could make a bit more by selling it direct instead of to the roundsman. I don't know, but it would be characteristic. Anyway, it was a lot of fun, like selling baby pork—suckling pig, a great delicacy. Of course we often killed a pig: there was a taciturn old chap who went round doing the actual execution—Oh, those endless squeals —and then there was the great to-do of scalding and drawing and butchery, the cutting up and hanging, the mysterious pre-cooking, the scratchings and chitterlings, all 'spoken for' in advance, the chawl and belly-draft, the trotters and chine and cheeks, the spare rib and loin and finally, prized beyond all else, the great thick legs. These were always reserved for the family: much was given away, and possibly we sold a bit. Our farming was on a pretty irreducibly retail basis, you see.

Yet, strangely enough, my real introduction to country pursuits came later, when we moved house and gave up both the farm and the factory. All in the future was the real country life. Despite our little farm, we were at this time incorrigibly townee, manufacturers, sort of suburban. Our domesticated fields lay within the ambit of the village-town, in sight of the factories, half encompassed by buildings new and old. There were no woods on the farm, and, more important, there was no water, neither stream nor lake. A bit of a dew pond for the cows— it held no fish. The mysteries of coppice and waterside were all to come. We walked on pavements and drove on made-up roads in the Model T Ford, dark gleaming red with brass radiator and acetylene headlamps and oil side-lamps and button-back upholstery stuffed with horsehair. Doctor Gilchrist *pished* and *tutted* around on a two-stroke Triumph motorbike. Life was urban, with a smack of something else, the impinging countryside.

Soldiers from the war returning called frequently: much older cousins, mainly, for my mother was by far the youngest of her family brood, her eldest sister might almost have been her mother, and some of our cousins were of an age to be uncles and aunts. This was a great family, Aunt Ginny's: she had eleven children and brought them all up on a miner's wages, and their vitality was one of the mainsprings of my early life. Aunt Ginny married George Smith, who liked his beer and smoked thick twist in a clay pipe and was of a different stamp from the earnest and abstemious Wiggins. I held him not only in affection, but in awe. He smelled different, for a start: a man's smell, I had no doubt.

There were abstemious, God-fearing miners, and there were miners like Uncle George who liked their beer and baccy and did not go to chapel. He lounged about wearing a thick flannel striped shirt and with his trousers held up on his paunch by a leather belt with a formidable buckle. He was fairly bald, and sported a walrus moustache of streaky grey. He was fearless, like all colliers, and did not mind what he said, or whom he said it to. I think I got my first real inkling of the nature of life as lived by others than the Wiggins—that is to say, the first glimmering of the social sense—at this house in Station Street, a tall, three-storied house in a row, almost next door to the monumental mason's and opposite the police station.

There we visited Aunt Ginny and Uncle George and their children: Beattie, Mary, Annie, Bill, George, Betty, Sam, Leonard, Rachel, and the twins, Emily and Lucy. That was the surviving eleven, a marvellous brood, full of energy and fun, physical vitality and mental alertness, good looks and good humour. Some of them did very well, as the world has it: none came to grief. To me they were infinitely kind and long-suffering. When you've got that many people living in a house you don't actually need an inquisitive nipper under your feet as well; but they were patient and gentle with me. Cousin Sam Smith was the nearest boy to my age, but really very much senior; he was in long trousers, and working, while I was a nipper. He was allowed to ride my pony, Star, bare-backed round the meadow, a dashing performance. Normally he harnessed Star in the trap and took us for a decorous drive through the lanes, to Shareshill or Laudywood, Wyrley or Brewood. I thought the name Sam Smith, so simple and manly, was the height of felicity, much nicer than Sam Wiggin, and later in life used it as a pen name, now and again. I was named Sam, after my father, and my mother had me christened Maurice to avoid confusion, but nobody ever called me anything but Sam until I became a writer and reluctantly began to use my first name in order to save my father from embarrassment. Sam Smith was one of my heroes, but perhaps the chief hero was his elder brother George, who was an infantry soldier in the war, one of the visitors who came and had tea in our front room when on leave from The Front.

There were quite a lot of them: the village did its bit, and more. I was awed by the rough khaki, the belts and boots, but always asked them how many Germans they had killed. I was six when the war ended and was already reading the war news in the papers. The name of German was a potent threat, far more so than the gipsies. 'The Germans will come and get you.' 'I'll send you to the Kaiser.' I don't mean that I absorbed German-phobia from the soldiers: it was the old wives of the village, no doubt, who propagated it most powerfully. But there it was: while still an infant I absorbed a horror of the name. It was the stuff of nightmares. Despite his age—thirty-eight—and his important war work, my father was eventually called to the colours. I remember seeing him, in a squad with my Uncle Enoch and Uncle Hiram, being drilled, in civvies, in the playground of Elmore Green School. I had it all off by heart at six years of age. 'Squad will move to the right in fours, f-o-r-m-f-o-u-r-s.' Then suddenly the rough rasping khaki came home. Dad was Quartermaster Sergeant Wiggin. Uncle Charlie, even, the religious non-Wiggin who married Aunt Mary and lived next door and was a headmaster, even Uncle Charlie was in khaki. But the armistice saved them, just in time. No more zeppelins going over, no more casualty lists. No more returning soldiers to tea. That night children formed a crazy crocodile which ran through the village screaming and singing, I hanging on to its tail. An old man came out of a house and drove us away, testily, saying his wife was ill. It put a damper on it.

Then everything seemed to happen very quickly and life changed key.

Chapter Three

In a real sense, for me at any rate, it truly began. For now we struck out on our own, just as I was really growing up.

I dare say the war enriched us, though by what amount I could not say. Not very much, nothing like the gross profits of gross profiteers, but now there was a little surplus in the bank, possibly as much as two thousand pounds, though again I'm only guessing, and now there came a stirring and diversification in the ranks of the clan. Of course the family firm went on, but some of the brothers withdrew to strike out on their own with their little bits of capital. Uncle Enoch went into the leather business in Walsall, about which he knew nothing. Uncle Hiram went into farming, of which he had no experience whatever. My father went into the building business, of which his knowledge was nil. Uncle Will, Uncle Joe and Uncle Noah remained at 'J & J's', and of their superior wisdom and discretion there can be no doubt. But the renegades had a run for their money, and while it lasted, they enjoyed the heady draught of independence. It didn't last any too long. Uncle Enoch and Uncle Hiram failed. My father struggled on for ten or eleven years before he admitted defeat, and though he never went bankrupt, ultimately he had to sell up and go back into 'J & J's'. Those were my formative years, lived on an elastic shoestring. Lived on a razor-edge, teetering between prosperity and failure. For my parents, years of worry. For us children, sensitive to that worry, years of alternating confidence and doubt. Speaking for myself alone, I can say I honestly never gave a damn whether we were rich or poor, for all or almost all my friends were poor, and I was soaked in the rough democracy of the Black Country, I really believed that 'a man's a man for a' that'. And I still do. But children are sensitive to stresses and strains in the domestic atmosphere, and we were really far more concerned for our parents' peace of mind than for ourselves.

Dad bought old Saml Wootton's building business when that worthy, whom I never knew, passed on, and we moved from Lichfield Road to

The Oaks. Thus once more we were living on the working premises, like proper tradespeople. The Oaks was a very old house, almost certainly eighteenth century, double-fronted, with a porch, and various oddments built on. It stood in an acre or two of ground on a windswept corner where five roads met: Wolverhampton Road, Sneyd Lane, Bell Lane, Broad Lane, and the Sandbank. Half the land was an interesting garden, half was the builder's yard, full of fascinating things like the limepit, piles of bricks, great stacks and wigwams of unplaned wood. The joiner's shop was opposite the house, across a yard which appeared to be made of red brick-dust, well rolled. There were various fine big sheds full of slowly maturing timber, a sawmill, stables, an unusual number of outside lavatories, and the coffin shed. For Saml Wootton had been an undertaker, too. We did not carry on this aspect of the business; it was enough to be learning one completely new trade. (For when he became a builder, dad did not know a dowel from a joist.) However, for years it remained 'the coffin shed', full of massive planks of the finest funereal timber. It was long and narrow and had no windows. Needless to say you only entered it on a dare, for the odour of funerals clung to it, it was known positively to be haunted. It was a cruel joke to trap some unusually sensitive child inside. I was so trapped myself, several times, and I can answer personally for the terrible nature of the ordeal. But cruelty was commonplace.

Do I really mean that? Perhaps I should say that a certain stoical attitude to suffering was commonplace; perhaps I really mean that courage was commonplace. It's another way of looking at the same thing. Life was not easy, for most people: economically and in every other way, life was inclined to be spare and rough. Margins were tiny. It was something to have a job, to be earning the basic necessities of life; anything over and above that was riches. I absorbed this so thoroughly that it stays with me to this day. Survival was something. Honour was inextricably and almost wholly linked to courage. Pared down to the bone, a matter of escaping starvation, life looks very different from life as lived on margins which suffice to buy you things you never need.

It came out, in practice, this unformulated attitude, as a dogged defiance of physical stress and hurt. There was not much room for softness. 'Big soft Nellie' was a term of baffled, almost incredulous abuse. Yet there was no really aggressive hardness, either. Bullies were rather few. If attacked, you had to fight: but you knew your neighbour's circumstances as well as you knew your own, you knew too well the buffets Fate could deal him to want to add to them. People who endured their own hurts stoically were stoical about their fellows' hurts, too: though a rough and ready kindness, a gruff and inarticulate helpfulness, were common, in fact obligatory.

Vic Parry was the local Scoutmaster. His family owned collieries, were leading lights in the moral regeneration of the place, and, I must say, staunch Anglican. Vic anticipated the Welfare State and the Health Service, as did several individuals, though none so thoroughly. If you were hurt, you went not to the doctor, whom you couldn't afford, but to Vic Parry's kitchen door. There he dispensed first-aid; bound up wounds, sterilised cuts, treated all sorts of knocks and sprains. 'As good as any doctor,' they said. You didn't have to be a Scout or ex-Scout, either. Many's the time I've assisted at the bloody scene at that back door: with bleeding heads, livid bumps, suspected fractures, the walking wounded supported by their mates turned to Vic for help and sustenance, and never in vain. Vic's brother, Harold Parry, was a poet, and a brilliant scholar, cut down in the war. Vic's life was Harold's memorial.

Whichever way you turned, you went down. And whichever way you turned, led to the water. The place was ringed by canals. Other boys grow up in a land of rivers, lakes or sea. I grew up in the land of the cuts. They had just the same meaning. They meant fish. I began to fish when we moved to The Oaks, when I was six. Fishing was the thread on which all other events and distractions were strung. It assumed an importance in life which outweighed everything else (except, in its season, sex). The moment when, all restraints evaded, all travelling done, you tackled up and threw your beautiful float out into the porter-coloured water of the cut—that was the moment in which life was transfigured. At that moment it became a different kind of life. As long as you could sit there, on the edge of the cut, watching the gently stirring float, life was wonderfully enhanced, more vivid, yet more tranquil. The essence of angling is this uniquely therapeutic combination of excitement and tranquillity. Some people never feel it; those who feel it never lose the sense of wonder that others can be content away from the water.

Absalom the carter was the last of his race. Even while I was a boy the local tradesmen and manufacturers were beginning to make their own deliveries in their own vehicles. The Wiggins had a lorry with chain drive, a Scammel I think, which may have been W.D. or even pre-war, or possibly both. It took a good man to start it and a mechanical genius to change gear, using both hands and feet. Still, it was a step in the wrong direction, the ghastly direction of 'progress' and speed and din and nervous exhaustion. So we were very pleased with ourselves. In their little way the Wiggins have contributed their whack towards making the world uninhabitable. We have been right there in the van of progress. May the Lord forgive us. Since we have mostly spent our spare time in praising Him to His face, succouring the afflicted, and generally spreading sweetness and light, the chances are that He will.

Of course, I didn't always think along those lines. I was dead progressive once.

Absalom had a covered wagon with a hooped canvas top, and a quiet old horse named Billy. There were still a fair number of horses in the village when I was a boy. Then they all disappeared. Now they have come back—but not the old work-horses. Nowadays there is a new population, a growing population, of play horses and show horses. All the young ladies want to ride a horse. It is the socially right thing, like owning a veteran car. Ah, well. In the days of my youth nobody saw any social advantage in horse ownership. On the contrary. To be horse-drawn branded you as old-fashioned. People were getting out of the horse age and into the motor age as fast as they could.

My pony Star was one of the very last trap-drawing ponies in the village, and even so, the trap was a 'second vehicle', almost a toy. There were still a few pony-and-trap outfits left, but when Doctor Gilchrist bought a belt-driven Triumph motor bike, and Doctor Mac engaged Billy Ison as his chauffeur, to drive him round in a Standard two-seater with artillery wheels and a yellow Cape Cart hood, the writing was on the wall. If it was O.K. for the doctors it was O.K. The doctors still had enormous social prestige and influence. This was when you had to pay them, or owe them.

The farmers still relied on horses. I can't just remember when I first saw a tractor, but it was long after childhood. On our little farm we made the hay and did all the ploughing and rolling and harrowing with the help of horses. Every milkman and baker had a horse, or hired one. You could still smell the sweet reek of stables as you walked round the village in the evening. And Absalom the carter had a quiet old horse named Billy.

I was full of the passion to travel. I loved setting out almost, though perhaps not quite, as much as coming home. Duration and distance were unimportant; what mattered was to be moving, however slowly, however humbly. To be perched high up on Absalom's van was a godly experience: feet stretched out towards the bracer board, jogging along the bony roads of the Black Country, watching the horizons slowly change, and the plump rump of Billy the horse heaving between the shafts. It was glorious to set off in the morning from the village, knowing that before sunset you would see the big town and some at least of the surrounding Black Country, the one-time villages that had merged into a gap-toothed spread of sooty brick. Best of all, perhaps, to come jogging home at evening across the waste land where the blast furnaces flared and smoked, monstrous against the sky, and you came at length, as to a frontier, to the Station Gates.

The Station Gates were almost literally the gateway to foreign parts. There was a level crossing just outside the railway station, which was itself quite inconveniently remote from the village, and double gates barred the way. On one side of the gates, a metalled road, houses, pubs, shops and street lamps; on the other side, the waste land, unclaimed, with mere tracks leading drunkenly across it, and rare little isolated houses, each with a tiny vegetable plot snatched from the heath, a few wandering cows and sheep, a tethered goat or two, roaming mongrel dogs and usually a few gipsy caravans. And dominating all, brooding over the waste, the monstrous great towers and caissons of the furnaces.

It was a scene which had not changed in its essentials since the Industrial Revolution came to blast the fair face of God's Island. Somehow, whenever you found yourself at large upon the heath that wandered undulant and vague towards the smoking skyline of the Black Country proper, you felt stirring the animus of the unavenged past, you felt the movement of ravaged ghosts and the deep unassuaged sadness of the ruined plain.

Many a time our way led us across this heath, and it was always at the end of the day, when Billy was tired and Absalom was even more taciturn than usual. He was a quiet man, a brooding one, not uncivil and not bitter, but sunk in his thoughts, which seemed sad. He had lived too long, he had seen the end of his epoch.

Now the heath was jewelled with pools. Some of them were black and brooding, reedless and unvisited by birds, but some were fringed with merry green growth, the haunt of moorhens. And these held fish. It is likely that some of the pools were artificial, even accidental: products of subsidence caused by long-abandoned mines, and other industrial calamities. But I expect that there were some natural survivors from the original waters of the moor, and these were probably the pretty waters that held fish.

Absalom the carter was not a particularly sociable man, nor an angler, but he was basically good-natured, and if his schedule allowed it he was willing to halt old Billy long enough for me to run across the tumpy grass and peer longingly into the water, and to interrogate such of my friends as I spotted in the distance, fishing. To pass by water without stopping and peering was unthinkable; it still is. I was an unpopular passenger on that account, if not other; but since I was always willing to hold Billy's head and feed him and generally make myself useful as carter's lad, one thing balanced another. Sometimes the carter would drop me at a distant pool on his way out in the morning, sometimes he would pick me up on his way home; I rarely seemed to fish the pools of the heath without a lift, coming or going, from old Billy and his van. So that particular fishing is associated for ever in my mind with the last of the carters.

It was surprisingly good fishing at times, though not so good as the legendary fishing in Pottall Pool, in Stubber's Green and in the great shining lakes of Gailey and Norton Canes. There were the usual roach and perch, and there were sizeable pike, and it was here that I first made the acquaintance of eels.

I went out one afternoon with Travesty Brown, who was *on the box*. Being *on the box*, Travesty had no right to be fishing, and we had to take diplomatic steps to protect his honour; and, what was more important, his bit of sick pay. In these strange remote times of which I am thinking now, long before the Health Service was thought of, a working man who was not well enough to work drew a pittance from his sick club, if, and only if, the doctor certified him as unfit for toil. The duration of payment was strictly limited. This condition was known as being *on the box*. Now nobody seems to recall the phrase, or its origins; yet it was a term in constant, daily use in the lifetime of men still far from old.

Being *on the box* carried one particular drawback: you must not be seen doing *anything* more strenuous than walking. The vocation of informer has a long history. If you were observed to be fishing, for example, some blithe spirit would feel it a social and ethical duty to inform on you, and your sick pay might be stopped, on grounds that you were malingering. Lead swinging was not entirely unknown. So when Travesty and I went fishing on the blasted heath, we were definitely sailing near the wind; and we knew it.

Travesty got his name from a habit of speech. Many of the miners and artisans of the district had some feeling for words (we produced more than our share of lay preachers and agitators) and there were several cases of men, otherwise practically without a vocabulary, who fastened on to one particular chance-met long word and used it on all possible occasions, with a fine disregard for suitability. Bert Brown's word was travesty. 'It's a travesty, if you ask me,' was his stock opinion on virtually everything under the sun. I recall, too, Immaterial Earnshaw ('it's immaterial to me'); Proletariat Wiseman; Phenomenal Cartwright; Chronic Parker; and (a slightly different case, of course) Reincarnation Reynolds. All good men and true.

Travesty was undoubtedly a malingerer; even at the time, *naïf* beyond belief, I was vaguely aware that he was a lazy and shiftless man. But at that period I had not learned to judge; certainly not to judge by the standards of commercial morality, if you will pardon the expression. I sympathised with Travesty's bad luck in being poor, and entirely shared his predilection for idling the time away at the water's edge. So I was only too happy to collect his rod and satchel from his little terrace house and carry them to the Station Gates, and beyond. It lent a mild touch of conspiracy to the outing.

We met at the water, as if by chance, and scanned the skyline pretty shrewdly in all directions before assembling Travesty's rod. Then we set to fishing. Travesty was a man who would fish with intense concentration for about half an hour, in total silence which I learned to respect. Then he would slowly relax and become human again; or as nearly human as he could. I learned that this odd habit was not simply the ordinary evidence of human frailty, lack of staying power. One marvellous morning Travesty had a great stroke of luck. He 'got among 'em' instantly. He missed a bite as soon as he made his first cast. His next six casts brought him six fish. In half an hour he landed thirteen, all exceptionally nice. Then the fishing went right off. He didn't touch another fish all day. Travesty was not an outstandingly intelligent man, and it stuck in his mind for ever more that the first half-hour was the likeliest. He began to fish with vast optimism and concentration. When the half-hour was up he felt it was fairly safe to relax. He felt sure that it was not going to be another red-letter day. Dense, perhaps, but pretty human.

As it turned out this sunny afternoon, sport was rather slow. When I say rather slow I mean that we didn't get a bite between us. Deadly long after Travesty's statutory half-hour was up we were still without a fish. This was slightly unusual at this pool, a pretty piece of water of about two acres. It was also slightly depressing. It always is. Let's face it.

I did not exactly feel that it was up to me to make a constructive suggestion, but Travesty didn't seem to have any ideas, so I plunged in with the only thing that entered my little napper:

'Mr Brown, d'you think we're fishing too shallow?'

Mr Brown considered this for a minute or two. Mr Brown was quite a fast thinker when it came to getting in a bit of fishing while technically *on the box*, but in all other respects he was a very steady thinker indeed. Not to say bone-headed. You could practically hear the rusty wheels whirring round beneath his black peaky blinder. It was Travesty who had set our depth to begin with, and obviously my innocent suggestion was going to be construed as a reflection on his expertise.

'No, I *don't* think we're fishing too shallow', said Travesty at length. 'What meks yer think that?'

'Well, we aren't getting many bites.'

'P'raps that's because we'm fishing too *deep*,' said Travesty with a triumphant squint. (His eyes, like mine, were rather too close-set for beauty). 'Never thought of that, did yer? I'm gooin' to slide *my* float *down* a bit.'

With which, Travesty hauled his gear out and set his float so that he was fishing about two feet below the surface, at most. This action of Travesty's touched off that nasty perverse streak in me. I should have been quite content to follow his advice, but a touch of high-handedness in his manner got the old back up. Even at a tender age the old back was notoriously easy to get up. Treat me on the level and I'll eat out of your hand; you can lead me around as docile as old Billy. Come the old acid and you've got an enemy for life.

So I heaved in my gear and rather ostentatiously slid my float right up the line. When I cast in again my bait was on the bottom and my float was leaning over at a sharpish angle. Not a word was said for a couple of minutes, but Travesty could not contain his indignation indefinitely.

'Yer float's layin' over, lad.'

'I know.'

'Yer bait's lyin' on the bottom.'

'I know.'

'Well, ain't yer gooin' ter dew nothin' about it?'

'Why should I? We caught nowt when it was off the bottom.'

'But it's a travesty of fishin'!' Mr Brown was beginning to get worked up. 'It's a travesty! Yo'll get nowt wi' yer float like that. 'Tis neether one thing nor t'other'

'I don't care.'

'Don't care was hanged, me lad. Doh yo forget that. I doh know wot kids is comin' to, knowin' better than their elders.'

Travesty was in a fair paddy, the calm atmosphere of the outing was quite ruined, and heaven only knows what might have developed as tempers rose. For he was a cantankerous man and I was a hot-tempered boy. But before we reached the point of exchanging unforgiveable (or, at least, unforgettable) words, something very interesting happened to my float.

It disappeared.

Even Travesty's ready flow of wit and repartee was stilled. I forgot all about our tiff. True, the float quickly reappeared, but obviously there was 'something at it'. It dipped and skipped and nudged and inched and trembled for a wonderful minute or so, and then it plunged beneath the dark surface of the pool. For a long moment we saw it vanishing, growing dark and distant, then it was out of sight, and I was on my feet, swinging up the rod. There was a solid resistance, a thrumming and quivering deep down in the water, and the line began to cut the surface and hiss and sing.

I shall never forget the sheer power and pull of that first eel, the vitality and rage. It was only quite small, about a pound, but it was my first intimation of the ferocious life-force of the eel. I landed it more by luck than judgement, and because my tackle was unduly stout. I gave it to Travesty, perhaps a diplomatic thing to do, and he was instantly appeased. Nonchalantly, talking about something else all the time, he slid his float up the line until he too was laying-on with his float heeled over at a drunken angle. Alas, he caught nothing, even then. But it was an afternoon to remember.

We had almost reached the Station Gates when the carter's van overtook us, plodding home.

I was a water baby from the age of six. A wonderful year. We had left Lichfield Road, left the farm, left 'J & J's', and I had left the dame's school and gone to the National School. The Nashnul was the C. of E. elementary school, next to the Park, on High Street, which was always known as The Street. 'Chop up The Street for a ha'porth of candles,' my maternal grandfather used to command his brood. He was a stern under-manager at one of the local collieries. He had a big brood of whom my mother was youngest, and he commanded them royally. His shopping was on an irreducibly retail scale. With so much free labour at his disposal, why not? He enjoyed exercising command and doling out his cash in ha'porths. He collected watches, which I have always thought a sure sign of something. When he lay on his death-bed, and he lay on it for years, the wall over the fireplace was covered with watches, hanging on pins, all telling different times. He used to tantalise us by promising this watch or that to current favourites, after he had 'passed on'. Most boys treasured a watch, but I never did, and still don't. I never remember to wind it, or even to wear it. Sometimes I don't even know what day it is, though I know the season. That's near enough. It's today.

It was a bit of a come-down to go to the Nashnul, I suppose. Some of my cousins went to private and even to boarding schools. But my father and his brothers had gone to the Nashnul. It would be quite a new school in their day, of course. Now it looked nicely old. It had those soaring Gothic windows, a soaring beamed roof. It was heated by great blazing coal fires as well as by 'the pipes'—a rudimentary sort of central heating. 'The pipes' ran only along the back walls, which meant that good scholars who sat on the back rows got some benefit from their goodness. However, very bad scholars who sat in the front rows got the benefit of the fire. As usual, it was the poor perishers in the middle who were mediocre, neither good nor bad, who got lumbered with a little bit of nothing.

Not only had my father been educated, until the age of thirteen, at the Nashnul. Mr Satterthwaite, headmaster in my father's day, was still headmaster when I turned up. He leathered my dad and he leathered me. He was succeeded, as headmaster, when I was in Standard Two, by his son. So two generations of Satterthwaites leathered the rudiments of English, arithmetic and Scripture into two generations of Wiggins. Far from there being any ill-will, there was a positive, not negative, a positive respect and admiration for the Satterthwaites. Why, if we were negligent or idle, should they *not* apply the strap? It was the understood thing. It was plain justice. I certainly never resented it. Not even at the time.

The instrument of retribution, in those days and in that school, was the tawse. It was a black leather strap about a quarter of an inch thick, with four tongues. Some say five. I think it was four. It was applied on the upturned palms of the hands, which tingled quite pleasantly. No masochist, yet I never feared the tawse, though it raised interesting red weals when applied in earnest. One on each hand was ordinary: two on each hand was severe. There is perhaps no portion of the anatomy better equipped to take punishment than the palm of the hand. Few boys wept, though faces went very red with the effort to stay manly. I got it once a week at least. 'Sam, fetch the tawse.' You left your seat and walked to whichever classroom the headmaster happened to be teaching in.

'Please, sir, Mr Hadderley's sent me for the tawse.'

'Oh yes. And what have you been up to now?'

'Made a blot, sir.'

'You've got to learn to take more care, Sam.'

'Yes, sir.'

You walked back through the rooms and corridors and handed the strap to teacher. It was a sort of ceremonial journey, watched by every eye. Surreptitious whispers as you passed:

'Yo'll get fower.'

'Chuck inkpot at the bugger.'

Some boys did chuck an inkwell at the bugger. It was the high point in an age-old ceremonial drama. The inkwells were sunk into holes in the desks. For generations—well, at least two—it had been a tradition that really bad boys, really daring boys, would, on returning to their places after having the strap, put a hand under the lid of the desk and ease or pop the inkwell up, then throw it at the master. I didn't really and truly see it happen very often, but several times it made a nice bit of life to wake up a dreary lesson. The consequences were serious. The erring parents were informed, called in for discussion. The boy was a marked man thereafter, hero and/or desperado.

Sometimes, even more interestingly, parents did not wait to be called in for discussion. Bellicose mothers, dads, even big brothers, occasionally called unasked, creating interesting scenes. Such as the time when one brawny scold, whose son had richly deserved his strapping, appeared dramatically at the classroom door in the later morning, that dread time when hunger gnawed and concentration was most uncongenial. She wore a hodden shawl, a hessian apron to protect her old black skirt; her bare arms, akimbo, were raw from wind and wash-tub. Wisps of hair escaped from the dragged-back bun. Lady Macbeth could not have appeared more appositely than she, flinging the door open so that it clanged against the roughly distempered wall on which the only decoration was a small framed copy of Haig's recent exhortation to his troops after the great German breakthrough in March 1918, when the Fifth Army fell back. The backs-to-the-wall message, in fact, which we all felt to be so English. The precise qualities of moral fibre which it called upon were now to be seen in action.

'Is that 'im, Jim? Is that the bugger as 'ommered yer?'

'Yes, mom, that's 'im.'

'Oi'll give 'im 'ommer. Oi'll 'ommer *'im*.'

And the burly virago rushed towards the fireplace and easel, where the assistant master, so sorely put-upon, went interestingly pale, I noticed, then very red. He seized her wrists and they wrestled for a time, quite inconclusively—we had some rare Amazons among us—until the clamour and tumult brought the headmaster and several other assistants rushing in to separate the contestants and restore the peace. Of course, it meant that morning school was virtually at an end, and if we were especially fortunate, one or more fights would develop among partisan bystanders, to be settled outside, 'after'. All fights were scheduled for 'after'. It might mean after school, or after work, or after Sunday School, or after whatever communal activity it was that was occupying the moment, such as a session at the pub, or a tea party. We were one-thing-at-a-time chaps, experts at getting the most out of the moment.

There were never prosecutions after these little affrays. It was felt that you settled your own disputes out of court. We were flown with a high sense of justice, but were not litigious. We were to some extent tribal.

I was more 'successful' at the Nashnul than ever before or since. There was no sense of strain and no competitiveness. One absorbed the basic elements of learning, quite naturally, or one did not. Either way it didn't seem to matter: the tawse apart, there were no pressures, either in school or at home. The strap was awarded mainly for arrant indiscipline, to teach us manners, or for culpable carelessness, such as my blots. This was generally understood and not generally resented. But it seemed an understood thing that some people picked up book learning, some did not, and though doubtless it was an advantage to be bright, it was no disgrace to be dull. Bright boys were not made much of: in fact their tiny precociousness was looked at quite coolly, they were emphatically not encouraged to get ideas about their cleverness. Conceit—conceit about so unimportant, trivial and useless a thing as book learning—was liable to be 'ommered out of swell-'eads, or as we said *swole-'eads*, peremptorily. But if you took your success modestly, without smirking or talking about it, it wasn't held against you, either; and of course it wasn't held against you that you were as dim as a candle in a crypt. It was understood that there were other qualities besides the ability to remember rather uninteresting facts. Indeed, the fact that one was quite good at istree or jogrufee had to be atoned for by unusual modesty and/or a demonstration of personal qualities which were held in higher esteem.

I had learned to read long before I went to the Nashnul, but it was in the Infants', under rustling and bosomy Miss Stokes, that I got my first taste of literature, and my first taste of the North. There were periods on winter afternoons when we read silently, or as silently as infants read; a murmuration of infants. Here in 1918 I got the taste of the North from infants' editions, in big type, fourteen point or Great Pica, profuse with line drawings of vikings, trolls, fair maidens, long ships, palisaded forts, beamed roofs like the roof under which we read, pine forests, lakes and wolves; dog-eared books which we read silently, or as silently as infants read, in dusky winter afternoons by gaslight, in a cream-and-brown-washed room with pointed Gothic windows and a soaring roof, like a chapel, or 'the Great Hall of Aud the Deep-Minded, mother of Thorstan the Red, conqueror of Caithness and Sutherland'.

Children are sold into bondage by the teachers who give them their first taste of literature (or possibly, now, by television which gives them their first taste of drama). When upon the first taste of trolls and vikings you superimpose Grimm and Andersen and then a solid course of Dickens, the least Mediterranean of authors, you have an imagination fairly unreceptive to South and summer. By the time I was ten I had assimilated northernness and wintriness; they remain, for me at any rate theoretically, a congenial climate, though I dare say I am too frail for them now. You can never go back. My early acquisition of a taste for the mythology of the dark North may have meant a lifelong failure of sympathy for 'the civilisation of the delicate olive', but I feel no unbearable sense of loss. The furniture of my imagination was undoubtedly barbaric and uncouth, but I was at home with it. Of course there is an obverse to the long nights of the North, endless dark forests, crags and torrents and wolves. It is cosiness. You can only acquire a taste for cosiness in a rough climate. Though an outdoor lad, I grew up preferring the cosiness of kitchen fire, shut casement against which the gale lashed, to heatwave and swimming pool.

Education was minimal. Of the teachers, Satterthwaite, Hadderley and Fryer were recently returned from the War; Colthouse was older. I remember them all with gratitude and affection. They leathered the elements of arithmetic into me; it came hard. But I was effortlessly afloat on reading and writing, jogrufee and istree. Scripture was murder: it was neither readin' nor istree, but a bewildering procession of inexplicable names and incomprehensible doings. Since we were a Church school, the vicar occasionally addressed us. He was treated with great respect by the staff, but to us, or most of us, he was a figure of fun. He wore a flat wide-brimmed canonical hat and had an impediment in his speech; probably a cleft palate. He stood there jabbering away, grinning fulsomely: it was deeply embarrassing. Double-dyed nonconformists among us regarded him as little short of diabolical. When, at family midday dinner, I told my parents that the Vicar had been to school, they sniffed.

'Ritual creeds and dogmas,' dad said pityingly, shaking his head.

'They haven't seen the light,' said mother.

Needless to say, we *had*. By now we were ardent practising spiritualists.

Chapter Four

This Spiritualism was a key factor in our lives in the Twenties. Up to and including the Lichfield Road days, we had been staunch Wesleyans. There was a particularly fine pseudo-Gothic Wesleyan Chapel in Bloxwich; they have just pulled it down to make room for something or other, a supermarket I'm told, and built another behind it which is also quite fine in its way, if you like a chapel that looks rather like a power station or carpet warehouse. But nowadays the one chapel will comfortably accommodate all the Methodists in Bloxwich. When I was a nipper there were three strong sects, all flourishing, bursting at the seams. The Wesleyans were in tremendous form, undoubtedly the aristocracy of nonconformity, with all the leading Methodist families attending. The Primitive Methodists, known of course as the Prims, had a ferociously ugly chapel near the Pinfold and a large lively congregation, including some of the brightest sparks in the area; but their *class* was a shade lower. Then there was the New Street lot, who perspired through their dejected rites in a smaller and even plainer chapel. Now, as I say, the spirit of union has done its work, strongly abetted no doubt by apathy, ecumenicity's ablest ally, and the one chapel is plenty for the lot. But in our day it was different.

We attended night and morning on Sundays, with Sunday School in the afternoon for good measure. Occasionally there was defection, owing to crisis in farm or factory, and I was sent up to chapel on my little tod, clutching a sixpence for 'the plate'. I never had much interest in religion in those days—who does, at six?—and I'm inclined to think that I was by no means alone in my indifference. But it was the done thing to show up, the badge of respectability. It was intensely boring, but one never thought that there could be any escape. The point about this sort of upbringing is that whether you have the slightest religious feeling, or not, you grow up accustomed to the forms. It becomes second nature to observe them. The hymns, the familiar phrases, a sense of the propriety of being hectored and sermonised, the names of

God and Jesus, above all the hymns, which for us Wesleyans were really rather glorious, simply looked on as songs: all this background you easily absorb when young, you take it for granted that there must be some sort of transcendental mystery, even if you can't quite divine it.

Spiritualism was grafted on to this quite strong and fervent religiosity about 1918, I guess. I do not know exactly the origins. But certainly, by the time we reached The Oaks, we were ready for the clean break. In this as in almost everything else, it was the climacteric move of our lives. Though the connections with the rest of the family were warmly maintained, we were on our own from now on. And we charted a singular course.

I think the infection of spiritualism had reached us from Walsall, where there was a well-established 'church'. But of course we were not content to be attached for long. I think my father always had a bit of an urge to act, and he simply loved organising and administering—did it very well, too—and frankly I suppose he preferred to be the big fish in a little pond, instead of just another fish in the ocean. I'm not criticising the old chap, whom I dearly loved. It is a quite common disposition. Anyway, he soon became by far the biggest fish in an exceedingly murky little pond.

Actually the Bloxwich Spiritualist Society was founded by my Uncle Ben, in 1920 or 1921. Uncle Ben was mother's only brother. He was extremely interesting, in a macabre way. His back had been broken by a fall of rock in one of the local collieries, and all the time I knew him he was a cripple. I must tread very warily in writing about Uncle Ben, for I never warmed to the man, to put it mildly. Anyone who has been down the pit and suffered a blow like that deserves and demands our sympathy. But deserving and demanding it, and getting it, are different things. Uncle Ben did his best to forfeit the sympathy of those who might have given it most willingly. For he was an ingenious and talkative valetudinarian, never without an interesting symptom, and a bit of a self-righteous humbug. I'm sure that if my back had been broken I should have been a darned sight more unattractive: suffering doesn't improve the character markedly, so far as I can judge. Not mine, at any rate. But whatever the theoretical rights and wrongs, the fact is that Uncle Ben's self-pity tended to inhibit the pity others might have felt for him. The poor old perisher simply asked to be teased, though of course we were sharply smacked down when we let the temptation get the better of us. Uncle Ben was held up to us as an example of the blind caprice of fate, and we were urged and enjoined and sometimes bluntly ordered to strengthen our spiritual quality by practising compassionate tolerance towards him.

I suppose it would have been easier if he had been less vain. But the poor old thing was eaten up with conceit. He was or had been an amateur watercolour painter. I've seen worse. But like all artists (what bores they are) he was satisfied with nothing less than the most unctuous, oily flattery of his work. He also saw himself as a 'deep thinker'—his own favourite phrase. If you could not see the point and justice of his argument—and he was an expert on everything—that was because it was 'too deep for the likes of you'. This endearing trait made him especially lovable in a family much given to philosophical speculation of the wildest and most uninhibited sort. We were extremely fond of theological discussion, the family was full of parsons and local preachers and really interested in religion. No holds were barred. Doubtless we were conventional in some respects, in fact respectable, but freedom of thought was a reality: it was not denied even to the children, indeed it was encouraged. The house was full of weird Eastern mystical crap in paper covers, supplied by enterprising publishers. My parents could not resist it then, just as the Beatles later could not. It was all utterly phoney, but it was usually couched in extravagantly high-flown prose, and for this we were ever suckers.

Uncle Ben used to come staggering to our place, several times a week, bent against the prevailing wind, gasping for breath, his parchmenty face tinged with blue from the cold and the effort. He wore in all weathers a greenish bowler, a hard high come-to-Jesus collar, button boots, several layers of mustard coloured cardigan, a black jacket and pin-striped trousers, a greasy mac, and two or three scarves. Wheezing and panting, the poor old thing would flop down in the grandfather chair by the kitchen fire, opening up his layers of clothing one by one, like an onion being peeled. No matter how inconvenient the time of his calling, mother would have a cup of tea laced with whisky in his shaking hand before you could say 'Bugger me Lucy it's perishin'.' Though we did say it, sometimes, in cruel mimicry, and suffered for it. She looked after him with endless and inexhaustible fondness. Like many in a similar condition, he was exceedingly pernickety and finicking about his food, and if any of us showed signs of fiddling around with what was on our plates we would be called sharply to order with the gibe, 'Uncle Ben!' It was enough.

Yet this was the man who got in ahead of us and founded the Bloxwich Spiritualist Society. I doubt if we ever entirely forgave him. True, we soon organised him out of the leadership, for which, indeed, he was but ill-suited. But for ever after, or long enough, the literature of the Society commemorated the interesting fact that it was Founded by Uncle Ben, and he was a Life Vice President. Few if any members of my family have failed to hold office in this organisation, at one time or another, save yours truly, a determined non-joiner. I joined the human race and that was enough to be going on with, without joining any clubs and societies. I'm a non-sectarian society of one, which is how, come to think, they bury us. Whatever it may say on the box.

The early meetings of the Society took place in a large cheerless rented room over the Co-op, which in Bloxwich was a quite splendid building. But this would never do for a family so root-conscious; we wanted the adventure all sewn up in a place we could really call our own; and in 1920 or thereabouts we took over The Orl. For more than a decade The Orl was a factor in our lives of the liveliest importance.

The Spiritualists' Hall, to give it its proper name (the Spirichulists' Orl was what everyone called it) was a pretty dire building, not interestingly old, but very far from new. It looked like a small garage, and it had been a small garage. Before that it had been a fruiterer's. Both enterprises failed. It was flanked by a fish-and-chip shop, a pub, the Spotted Cow, and some old cottages. Across the road, most conveniently, stood a three-stall urinal. We threw ourselves with fervour into converting this rum old place for the purposes of worship. We cut a small door in the double doors which faced the pavement, through which an older vintage of broken-down motors used to pass. Downstairs was a large, dark cold room with a floor of bricks. This was not holy ground; it was social territory. We put up a wooden partition, creating a small back room used for passionate committee meetings, small intimate séances, and just possibly a little furtive spooning. A flight of remarkably creaky stairs on one side led up to the main worship room above, which ran the full though not excessive length of the building. This was the Temple Of Light. The far end wall was painted, by some obliging amateur genius in the direct tradition of Michelangelo, with vivid gold and blue images; mainly, as I remember them, rising suns and angel wings, which represented eternal light and brotherly love, on which we were quite hot. In a tasteful derivation of the black-letter, the words TEMPLE OF LIGHT dominated the whole.

Here, at this far and sacred end, we built a raised platform—The Platform, in fact—with a rail in front. On the platform was set a table draped with a red plush cloth, that same cloth, I doubt not, on which I read the *Children's Encyclopaedia* down in Lichfield Road, and some hard chairs. A piano stood at one side. The congregation sat on kitchen chairs bought as a job lot, with an aisle dividing them into sixes and fives. Downstairs, we installed facilities for making tea and sandwiches. Spiritual though we were, we put a proper value on the things of the flesh, and foremost among them came a soothing cupper. The Orl was used at least as much for sociability as for worship. This was before radio, television and bingo. 'As good as the pictures—and you can get a cup of tea,' was one stranger's generous tribute after his first visit. There is no doubt at all, we filled a long-felt want.

The social function of The Orl was beyond argument excellent. It provided a succulent social life for poor people in a time when they had no alternative on offer at anything like the price. The Orl was in use about five nights a week; there were socials, with games and songs and tea and fish-and-chip suppers fetched from next door, and mounds of tinned salmon sandwiches and buns. There were séances, circles, healing circles, committee meetings, all sorts of big and little get-togethers. There were even afternoon circles, matinees, though these were less well-attended in a working-class village where most were either chained to the bench or on the dole. There was a Sunday School, though it was called the Lyceum. But when all's said and done, and glorious though the social contribution of the Orl was on weekdays, it was the big Sunday services, particularly the evening service, which put it apart from every other competing attraction. There was nothing quite like it.

The basic fact is that we were amateurs in religion, and, as amateurs, a good deal more enthusiastic than mere pros. There was an old tradition in the Black Country, deriving no doubt from Wesley but possibly going back even farther still, that salvation was something profoundly personal and man-to-man, like fighting; that religion was far too serious a business to be left to parsons. The place abounded with local preachers: at one time every adult Wiggin was 'on the Plan'—i.e., his name appeared in the list of local preachers, with details of where and when they would be holding forth, which was published for the delectation of the Methodist flocks within 'the circuit'—an area of several miles. So strong was the tradition of the extempore lay preacher that for a long time I believed Wesley, who was a living figure in our lives, to be only slightly senior to General Booth, or Grandpa Wiggin. And this readiness to be preached at was nourished and supported by the classless democracy of the system, if you could call it a system. A man might be poor, propertyless and unlettered, but if he had the gift of the gab, if he had the spark in him to get up and exhort us, why, we recognised it as a gift and gave him a respectful, or at least a polite, hearing.

41

If practically anybody was good enough to have a go, practically anywhere was good enough to have a go in. Without the slightest visible provocation, natural preachers would burst out in the oddest places: in the best parlour, at the barber's, on the pavement, or in any one of the chapel pulpits which kept an earlier generation of joiners gainfully employed. It made no odds. Uncle Joe was perhaps our most eloquent, certainly our most emotional, preacher. He could be relied on to draw tears, at any rate from his own eyes, within five minutes of the starter's gun. A gun, I may say, inaudible to anyone but himself. But my own father ran him very close; on a good day his sheer poetic flights took a lot of beating. It has taken me close on half a century to purge my style of the purple rhetoric which I inherited, like a disorder of the blood. I'm not sure that I've succeeded, even now.

With a background like ours, it was no trouble at all to devise an order of service for the new church. We were simply permeated with the stuff; it was part of the texture of our lives in and out of chapel. We took it home with us. For example, every Saturday evening during my boyhood there was a family gathering at Grandma Wiggin's house. Soon after Grandpa died, and we moved, she was installed in a nice new house in Lichfield Road—actually, one of the first that dad built—with a companion to look after her; and from this central and hallowed croft she ruled the ever-widening family circle with every apparatus of matriarchy. And here, every Saturday after tea, we tooled round for a training session which must have come in very handy.

Remembering Grandma, I am reminded that I grew up in the shadow of a living Victorian tradition; yet she died but a generation ago, when I was 21. She always, in my memory, looked immensely old, creased and withered, dark of skin; old people do not seem to look like that today. Grandma was as Victorian as Victoria. She wore a going-out bonnet of black straw, with small purple flowers and sillk ribbons, and a loose coat of black watered silk, and elastic-sided button boots. You could search the shops for a black bonnet today.

The Saturday evening session, which was obligatory, 'kept the family together'. For us of the younger generation it was an unalloyed pleasure, however it may have appeared to the grown-ups. It was a habit which seemed timeless and unbreakable; no doubt the adults knew better. We all arrived in our various motor cars or on foot, in the family crocodile which had not yet disappeared from the pavements, and foregathered in the front parlour. We drank strong dark tea, the Wiggin special (it was no different from anybody else's special, of course, but families prided themselves on a good cup) and we ate plentifully—Grandma would be down on us if we did not—of thin bread-and-butter and pork pie. Since we had a little while before eaten Saturday high teas, often enough of pork pie and bread-and-butter and strong tea, it is plain in retrospect that the family was generally speaking blessed with good digestive tracts. Or, alternatively, that we could never pass up a free meal.

Unfortunately all the family gossip which flowed with the tea was above my head; the social world of adults seemed then extremely boring, even more so then than now. But the real business of the evening was not gossip, but hymn singing. If this seems dreary, someone has been misinformed. It was rather thrilling. Grandma's harmonium, known among us as The Organ, was a prized piece of furniture. No-one among us could actually *play* it, I fancy, in the sense of actually reading music; but my dad and several uncles and aunts and even cousins were considerable improvisers. They played by ear, but their ear was not at all bad. To me this all seemed brilliant. I much preferred the harmonium's thrilling wheezes and blares and tremblings to the correct thin music of the piano, which was *de rigeur* in slightly more modern homes, such as ours.

We played no secular music. Enriched as we were with the rowdy and poignant revivalist hymns on which we had been brought up, we felt no need for the trumpery personal music of unbelievers. Much the same foundation underpinned our indifference to the playhouse. We were passionately fond of drama, actually, but found it abundantly in real life; everywhere, but especially in our religious activities. So we all sang with fervour, including to my certain knowledge some whose mouths were still not empty of pork pie. The brothers formed a sort of unofficial choir, a nice mixture of tenor and baritone and even a tentative bit of bass; the aunts included fresh sopranos, fruity altos. The point is that everyone sang loud and clear, utterly without inhibitions. In our own homes we sang all sorts of popular songs, equally fervently, but at Grandma's we let ourselves go only on the hymns. I've heard a fair amount of music in my life, one way and another, but nothing has ever affected me quite like these sessions under the pink shaded lights of Grandma's parlour; rich, fruity, earnest, sincere, a combination of well-oiled voices and well-loved words.

Bearing in mind this background of religiosity, it is perhaps not surprising that we retained the elements of familiar forms when it came to devising an order of service for our new church. We must have had an enviable freedom, but we chose to retain the best of the old alongside what we believed to be the best of the new. Some spiritualist societies were less religious, some more: some more scientific and almost secular, some more mystical and devout. Our own variant was emphatically a religion first: I heard many sad and superior references to 'mere spiritists', meaning, I think people who put the psychical phenomena first. We called ourselves Christian Spiritualists, at any rate for a time, and although the psychical phenomena were in fact the kernel in the nut, the juice in the grape, we took some care to preserve traditional outward forms. When I say traditional, I mean traditionally untraditional—the young tradition of nonconformity.

So we began and ended our meetings with prayer. The movement had a spiritualist hymnal, and a shocking thing it was, a truly dreadful production. The old battle songs of nonconformity (and a few Anglican ones, if truth be told) were grossly tampered with; watered down, theologically bowdlerised. A great many new spiritualist hymns were included, all written in doggerel, some plumbing new depths of puerility and bathos. Still, we had hymns, we had prayer. But needless to say, we did not have a Prayer Book.

Prayer, indeed, was the prerogative of anyone who happened to procure an invitation to sit on the chairman's right hand. The chairman was the M.C. of the proceedings, a sort of compère. He sat in the middle and he was usually my dad, who had quite a presence and did not find the sound of his own voice repugnant. Well, it was a good voice, at that. With him on the platform, arranged purely to suit his whim, sat the secretary, the speaker, the clairvoyant (sometimes the same person as the speaker, sometimes not) and the prayer-maker, if any; though quite often dad would throw in the prayer as an extra to his central duties. The whole set-up was elastic. The chairman could invite just anyone he fancied to take a seat on the platform whether active in the meeting, or not. It conferred status, and a good view of the flock. I think it was highly regarded, even sought-after. Mother did not consider the day was going well unless she had between twelve and sixteen people sitting down to Sunday tea and supper, and Sunday tea was often enlivened by whispered canvassing on this very subject of who should be elevated to platform status. Mother had no bump of diplomacy, and often embarrassed father by promising things she could not really perform, such as a seat on the platform and even the right of offering up prayer. There is no doubt she could make things awkward. I think she enjoyed a bit of fun. With (say) fourteen people in the house it was none too easy to find a quiet spot for a heart-to-heart, and I recall pretty frenzied whisperings in odd corners, such as the pantry.

'Sam, I've told Mrs Hankey she can give the prayer.'

44

'What in the name of faith d'you want to go and do that for, our mother? You know I've invited Mr Pankey to give the prayer.'

'I didn't know! You never told me.'

' 'Course I told you. I told you at dinner time. Now you've gone and put your foot in it again. Well, you'll just have to tell Mrs Hankey the position's already filled. She can give the prayer next Sunday.'

'*I* sha'n't tell her, our Sam! *You*'ll have to tell her. She won't *half* be offended!'

In the end Mrs Hankey would be offered some other supernumerary role, such as announcing the hymns—a bit carved off the chairman's chores and a bit he keenly missed, for there were few things dad enjoyed more than reading out the first line or two in his rich and vibrant dark brown voice. Sometimes he was so carried away he went right on and read the lot. He suffered a good deal from mother's impetuosity, which I'm afraid I inherited. But I don't think I inherited a certain tendency to moral blackmailing. Ma was a great one for getting her own way; no-one ever said that of me. She was only intermittently practical; half the time she was sunny, easy-going, almost dreamy. But when she did come down to earth and decide that there was something the world owed her, she could be quite a handful. Dad spoiled her hopelessly. But when things were *really* going wrong, and they quite often did, she was marvellously insouciant and gay.

The prayer, whoever gave it, often contained theological innovations of considerable daring. These passed unremarked: after all, we were innovators, rebels, reformers and radicals. Everyone looked at us askance, so we might as well give them something to look askance at. If God had any capacity left for surprise, he must have been surprised twice weekly by the prayers, and the addresses, that were delivered in Wolverhampton Road in the Twenties. I only wish I could recall entire some of the gems of free thought that were hurled at us, and the deity, in those happy far-off days. That oriental crap which I mentioned was widely read, if imperfectly assimilated, and we maintained a library of paperbacked gems, vilely printed, which passed from hand to hand, mind to mind, and must have had a more potent, and perhaps more unfortunate, effect on the thought of Bloxwich than anything else in the mass communication line before the coming of television. Speakers barely literate, but far from coy on that account, commanded us to accept the reality of Karma. Transubstantiation had a vogue. Discontinuous reincarnation was popular. Actually most of us were polytheists, whether we knew it or not. We praised a remarkably free-and-easy Lord.

However, you don't want to be bored by theology, and anyway I am getting rusty about it now, and would not like to swear to this or that in the theological stakes: though you may take my word for it, we were way out. But the address, after all, was only a polite token substitute for the conventional sermon: it wasn't what we went for, by a long shot. This was a sad fact of life which some speakers never cottoned on to. What we went for was the clairvoyance: the fun: the thrilling extra which the other churches and chapels didn't have.

As soon as the speaker got his or her behind back on the chair, you could detect a change in the atmosphere. There was that squirmy rustling that betokens interest. At this well-chosen moment the plate went round. It wasn't a silver collection; seventy-five per cent copper, I should say. One evening a rich well-wisher, visiting from another area (it might almost have been another planet) put a ten shilling note in the plate. The collector was so overcome, he could hardly carry on. And the effect on those still to receive the plate was pretty terrific. Twopence was acceptable, threepence quite good, a tanner a sign of prosperity and/ or devoutness. While the collection was being taken up the secretary came into his own and read a pessimistic account of our financial situation, which was always parlous; enlivened by optimistic commercials or trailers for future attractions, such as mediums known for their psychometry, or the laying on of hands, and speakers known for their erudition or the depth of their thought. Then we sang a hymn, usually curtailed, in deference to the rising tide of eager anticipation, to first-and-last-verses-please. Then the lights went down.

Not in a physical sense; but that was the effect. This was the big turn. This was where the shiver ran through the congregation.

There were mediums who operated without going 'under control', but they were heavily outnumbered, I think, by those who worked under trance conditions. To see the medium slowly going under was quite a thing. The timing was delicate. Usually the going-under process took about five minutes, during the collection and the hymn. First the medium nodded off. Then the jerks and twitchings started. If we were in luck, these culminated in fearful shuddering spasms. There were those who wrung their hands, others who waved their arms. But if you've ever seen anyone going into an epileptic fit, you have the rough idea.

But it was the first sounds that were most keenly awaited. These gave us a clue to which guide would be in control. Every medium of consequence seemed to have the choice—no, I mustn't say choice—seemed to be served by several spirit guides. They usually came from sharply differing earthly backgrounds and periods. As I understood it, the medium had no say in deciding which of his familiars should come through, at any time. Some mediums gave us a clue or two, engaging while still imperfectly entranced in a sotto voce conversation with their guides. 'No, Trixy, there's a good girl, be *quiet*, Trixy' (accompanied by a playful slapping movement of the hand) might mean that Trixy was going to come through. On the other hand, it might equally mean that Trixy was being kept out, though only just, in favour of Mr Gladstone, or Sitting Bull. Speculation was intense and enjoyable; those in the know exchanged knowing nods. I wish I'd made a book on it, as a regular thing; but was held back, then as now, by diffidence and bad arithmetic. This, of course, was when we had mediums known to us. Strange mediums facing us for the first time were unknown quantities. Still, there was always the exercise of wondering whether their guide would turn out to be a Red Indian chief, a Chinese or Greek sage, a cotton-picking negro closely resembling Uncle Tom, or a mentally defective little girl of dubious nationality. It might, of course, turn out to be a disappointingly ordinary English person. Ex-person, I should say. But such disappointments were uncommon. The survival rate of the plain English cannot be high. 'Oi am the great So Kraits,' a burly Black Countryman once declared in my hearing, thumping his chest. That was not the only occasion on which I regretted that I had not learned Greek. The more eminent the public figure that died, the sooner he or she 'got through' again. I have been warned to mend my ways by Clemminsaw, Lord Kitchener and Horatio Bottomley.

The sight and sound of the medium going under control were enough to make a stranger to these proceedings goggle. But it was when the medium, fully under, got to his or her feet and began to sort us out that we really got our money's worth, and knew we were getting it. Faint-hearts tended to cringe a bit when the medium pointed right at you and declared in a ringing voice, 'I see with you a tall dark man...' or 'Standing behind you, dear, with his hand on your shoulder...'

Still, fainthearts were outnumbered heavily by those who simply gloried in being accompanied by the tall dark man, etcetera. Indeed, there was sometimes keen competition to be on the spot. I have known the time when two or even three would claim to recognise the tall dark man, etcetera, and considerable huffiness might result. The medium at this point had to make a friend for life, at the somewhat extravagant cost of losing two, by defining the visited one more precisely. 'Ze gentleman third from the left,' or 'Dat's de friend I'se talking to, folks —de nice kind-looking friend wiz de goitre.'

Some mediums were dab hands at describing the lineaments of the visitor from another world, some were less skilled; as in literature. Some, confronted with dubiety, switched from description of the face and figure to a recital of sympathetic ailments. 'I get a condition of . . . H'm. Don't rush me. O what a pain I get here' (clapping a hand to the affected part). 'I get a condition of—what is it?—*heartburn*. Does heartburn mean anything to you, friend?'

It usually did. There was rarely any unbecoming reluctance to recognise the visitant—usually a departed member of the family circle, but sometimes, though more rarely, a phantom from a different earthly situation who, presumably, had no relations of his own to haunt, or possibly did not care for them very much.

Generally speaking it was considered rather bad form to refuse to recognise the dear departed. But there were sometimes one or two perverse souls who held up the proceedings by what we frankly considered an unbecoming reluctance to clinch the deal and get on to the message. The message was the pay-off. For, after all, though it must be comforting to know that your every movement is under the unflinching scrutiny of one or more revenants, it is difficult not to feel that they are wasting their time unless they can use their powers to pass on a few tips for the future—preferably the immediate and highly mundane future.

There were three basic messages. The first and least exciting simply told the flattered recipient that Uncle Ern was with him and everything in the spirit world was just fine. More to the point was the message which added some modest tidings of trifling good fortune in the not-too-closely-specified future. But the message which really hit the charts was the message that prophesied woe, dire and inescapable.

Strangely enough, this third message was popular with everybody—the recipient as well as the audience. It really set 'em up. Perhaps the reason is deeply buried in the quicksands of human nature. Perhaps it is simply that we would rather know the worst; that we prefer the precision of categorically foretold misfortune to the vague brooding sentience of misfortune which informs so many lives. Actual misfortune is news, it enlists sympathy; is therefore preferable to the plain absence of good fortune, which is commonplace. Is that it? I do not claim to know. But I do know that specific predictions of calamity were immensely popular and did a medium's rating no end of good.

Love and health were, needless to say, the most popular subjects for prediction. I heard more than one plain party (and the standard of beauty among us was not high) fervently advised to take great care when in the company of good-looking men. How they bridled and simpered! How lovely it was to see some deeply unattractive old bag virtually renewed and fulfilled, as much as she ever would be, by being warned of predators lurking in wait to deflower her virtue. I have known women stay indoors, for days, at the cost of no small inconvenience (to others as well as themselves) sooner than venture to the shops after receiving a message that 'next week is dangerous for you, dear. I have to tell you to avoid crowds'. Not everyone possessed the natural scepticism, or perhaps it was plain irresponsibility, which buoyed me up when my mother was assured that I should fail every examination for which I sat. Mother believed them all. If the spirit friends said I was going to fail, I could not possibly pass. I did pass, in fact; I scraped through the lot of them: the 'eleven plus' (not that we called it that, in those days), School Certificate, which we now call O Levels, Higher School Cert., which we now call A levels, the university scholarship examination, Moderations, and Final Schools. I somehow got through them all, but in the teeth of categorical predictions to the contrary, from a flatteringly wide and unanimous variety of spirit friends. After each modest success on my part, which was also a failure on their part, a discreet silence reigned for a little while. But the tension built up again as the next hurdle approached. Boys less well fitted by natural irresponsibility to ride out these howling storms of doubt might conceivably have suffered some mental discomfort. Since I did not give a damn, one way or another, and on the whole rather hoped to fail, so that I could get out and get on with the life I much preferred to any academic career, I was unmoved. I may even have tried a bit harder than I had intended to try.

But the injuries suffered by the impressionable were doubtless severe. For some helpless souls, the whole of life was coloured by messages given and *not* given. Some modified their lives quite drastically in response to promptings from the spirit world; others modified other people's lives instead, as my mother would have modified mine. But if all this seems a shade irrational, there must be set against it the joy of those who to their own satisfaction re-established contact with those of whom we sang, who had been 'loved long since, and lost awhile'. Some might consider the evidence on which this joy was based to be insufficient. It made no difference, it never does make any difference. The joy was real.

Such, then, was The Orl, a central fact in our lives during the Twenties. It remained a central fact in my parents' lives through the Thirties and Forties and Fifties, too, but I quit when I began to grow up. Later on they built a fine new church, with an organ costing eleven hundred pounds, and The Orl was abandoned and perhaps forgotten. A sort of respectability began to grow around the cult—possibly a sign that the rational basis of life was being even further eroded. But during the Twenties, the years of The Orl, we throve on suspicion. We were considered a bit cranky, even by the standards of the district, and knew it. We resented it, yet found it thrilling. This is how oppressed minorities feel: resentful yet somehow thrilled. We knew they envied us our spooks. They envied us our direct and manageable contact with the uneasy dead. So we convinced ourselves, and possibly there was some basis for the conviction.

All this time we were furiously active in the spiritualist movement in its wider aspects. My father held some sort of honorific appointment in the wider Midland area; the net was cast wide. We were always on the trot to far-flung spiritualist churches, and mediums from far afield were always coming to stay with us at The Oaks. We ate it and drank it, breathed it and slept it. It was our hobby, our faith, our obsession. I am speaking of my parents, of course. My sisters tended to follow them closely. I accepted it all as normal and natural while a boy. Indeed, I'm by no means absolutely sure that there isn't 'something in it', but what there is in it, I don't care to find out, until I have to. At the time I let it swirl over and around me: it was our natural and native air.

We had a 'home circle' at The Oaks every Thursday night. The small group of faithful friends sat in a darkened front room, around a card table, which told them this and that, often something to my disadvantage, it seemed. There were certain treasured props: an aluminium trumpet, which floated around, I gathered, and occasionally gave voice; a small harp, which also levitated and occasionally was sounded by ghostly fingers. It must have been exciting, sitting there in the dark, summoning up the dead. I was not allowed to take part, being too young, and flighty. My elder sister (seven years my senior) joined in due course. It was a small select circle, of which my father was the medium; but I fancy it was my mother who was the powerhouse of faith. The two or three close friends who 'sat' in the Thursday circle were also pretty full of faith, though.

The slightly smaller of our two front parlours, which was reserved for the Thursday circle, tended to retain a touch of the numinous quality, for us nippers. I don't say we were actually afraid to go in, by any means, but after all, it was *there* that the trumpet floated and spoke, etc. But we were throughout encouraged not to be nervous of 'the friends', and I really don't think we *were* very nervous of them. 'The friends only want you to know they're looking after you'—standard reassurance when any of us complained of rappings, picture-twitching, creaks and knocks, during our parents' frequent absences at The Orl, on long winter evenings. None of us was 'psychic', except dad, or it might have been worse. I suppose I absolutely *believed*, up to the age of about twelve; did not really wholly believe, but kept it dark, from twelve to, say, fifteen; thereafter disbelieved openly. But disbelief even when avowed was never allowed to mess up the harmony of the family, which was considerable. We got on well, with a useful working mixture of affection, diplomacy, and hypocrisy. The fact that we were spiritualists, marked men, members of a semi-secret society, a persecuted (or at least despised) minority, gave a curious flavour to our life together at The Oaks, in the rocky Twenties.

Chapter Five

When you were fishing the Broad Lane cut you sometimes saw colliers on their way home, half-way through the afternoon. But you couldn't tell one from the other till they spoke. Their faces were black with coal dust, their eyeballs staring white, their 'nigger' lips strangely pink. These were men whose wives had got them up in the middle of the night, to set them on their way with a packet of snap and a bottle of tea. Some walked or cycled several miles to the pit, worked a full shift for about ten shillings, and walked or cycled back. All on a bit of bread and bacon, or bread and cheese. They were the most stoical, cheerful, splendid of men. The deal they got from life was absolutely rotten, but they reserved their bitterness for the bosses, the coal owners. There was nothing they would not do for one another, or for us kids. Most of them were keen fishermen, or pigeon fanciers, or whippet breeders, or ferret men, or gardeners. Cooped up down the pit all day, it was as if they were ravenous for the open air and its immemorial pursuits. Flaked and famished as they were, one or two would usually pause on the bridge.

'Worroh, then. Copped owt?'

'Ar. Got three roach.'

'Giz a couple for bait then, kid. Oi'll 'ave a goo at a poike, when Oi've 'ad me tea.'

There was Pratts Bridge cut, Little Bloxwich cut, Broad Lane cut, Stafford Road cut, Fishley cut, Long Lane cut, and Sneyd Lane cut. At times we fished them all, but Broad Lane and Long Lane cuts were the nearest and most favoured. Actually it was all the same canal system, but local patriotism lent special virtues to this or that stretch. Access went by bridges.

Practically the whole mileage of these canals has been filled in now, more's the pity. In my day they were just beginning to slide into obsolescence. There was a little occasional traffic of long boats, but so rarely that weed growth was abundant and fishing at its best. During the bad days, perhaps in 1926, I saw two men towing an empty barge on the canal. Two men doing the work of a horse. They were half starved before they started. About the same time I saw a man on the top deck of a tram going to Walsall who took a snap packet out of his pocket, unwrapped the newspaper, and began ravenously to eat—two rounds of dry bread. One day mother sent me out to sell tickets for a Grand Concert in aid of some good cause. They were Ninepence and One-and-Six. With a child's sublimely tactless effrontery, I knocked at the first door I came to, on the Sandbank—a blackened redbrick cottage where one of my schoolfellows lived. His father came to the door. I cried my wares, winningly as I thought. The man looked at the tickets and then he looked at me. His face worked a bit, and he handed them back.

'Eighteenpence,' he murmured. 'If I'd got eighteenpence I'd be able to get summat t'eat for the missis, lad. No, lad, we've got sickness here.' And he closed the door. I went straight back home and threw the tickets on the kitchen table, utterly ashamed. Mother told me not to be silly. I should have had more sense than to start on the Sandbank. Why didn't I try down Stafford Road, where the money was? But that threw me into a fury. 'If they can afford eighteenpence for a ticket for a concert, they can afford to share with poor people.' It was no good arguing. Dad comforted me. 'Your feelings do you credit, lad. But if all the money in the world was shared out equally today, tomorrow there'd be rich and poor again just the same.' This was the first time I heard that, though not, of course, the last. Dad was sympathetic to the point of being tender-hearted; later he served for years and years, selflessly, as a socialist councillor. But from his lips I first heard that catch-phrase, so true, of course, so obvious and undeniable; but used by so many to excuse their hardness of heart. In a queer way it *did* comfort me. It took me aback. It burst in my consciousness like a bomb. Weary old cliché as it is, I was hearing it for the first time, and from my number one man, he who knew everything and could do no wrong. It must be true.

So if that was the case, who was to blame for the wretchedness of the poor? Look which way you like, you always came back to the same point. God was to blame. 'Bugger you, God,' I muttered, walking round and round the tall wigwams of planks in the builder's yard. Then I was frightened. I hopped over the wall and ran down to Jim's. He was cleaning the family's boots. I told him in a whisper what I had said about God, *to* God. Jim was appalled. 'God almighty,' he whispered back, 'yo'll cop it.' 'What can I do?' I begged. Jim couldn't think what.

He was so shaken he didn't want to be seen near me. I got the drift of this unease. Jim thought if God saw him hobnobbing with me, Jim might cop it too. I left him and trotted home. The mission bell was ringing, bong bong bong. I was half afraid to pass the little redbrick mission. I thought God would be waiting for me there, at least He'd see me slinking past. I swerved to go down Parker Street instead. It would be a long way round but at least I wouldn't have to pass His house, with the door open and Him waiting to watch me go by. Parker Street was quite dangerous. Several local boxers lived there, and about half the boys from Parker Street were going to be boxers when they grew up. Meanwhile they liked to get some practice in on the likes of me, a little boy trotting the long way round. Half-way down Parker Street I began to be more afraid of the boys who were going to be boxers when they grew up than of God. I swerved off to the left and crossed the bit of waste between Parker Street and the Sandbank. It was rough going and I caught my foot in a tumpy hole and came down, spraining my ankle. It was agony. I limped home in black despair, convinced that God had punished me. But when I had my ankle soaking in a bowl of warm water and being strapped up, suddenly I felt pleased. Maybe this was God's way of squaring it. I'd had my go, He'd had his go: fair do's.

I was in bed when it suddenly struck me that the man who couldn't afford eighteenpence for food for his sick wife *still* couldn't. All this evening of black blasphemy and agony of spirit and the final squaring-up between me and God had made no difference to *his* situation. It had all been wasted. What could I do to help him? Direct practical help was what he and his family needed. Our family were holding a circle downstairs. I crept down and got into the pantry. What would he like most for his sick wife to eat? I couldn't see anything very interesting. I wasn't sure what a sick wife needed most. What *I* liked best, of the food I could see, was red pickled cabbage. Mother put down gallons of it, every year. I took a stone jar and slipped out quietly. It was dark now. I limped up the Sandbank with the jar and put it down on the step of the man's house. It seemed in darkness. I gave the door a good rattle and hurried away home. I got back in all right. The pickle wasn't missed for weeks, we made so much. I never heard any more about it, from any source.

Mother pickled red cabbage, shallots, and cauliflower. She made cake including of course the Christmas cake, and her own puddings including of course the Christmas pudding, and she could bake bread though she didn't, except once in a blue moon. She also put down eggs in water-glass; a great stone or earthenware bowl of them, hundreds at a time.

Sometimes we had to go down into the cellar, which was pretty eerie, to turn them, and of course to fetch them up. Mother kept fowl right up until she grew old. We always grew our own vegetables. Father was too busy to be a good gardener but he knew about gardening, and there was always a man only too willing to earn a few shillings by doing the hard work in the garden. For some years we more or less kept a handy-man named Edgar who was really a bit too thick to hold a real job. He did odd jobs for mother and killed a fowl or two when she needed them for dinner. I used to help him. He had a rather slow way of killing a fowl by bleeding it. I was uneasy about it, but it was said to make them better eating, with whiter flesh. When the fowl was dead either Edgar or I would pluck it, sometimes we plucked one apiece, sitting with a galvanised iron bath between our knees, in the outhouse next to the back kitchen. Then we would draw it. Mother had shown me how to draw a chicken, shoving your bare hand up its behind and dragging the innards out, then sorting out what was good of the giblets for making gravy. I was quite competent and not often nauseated, though the smell was strong. There are quite a few things I could do then a sight better than I can do them now. Not that I'm keen to do them now.

All the merriment, gaiety, love and faith, the fun and games and the staunch family feeling, were mixed up with daily intimations of the fearful inequality and uncertainty of life, its cruelty and caprice.

Walking home from up The Street one afternoon I came across a big boy lying on the pavement between the Spotted Cow and the Turf Tavern, not far from The Orl. It was a wide pavement here, half its width packed dirt, half tarmac. This big boy, he was a big boy to me, by which I mean he would be thirteen or even nearly fourteen, and wore long trousers, was lying stretched out on the pavement and weeping bitterly. He did not bear any marks of violence so far as I could see. He was just lying there, rolling a bit, and crying, with his eyes shut tight. His face was wet with tears and his sobs I thought would never cease. I suppose they must have ceased, some time. I looked down at him for a minute, but what could a little boy do for a big boy lying there weeping his heart out? I had never seen a big boy cry before. He wore hobnailed boots and his trousers didn't come much more than half-way down his calves. His coat was rough. He had fair hair and needed a haircut. I hurried away, stricken to the heart. I know no more about this boy than I have told you. I never saw him again. I never forgot him. God let it happen, that was all I knew.

When you needed a haircut you were sent to have Old Hall's tuppenny. There were two barbers in the village, one at each end. Old

Hall had a little house in a terrace in Wolverhampton Road, next door or near enough to Percy Lawrence's, the cycle and motor place. A shave was twopence, a haircut fourpence; half-price for lads under fourteen. But few lads patronised Old Hall. If you were poor enough to feel the loss of twopence, you sought out somebody in your road—there was always somebody—who would crop your head by putting a basin on it and cutting round. No basin would fit my head. The regulation haircut was a Prussian tonsure; you emerged virtually bald, with a forelock.

I had a rather tender scalp for years, and this for an unusual reason. I was born with fair hair. Some said fur hur, some said fair 'air. It was a brace of words that seemed to give trouble. When I was about five, and we were living at the farm, messing about in pig-styes and hovels, I caught ringworm. There was a lot of it about. Mother, who always had her own ideas about medical treatment, poured a bottle of iodine over the raw scabs that covered my skull. I fainted with the pain. That was the end of my fur hur. It grew again, abundantly, as if fertilised by the iodine treatment, but it grew dark brown. The scalp remained unusually tender for years.

It took a lot of knocks. One day in the playground a big boy was swinging a little boy round, not to hurt the little boy, who was enjoying it, but to show his strength. The little boy's hobnailed boots were whizzing round several feet off the ground. I had to get too nosey, of course, and in fact I got so near that the whizzing hobnail boots opened up a real nice cut in my scalp. I have the scar to this day. It wasn't the only time I was kicked on the head, by a long shot, but it was the only time I was kicked on the head while standing up.

At Old Hall's you had to kneel upright on one of his hard wooden chairs. There I picked up a distaste for having my hair cut which has lasted to this day. It's a wonder that's all I picked up; the place was not over-clean. But there was a certain amount of indiscreet talk, which was well worth overhearing, about pay rates and pregnancies, pigeons and whippets and fishing. It was while waiting in Old Hall's that I learned how to breed my own maggots.

I know now that you can go fishing quite cheerfully with a bit of bread for bait, but in those days, and indeed for years to come, I suffered from the common fisherman's delusion that my lack of success, or other people's abundant success, or both, was solely due to their owning the secret of some special lure, denied to me. The most desirable bait was maggots; what in the south are known, gently, as gentles. Although in fact our worms and breadpaste and elderberries and stewed wheat were splendid baits, we tended to regard people who had maggots as taking an almost unfair advantage of us. How could you come by maggots? Nowadays they are sold, indeed manufactured on a vast commercial scale; not then, or not in Bloxwich, at any rate. Now in Old Hall's a collier told me how to go about it.

'Yo gerra fish as yo doh wanta eat, see,' he said. 'A roach or a gudgeon'll do. Then yo put it in a cardboard box and bury it in the gardin. About six inches down'll do. Leave it a wik, mebbe a couple o' wik—depends on the weather, see. Yo'll find it'll tern. Oh, I was forgerrin—yo want ter 'ang it a day before yo bury it—let the flies gerratit. But keep yer eye on it—if yo leave it too long, the maggots'll escape.'

Thus I became a private maggot breeder. The family did not take it any too well. I was keen, but careless; sometimes the little fish was left in the sun, on the outhouse window sill, a little too long for their comfort; once or twice my little cardboard coffins were dug up before their time, by the dogs, or even by mother, who did not much like having a maggot-breeding roach buried lightly among the Sweet Williams. But by and large I bred some fine maggots. My fishing did not improve, though: I did much about the same as before. Even so, I acquired a little prestige among my fishing friends.

Joe Harper taught me to mix custard powder in my breadpaste. The maggots were not the end of credulity; for many years after Joe swore me to secrecy about the custard powder I believed as an article of faith that it was *the* special ingredient which turned an ordinary angler into a sort of magician, a Merlin of the reeds. Joe was a spiritualist; that is how we came to know him. He was also a checkweighman at the pit, like Uncle Tom Westwood. Checkweighmen, as the name indicates, were models of sobriety, responsibility, and judgment, respected and trusted by both management and their fellow colliers. I knew several; indeed, my maternal grandfather had been one, before he became a manager. They represented the very best of the Victorian ideal of the working man devoted to self-improvement. They were the men the Institutes were built for, and the public libraries. They were upright and thrifty. They took extra responsibility—N.C.O.s of the industry—and thereby earned an extra few shillings. They worked shoulder to shoulder with the working miners, but aspired to a quality of life a little higher than the bleak terraces provided. There was no question of being 'traitors to their class', but they accepted that a man could haul himself up by his own bootlaces, and that he had a responsibility to do so. They were pillars of the chapels and the temperance movement.

Dad built a bungalow for Joe, in Long Lane, Essington. It was a rare miner indeed who could afford to build his own home. Joe's thrift was a way of life, and his buxom wife did some small jobs, I forget what. The bungalow was a pretty irreducibly economical affair of pale red brick, but set in a whole acre of vegetable garden: land was cheap. I suppose the whole establishment, land included, cost about £300 to £400, at the very most. I remember being there with dad the day it was finished and handed over. We all stood in the middle of the lane looking at it.

'Well, there you are, then, Joe', dad said. 'An Englishman's home is his castle.'

'Why, so it *is*, Sam,' Joe said. Perhaps, like me, he had not heard the phrase before. It struck me as wonderfully romantic, and The Oaks immediately became a sort of moated keep. When we got home, after brooding all the way back in the Tin Lizzie on this stroke of luck that had made me custodian of a keep, out of the blue, I went across to the joiner's shop and had a word with Fred Southey. Fred was in charge of the machines downstairs, the big circular saw, the bandsaw and planing machine. The old-style carpenters worked upstairs with hand tools, in a traditional way, at long benches with shavings up to their ankles. They made the window frames, doors and door frames, staircases, and so on, for the houses which dad built, at a price that did not always allow much of a profit, if any. Times were dicey. True, houses were much in demand, but there wasn't much money about, or so I was always hearing, and I dare say my father was not really a good business man. In fact I'm sure he wasn't. Like me, he got on fine with people he liked, but lacked the robust commonsense which overrides sensibility and allows you to make a go of working with people you cannot stand. He had the gift of leadership, without a doubt, and thoroughly enjoyed using it. He could impart enthusiasm. He had drive and he worked hard. He was several sorts of idealist. But when it came down to managing men who possibly lacked all those qualities, and to costing a house for people whom he knew or suspected couldn't really afford it, I'm afraid he made allowances which endeared him to many, but put no money in the bank. He wasn't such a fool in money matters as I turned out to be, but he was much too nice a man to get rich.

Fred Southey was a dashing ex-soldier whom I privately thought to be the handsomest man I had seen. He had those clear blue eyes, fur hur, open countenance and fine strong jaw—all those details of physiognomy, in fact, which I lacked and admired. I'm afraid I was a burden to him. For one thing, I insisted on being allowed to 'help' start up the gas engine which powered the machines, and I liked to be in charge of the oilcan, too. Fred was visibly relieved when dad listened to his exhortations, tore out the obsolete gas engine, and went over to an electric motor. I was not just disappointed, I was grieved. What glamour was there in a goddam electric motor, of which you could see no moving parts? However, the grief was soon assuaged. It dawned on us that even little boys, if they had nerve enough, could start an electric motor simply by throwing a switch—whereas starting a gas engine was physically beyond us, apart from the telltale noise it made. Thereafter on Sunday evenings when the family were safely at the Orl we often had all the machines going—circular saw and all—and did considerable damage in the course of providing my little friends' homes with various much-needed items, such as dog kennels, chicken coops, even the odd door, cradle, and chair. Perhaps this was an unsuspected factor in dad's economic difficulties?

Anyway, the long-suffering Fred at my instigation drew a shield and cut it out on the bandsaw, from a lovely thick piece of oak, and on the front he painted a black Maltese cross, which I adopted as my knightly symbol. With a wooden sword of which the point had been charred to give it extra hardness, I was fully equipped to hold the keep. Fully except in terms of actual physical strength, that is. I grew up a thin and puny boy, always sickly. My heart was sound, but there was something not quite right with my stomach. I had a bilious turn at least once a week, if not oftener; was prone to stomach-ache, sickness, nausea; could not digest my food properly; and loved all the acidulous things which did me most harm. I grew up flat-chested, undeveloped, spindly. Eventually my legs and stomach developed reasonably fair muscles— with all the cycling and running about I did, they had to—but the torso and arms remained pretty puny. I had little or no strength to outgrow and was always outgrowing what I had. I tired easily. When at length I was involved in a second war against the Germans—an event which I had felt coming, inevitably, from infancy, when those soldiers on leave from Flanders visited us and I was threatened with 'the Germans'—I worked like a slave, led a strenuous physical life, survived five and a quarter years in the ranks: and still didn't develop much muscle. But I had grown quite wiry, and although still lacking in actual muscular power, could do quite surprising things, in the lifting and humping line, by virtue of sheer nervous energy. Well, what a bore people's ailments are. None of this deterred me from living as physical a life as could be. Though a great reader and a full romantic, I saw life in terms of physical happenings—coloured, of course, by emotional values. I suppose I still do, though now the emotional values are pretty well flattened out. I never really knew what intellectual life meant. Clever as quicksilver, precocious with words and images, a bright little scholar, as they said, who found it easy to learn anything interesting, I yet had no notion what the thinking life meant. I could work things out. I was inventive. But the little brain only worked when it was presented with a problem. The moment the problem was solved, the brain signed off, clocked out. I was a dreamer, an unregenerate day-dreamer. I suppose I still am. I hate using the loaf, and never think a thought unless compelled by stark necessity. Thinking is real hard work.

The knightly shield was much envied, despised, and resented by little lads who didn't happen to own one. The first foray I made armed with my new shield and sword led to actual bloodshed. I should say that other boys also had wooden swords; it was my shield which triggered off those nasty feelings. Later on, the bandsaw was pressed into use, illicitly, to cut out several more shields. Several boys came within an ace of losing a finger or two, in doing so. One strong lad tried to smash my shield over my head, but it was far too robust. I had caught him a shrewd one in the earhole with the point of my sword.

I suppose the shield was used for carrying home fish and chips, as much as anything. Just across the road from The Oaks there was a little blackened terrace of workers' houses, of which two were shops. One was the fish shop, run by Jack Smith. There were six fish and chip shops in Bloxwich, but we counted it a great good fortune to live so near one. Jack's vats were heated by coal, or rather by slack (sleck). He had a little iron door which he would open to rake up the fire and throw a couple of shovelfuls of sleck on. I frequently assisted him at this, which had something in common, one felt, with being a fireman on a railway engine, or a stoker in a ship. At that time you could get a ha'porth of chips, though during our residence at The Oaks a penny-worth became the standard minimum helping. I had one of my heart-broken goes through this. Two little lads came in while I was waiting for a fish to be fried and asked for a ha'porth of chips.

'Sorry, lad, we don't mek 'a'porths no mower.'

'Yo doh mek 'em?'

'No, lad. Tell your mom we car mek 'a'porths no mower. It's gorra be a pennuth now, see?'

The two little lads obviously had only a halfpenny between them. It seemed like the end of the world. Their eyes grew round with wonder and dismay. They shuffled off without a word. What was there to say? The rising cost of living had caught up with them. The uses of a ha'penny had been drastically reduced, within their experience. It might still buy a paper screw of khali (sherbet sucker) at Jack Keay's, but it would no longer buy a little paper of chips.

I felt outraged and sickened and thrown clear out of kilter on their behalf. I didn't blame Jack Smith, who hated the moment himself; I didn't blame their parents who could only give them a halfpenny; I didn't know enough to blame the bloody war profiteers, the hard-faced bastards in London and elsewhere. I just blamed God. Once again I had been vouchsafed an insight into the total injustice and unreasonableness of economic life. I was never going to get on top of this. There was nothing in this world I liked much more than chips, and the thought that two little lads could no longer have a taste for their supper because poor Jack Smith could no longer afford to 'make' a ha'porth depressed me like a sudden sick headache of a bilious qualm.

However, some of the happiest hours of my life were spent in Jack Smith's. He let me stoke the fire now and then, and use the giant salt and vinegar shakers on my own purchases. While we were little it was possible to buy a penny fish, admittedly a pretty small sliver, but wrapped in a lovely crisp envelope of batter. The twopenny fish was standard, the threepenny fish considered rather ostentatious, or gluttonous. Hake and plaice were the standard fish, though I fancy some of the 'plaice' were dabs and some of the 'hake' was cod. Occasionally, if I had peeled a bucket of potatoes, Jack allowed me to use the chipper, though he was always nervous that I might include a finger or two in the bucket of chips. It was deeply satisfying to put a big spud on the grid and bring the lever down, bash, creating those chip-shaped pieces which made the potato so much more thrilling than in any other form. I was too small and puny to use it properly, though. But I sometimes dipped the fillets in the enamelled bucket of batter when Jack was pushed, and tossed them into the bubbling, seething hot fat. This was very nearly as satisfactory as tossing lumps of iron into the cupola of the foundry. You felt you were really assisting at production, part of the merry and strenuous creative world. Foundry and fish shop were two of the nodal high points of my young life, which revolved around fish and fire.

Nearly next door, just across Broad Lane from The Oaks, Jack Keay the part-time postman ran a general shop. I shall never forget the smell of it as long as I live. He sold sweets, cigarettes, tobacco, sausages, groceries, some cuts of meat especially pork, a little hardware, boot laces, brushes, paraffin, vinegar, bread, milk, string, and stamps. It was in Jack Keay's that I first made the acquaintance of the toffee hammer and the twist slicer. Most toffee was locally made slab, poured into a tin tray and broken out by a little bright iron hammer, utterly fascinating. Thick and thin twist, which I often fetched for my father's workmen, was pulled off a lovely rich dark coil, like odorous rope, and laid on the thick little board of the slicer. Down came the blade, which was pivoted at one end, *thwack* through the tobacco on to the board. Half an ounce of thick or thin twist cost threepence-ha'penny in my day as an errand boy. It was not necessarily the cheapest tobacco, but it was by far the most manly.

I never managed to smoke twist, though I wanted to. One whiff and I was queasy. But it was an understood thing that men smoked. Tobacco was firmly established as one of life's manly pleasures, though alcohol was not. We were teetotallers still, and virtually our only drink was tea.

Chapter Six

The stubble glittered under a pearly sky. It was a treat to walk over it, walking free where not long ago the corn had swayed and no man dared to walk. It crunched and crackled under our hobnailed boots. We reached the boundary of the wood and entered its density. In the cool dimmity of the wood life was different. Robin Hood and Red Indians, Alfred and Hereward the Wake were our exemplars; we wished to live as we imagined they had lived, free from town law, town ways. We had a hide in this wood. It belonged to the Old Squire, a man unimaginably remote and aristocratic, a survivor from feudal times. He was no nearer to our daily lives than the Bishop of Lichfield; not a lot nearer than the Pope of Rome. In a vague unformulated way, we realised even then that he was an anachronism, in this land of factories and mines and trams. He lived on the fringe. In a literal sense, his domain lay outside our lives. And his whole life was centrifugal, flying away on the rim of what we knew to be real life. Yet magical, ever luring, was the land in which his estate lay, on one side contiguous with the Black Country, on the other marching with the wild free uplands, the wooded common lands where all could roam, of Cannock Chase.

The whole quality and feel of life was different within the dark wood. Where we were trespassers. The Old Squire kept game and a gamekeeper; occasionally the scarlet of the hunt flashed across those sloping fields, the baying and the bray floated incredible in the incredulous air. But it was unfashionable country; such things were rare. Mostly we poached for smaller game, rabbits, pigeons, and hares. Poor men with ferrets and snares entered the domain, stealthily; poor men with whippets walked airily, armoured in nonchalance, along its borders. We little 'uns armed with insolence, bows and arrows, and catapults, did little damage to the game, great or small. What we really sought was sanctuary, from the workaday world and its finite propositions. We eluded the keeper simply because he was there to be eluded, and eluding him was a game. We had no vainglorious designs on his game, though an occasional pheasant came down to our weapons and into the pot. But it was the hide we gloried in, the little shack made roughly of branches covered with bracken. There we snuggled down, to smoke and plot. Once we set fire to his bracken, and fled, aghast at our crime. But the fire went out.

The Little Brook ran through the Old Squire's domain and out and under the lane through an iron pipe. A boy could hide in the pipe and with weird magnified noises astound passers-by, who were few. Once Uncle Joe Simpson Hall took off his shoes and socks and crept right through the pipe from one end to the other, for a dare. He was one of the great men of my childhood. He was a Wesleyan minister of the finest kind. He had come out 'top of all England' in his theological college; I believe it was at Durham, or thereabouts. He had a fine mane of black hair, a noble forehead, twinkling eyes. He had a huge appetite for life, and the wonderful gift of connecting life with literature. In one sense I owe almost everything to him. At the very least, he confirmed me and fortified me in a natural bent—this bent for taking literature literally, connecting it with life. He was a romantic, I suppose. His appetite for literature was as enormous as his appetite for life: with Simpson, the two became one thing, a communicable fervour and glory.

He was a great reciter, easily our greatest in a circle very much given to reciting. Hardly a day went by—sometimes I am inclined to say not a day went by, but there must have been bad days, blanks—when one or other of us did not stand up and let it rip. We sang together and singly, and we recited together and singly. We had not discovered John Donne, or the Metaphysicals, but, those apart, anybody up to and including the Great War, we knew him and we read him and we recited him. But Uncle Sim knew more than anybody else and recited far better. He was an actor, of course. His pulpit manner was extra-ordinarily fine. His view of Christianity was certainly romantic. He gloried in the struggle. Naturally he disapproved of our spiritualism, but we never let doctrinal differences come between us. Fiercely the arguments flowed and ebbed, but neither party ever intended that theological differences should divide friends. We agreed to differ. Great the days when Simpson stood with his back to the fire, at The Oaks, letting rip with the *Lays of Ancient Rome*, Whitman, Whittier, Emerson, *Hiawatha*, Tennyson, Shelley, even Milton. Milton was a sore point; universally recognised as great, but privately considered incomprehensible and dull. Difficult, that is, to recite. With the publication of the English Association's series of 'Poems of Today' we came up to date with a bang, loving equally the great war poets—

Siegfried Sassoon, Wilfrid Owen, Edmund Thomas—and the romantic Georgians like De La Mare, who simply hypnotised us. But by and large, we were Tennysonians: he made us dilate, weep, quiver. When I got to Oxford I was astounded to hear a don say that he thought Tennyson had been wrongly discredited and was due for a revival. No-one had ever discredited him in my hearing; to me he was still going strong as the chief poet. Much of this was due to Uncle Joe Simpson Hall.

But Oxford, even the dream of Oxford, was infinitely distant when Simpson became an honorary uncle—we had quite a few of those—through his remarkable runaway marriage with our cousin Beattie Smith, eldest of the Smith girls, whose mother was my mother's eldest sister, Ginny, and whose father was the earthbound miner, Uncle George of the buckled belt and clay pipe and pint of beer. These Smith girls contributed much of the élan and vitality to our days: they were in a manner of speaking our antennae stretched out tremblingly towards the outer world of materialistic fun. I'm sure it was through the Smith family, and perhaps especially through the Smith girls, that I became very early and vaguely and excitingly aware of another sort of world beyond our domestic horizon, beyond the secure serenity of our particular family circle, with its inbuilt guarantees and acceptances—religion, literature, learning, sobriety, a calm and contented respectability, a curious and paradoxical sort of gregarious seclusion.

The Smiths, let me say at once, were just as respectable as the Wiggins. No breath of scandal ever touched them. They were honesty incarnate, hard-working, utterly decent, exceptionally intelligent. But there was this big difference between the ethos of their household and ours. Many of them went to chapel, just as we did; but somehow they seemed to be reaching out to a livelier life, they simmered and seethed, they brought back rumours of an outer world—a world of action, gay and unpredictable, limitless and dangerous, above all dangerous—which was so different from the fundamentally staid atmosphere which my parents had created for us, in our little hermetically sealed enclave or cocoon where everything was said to be under control.

'Our Sam, have you been fighting again in your dad's best shirt?'

Believe it or not, that was one of the formative phrases of my childhood. No, it wasn't addressed to me. Aunt Ginny said it to my cousin Sam Smith. 'The boys' were washing, sprucing up for the evening out— Oh, the so mysterious, unknown, unimaginable and infinitely alluring evening out. The ablutions of the entire family took place, of necessity, in the 'back kitchen', where the amenities consisted of a cold water tap over a sink, a kettle on the stove. There the boys and girls, taking it turn and turn about, prinked up for the big moment of the day's exhausting twenty-four hours—going out. Sam's shirt, or presumably Uncle George's best, was seen to be bloodstained. Hence Aunt Ginny's reproach. It conveyed a lot of new information, some of it still highly speculative, to my little mind. That a young man, no longer a boy, should fight, like a boy. That in some families a young man should wear his father's shirt. It hinted at modes of living quite beyond our ken, adventures and shifts we never discussed. It was one of a good few phrases on which I eavesdropped during childhood which sowed in my mind exciting, disturbing seeds of doubt. By the time I was twelve (at which late age, by the way, I first learned the facts of sexual reproduction) I had acquired a goodly stock of reasons, satisfactory to me, at any rate, for doubting if things were ever just what they seemed. Not that I really minded if they weren't. I enjoyed a bit of mystery.

From two of the Smith boys, George and Sam, I learned the very lineaments of manliness. George was really old enough to be an uncle. He had fought in the Great War. We were never intimate, the age-gap being what it was, but I sat at his feet when I could, hearing about fighting and motorbikes, war and peace. Sam was nearer my own age, though still so much senior that really close companionship was hardly possible. But apart from riding my pony Star bareback round the meadow, and driving us to Brewood in the pony and trap, he taught me about horses, and, later, we went for motorbike rides together. Again, the difference in years forbade real close friendship in the intimate boys' sense, but from Sam, as from George, I acquired that certain knowledge, which can never be counterfeited, of what being a man really means, in terms of gallantry and clean-limbed, clearcut acceptance of life's inexorable demands and stresses—a splendid combination of gaiety and stoicism. Both George and Sam worked at the factory.

The Smith girls were as feminine as the Smith boys were masculine. Of course they, too, were so much older than me—their mother was the eldest Miss Haycock, my mother the youngest: at the very least, twenty years between them—that they were almost aunts. But not quite. When I was a little boy I was very sexy. I don't know at all if this was uncommon precocity, but rather doubt it. As I say, I didn't learn the facts of life, in a technical sense, until I was twelve. But femininity always disturbed and affected me, delightfully thrilling: this from the age of five or six. So when the Smith girls came, wafting their perfumes and swinging their skirts, into our sedate and decorous society, I caught a thrilling hint of things improperly understood but plainly of enormous import, possibly of peril, but undoubtedly of delight.

I remember walking home from chapel one Sunday morning with my father and mother, and meeting two or three of the Smith girls walking in Lichfield Road. They were wearing the latest thing in short skirts, and silk stockings. I don't suppose the skirts were really all that short, but everything, thank God, is relative, there are no absolutes except loyalty to your nature and your word. I really do remember a gasp going up. I forget exactly what dad and mother said, though there was certainly some such expression as 'Oh my goodness!' Briefly we dallied while dad and mother gently reproached the girls for being so abandoned, so wanton. Yet I didn't exactly get the impression that dad was utterly sincere. But the short skirts of the Smith girls were a topic of conversation at Sunday dinner that day, and in a way this incident set the tone of our relationship. The girls were often in and out, to discuss their courting problems and matrimonial chances. 'I should hang your hat up for him, dear,' I heard dad say once, to one of them. They brought a sense of frou-frou, of scent and frills and dangerously delightful flashes of silk. I became a mild fetichist about this time, a keen student of underwear advertisements, relatively unmoved, then as now, by the white nude, though later I learned that the honey-coloured, yellow, or brown nude can also be attractive.

The main thing, though, was that these boys and girls, but especially the girls, opened the dark casement one little chink on to the winter evening out. As opposed to the predictable and secure evening at home, of course. 'Something' was going on, out there, in the dark, and the artificial light, away from the security and decorum (and heavenly haven) of home. Boys and girls—young men and young women—went out in the evening, for some utterly thrilling, vaguely disapproved of, yet obviously human and accepted, purpose. One day I was going to find out.

The Smiths did well. None came to grief. They were basically sound as bells, good as gold. But the sensation of Beattie's runaway marriage to the Rev. Joe Simpson Hall rocked the village, split families, formed camps, created partisans. Alas, I was just too young to get the real drift of it at the time, though of course I was vaguely aware of *something*, and later learned all. Beattie was the eldest Smith girl, and not so very far off as old as my mother. It followed that we treated her as an aunt. She was a high-spirited, high-coloured, raven-haired young woman of keen intelligence and considerable dash.

She had become engaged to Ernest Philpott, a tailor of Bloxwich, whose sister, Edith Philpott, was already our Aunt Edie—she married Noah, the youngest of my father's brothers. The Philpotts were a well-established Bloxwich family of much rectitude, quiet people, who made quite a bit of quiet money, one way and another. Suddenly, out of the blue, one fine Saturday morning, Ernest received his engagement ring back from Beatrice—with the message that she was at that moment being married to the Rev. J. Simpson Hall. As you see, there wasn't really any element of the scandalous in it, but of course it rocked everybody, and 'running away with' a parson, a strange parson unknown to the village, that gave it a rare spice.

Uncle Noah 'took Ernie away', as they said—went away with his brother-in-law and close friend, for a period of recuperation from the shock. My parents were deeply involved, in some way—I don't know if dad was actually best man at the wedding, but he was certainly aiding and abetting in some manner—and Simpson and Beattie became thereafter, and remained, among our closest friends, tied by the bonds of mild complicity as well as natural affection.

They spent long holidays with us, and we spent long and frequent periods with them. Thus I came to know the feel of the manse. I was left at the manse for long periods every summer. The first manse was at Kidsgrove, and while staying here I got the feel of the Potteries, heard about Arnold Bennett, and, gazing on Lake Rudyard, first heard about Kipling from the lips of Uncle Sim. (Kipling never 'took' properly with me, except perhaps as a poet: the jungle stories, Kim, and Stalky, never went home under the skin. India never got home under the skin: all my life I never wanted to see India or Africa, only South America and China, and of course the South Sea islands.)

Uncle Sim rose in his profession, becoming Superintendent of wide circuits. The next manse was on Portland Bill, the next at Penzance, and he ended up at Llandrindod Wells. Portland was a marvellous place for holidays, with fishing in the harbour with a handline from a little boat, alongside the wreck of the battleship which was turned turtle to block the southern entrance to the breakwater, in the Great War. Later, the thrill of climbing the lighthouse steps, looking up the skirts of girls and women going up ahead, and gazing longingly at their silken legs on the putting green of Weymouth. At Penzance the fishing was even better, but by then one was growing up and longing to be off on one's tod.

Beattie and Simpson were staying with us at The Oaks when the affair of The Whistler occurred. Next door to us in Broad Lane, down past the bottom of our plot, lived a tragic figure who had been shell-shocked in the War. His neurosis took a mild and useful form. He was convinced of the extreme perilousness of the crossroads by The Oaks, where the five roads met. God knows it is perilous enough today— they've just erected traffic lights, and now The Oaks has been demolished and a great big garage and filling station stand where we lived, all our history and living wiped away.

But at the time there was little enough traffic, and only one ghastly accident in all our days there. However, this poor man conceived it to be his duty, almost every day, to guide and control the meagre traffic on a voluntary basis. Scrupulously turned out, neat as a new pin in a blue serge suit and cap, he marched up in the morning and took up his stance. To control the traffic he used a referee's whistle, doubtless following a pattern he had seen set during his time in France. When Fred Southey made me that shield and sword I trotted out to show them off to him. He was terribly upset, and complained to my father that I shouldn't have dangerous weapons like that. But no-one took him very seriously: he was harmless, and possibly did a bit of good.

But one morning something broke in that poor dear mind. Pursued by his sister, who looked after him, he left their house carrying a double-barrelled shotgun. Perhaps he dropped the gun, perhaps his sister managed to snatch it from him: anyway, she threw it over our garden hedge, and screamed for help. Dad ran out as The Whistler ran round to retrieve his gun. It was breakfast time. I saw dad wrestling with him for the great gun, and fled to the workshop to get help from Fred Southey and the men. Simpson shot out to fetch the police. He began to pound up The Sandbank, but got a lift on a milk float. The milkman whipped his astonished pony to a gallop. Even now the sound of galloping hooves sometimes brings back the stirring picture.

The gun was loaded: Fred showed me the shells. There was a quiet circle of men, standing around, looking all of them very strange, unlike their usual selves. The Whistler was explaining to them, with great amiability and a sort of pedantic precision, how the gun worked. Then the policeman arrived, with Uncle Sim, and took him away. I never saw him again. But I had learned that a mind could take a wound.

Great man as Uncle Simpson was, I could never get him interested in fishing. He followed football, as we all did, but that was the limit of his interest in games and sport. My fishing was done in the company of Joe Harper, who really taught me to fish, and any of a number of miners, who led me on up to pike fishing; or, of course, in the unsatisfactory company of my contemporaries. It was unsatisfactory only because they were heedless lads who didn't much fancy the quiet, brooding stillness which accompanies good fishing. I was a fidgety lad, in a general way, but at this one thing, this absorption called angling, I sloughed off my integument of dancing, twitching, jumping nervousness and became a tingling rock. At this and at this alone I could sit for hours, quiet and absorbed, not exactly relaxed, for I was tensed up for the bite, but totally immersed in the pursuit.

For this reason I was welcome as the fishing companion of grown men, dedicated anglers. I did not know the meaning of disappointment —just to be fishing was enough, and any catch was a bonus—and I lacked the competitive spirit, the mean and envious streak, the tendency to belittle and to boast, which makes the choice of fishing companions so exceptionally hazardous. Later on I acquired two splendid fishing companions of my own age and absorption. With Hardy and Eddie I got farther afield, fished strange waters. But that was in the Grammar School era, when life had changed.

I wasn't a bit keen to go to the Grammar School, though on the other hand I didn't give a tinker's cuss one way or another. There was some talk of awarding me a Scout's uniform if I passed the eleven plus (we didn't actually call it the eleven plus then, but it was the same thing exactly, except that we sat the exam when we were ten) but I didn't know that I particularly wanted a Scout's uniform anyway, so I certainly didn't try hard on that account. The Scouts were all right, but a bit too pure. In those days there was none of this ghastly neurotic excitement about it all: you sat the exam, passed or failed, and that was that. Who cared? Our grammar school was at Walsall: a four hundred year-old foundation of considerable local renown, called Queen Mary's Grammar School. It was definitely all right. It had a terrific record of scholarship successes to the older universities, a distinguished list of Old Boys though I'm damned if I can recall any of them now, except one named Somers (or was it Powys?) who became Lord Chancellor of England. Anyway, it was all right.

It was a day school and you could go as a fee-paying boy—only five guineas a term, isn't it absurd?—and doubtless my parents would have sent me anyway, or at least I think they would, now. But at the time I knew for certain that they wouldn't, for they said so. They were quite emphatic. Pass for a free place, or you don't go at all. Well, who cared? I was totally indifferent. On the appointed day we all trooped up The Street in a crocodile to sit the exam at Elmore Green school: I suppose this was to prevent favouritism or crookery or something. I know the pen I was issued with had a crossed nib. I went out to the invigilator and showed him. He accused me of dropping it on the floor. I denied it, and what's more I was telling the truth.

Anyway, by the time the mean old bugger provided me with a replacement nib, which he did very grudgingly, I didn't have the slightest remaining interest in any aspect whatever of the examination or indeed entire educational system. Not that I'd started out with much. The day wore on, I knocked off the composition and the English paper and the sums—that's really all I remember about it—and thought no more about it. They asked me at home how I thought I had done, and I had to tell them that it was a doddle. For so it was.

The news came in due course that I had passed and dad and mother took me down to Ennals's of Walsall in the Tin Lizzie and bought me the Scout's uniform as promised. They seemed quite bucked up. I was glad to have the lanyard and the clasp knife, but otherwise did not give a monkey's lunch. All school was just something between you and your real life, the adventure of outdoors, the water and the wood, the romance and excitement of the chase, and the loving. I could already read, in fact I loved reading. What else was there to learn from school?

I found out what else when I duly turned up at Moss Close, a huge old house built in a megalomaniac outburst of Victorian Romantic, by some rich burgher, on the outskirts of Walsall (well, it was the outskirts then) where at that time the first year or junior school was housed. I discovered that the outstanding little boy scholar of the Nashnul was just another so-so mediocrity at the grammar school. I still held my own at English, I was a champion speller, I could cope if I chose with history and geography: but what was all this algebra crap? It stunned me. And French—couldn't make head nor tail of it, didn't want to either. Since I couldn't really pronounce my own native tongue, I didn't stand much chance of pronouncing a language where they spelled wazzo oiseau and feeya fille. I promptly opted out of the educational system in a big way. There were some wonderful little boys at the new school—I was instantly lost in the wild marvellous life of friendship—but the masters gave me earache. They were Oxford and Cambridge graduates, almost to a man, and their accents operated on my delicate ear very unfavourably. Poor men, they really did have a bellyful, with some of us, nasty little recalcitrant dissidents. Patiently and diligently they set about, first of all, educating us in the pronunciation of our native tongue. Before every class we had to recite various runes designed to improve our accents.

> O my, cried Dai, I should like to fly, five
> miles high in the icy sky.

> O moi, croid Doi, Oi should loike to floi,
> foive moiles hoi in the oicy skoi.

> Herne the Hunter wound his horn on yonder
> haunted hill.

I could cope with the aitches, and in fact I wasn't at all bad at the 'I' sounds, but the 'u' sounds had me beat. To this day I occasionally get trouble with them, though otherwise my standard English is pretty standard, I think. We had a perfectly shocking little rune which ran like this:

> The brutal butcher crushed the nut
> under his clumsy foot.

This just creased me. All my u's tended to be like the one in brutal. In the effort to distinguish between the light and the heavy u's, I overdid it and got into fearful tangles. I wouldn't, even today, care to have to recite that rune in public. It tends to come out

> The brootal batcher crashed the nat
> oonder his clamsy fat.

because what I *really* want to say, by nature, is

> The brootal bootcher crooshed the noot
> oonder his cloomsy foot.

Talk about U and non-U.

Of course, although that heavenly idiocy had not yet been invented, U and non-U was what it was really all about. I discerned this at an early age. I knew that what it all amounted to, really, was social segregation. O yes, I did. This accents lark gave the show away. I began to nourish a doubt about the purity of people's stated intentions. Did they really and truly care about learning, or did they care still more about accents and other niceties of behaviour? Rightly or wrongly, I decided that it was the latter. I was being got at. That would never do. Of course, I *was* being got at. That's the whole point of education—they get at you in a well-intentioned effort to transform you from a slavering foul-mouthed illiterate little yobbo into a reasonably literate, reasonably articulate young man with decent manners and morals and some slight superficial knowledge of what the world is all about. Of course. I am absolutely all for a bit of education, even a modicum of polish. But the shock of immersion in the icy waters of Moss Close set me back a year or two.

Actually I was quite a nice little boy when I went there, at any rate on the surface, and when I finally emerged from the grammar school I was quite a nice young man, alas and alack. But in between there were painful adjustments to make. That first shock of accents, algebra, and French sent me into my shell for something in the region of three years, if not four. I lingered in the bottom third of the class until I reached the Fifth Form, when I more or less woke up and put away childish things, well, to a certain extent, I've never put them away for good, thank heaven. From fifteen onwards I rose effortlessly to my natural level as a fairly bright average lad again. But the years between were quite horrible in a way.

It must sound silly, in fact it probably is silly, but it really was this business of accent and intonation which threw me. Until I went to the grammar school I had not the faintest notion that there was any other way to speak than the Bloxwich way. Or perhaps that is a shade too simplified. As a comfortably placed Bloxwich boy I knew that there were two ways of speaking, what we might at a later stage have called posh and vulgar. I knew that at home we spoke posh. That is to say, standard English, flavoured a little by native intonation. Really, aside from that u sound trouble, which was mine alone and never affected any other member of my family, we spoke excellent plain standard English slightly inflected, or infected, by Black Country, and our habit of reading, especially of reading aloud, at all times of day and night from all the very best in English literature, plus the pulpit tradition—well, of course, all this maintained our speech in quite good condition. Ah, yes, but there is posh and posh. Our home language was good, accurate enough, intelligible anywhere; but it wasn't posh, it wasn't put on, it wasn't for effect, we didn't adopt it to impress and drop it with relief. In the factory we relaxed a little out of courtesy to our less fortunate friends. That is a literal statement of the truth, not a snide joke. We spoke the dialect as a natural courtesy, when conversing with people who spoke nothing else.

'Worroh, Sam. Gorra minnit?'

'Ar, Jack. 'Ow are yer?'

'Gorra birra 'eadache, but yo mustn't grumble. Ay, Sam, them pidgins. Yo know, wot 'Lijah gimme. One of 'em's a tumbler, did yer know?'

'It ay, is it?'

'It bloody is, mate. Ar rommed it in a pen by its bloody self, but it wo mek anythin'. Think 'e'd tek it back?'

73

'Rom it back in '*is* shed, Jack. Doh yo ave no ankey-panky with it.'

Very nice, too. I regret the passing of the dialect. It coloured communications wonderfully. But you see, here we were already on a double standard of speech, and now these perishing Oxford and Cambridge men, descending from an Olympus unimaginably lofty and remote, wanted me to talk posher than posh, to talk *fancy*. It came hard. I ended up talking quite fancy, but it came over me imperceptibly. And this was the starting point of a certain rampageous intermittent radicality.

Bloxwich was good enough for me. (I knew no better.) If those perishers found something funny in a Bloxwich accent, the worse for them. And since it was those same perishers who inflicted algebra and French on a chap, those subjects were tainted too. How absurd it all was. But there was a little bit of something else, besides. I really did love my rough little mates, and losing their company was a blow from which I never recovered. Ragged, snotty-nosed, and valorous, my little old mates were part of me, part of the ethos in which I had grown up. Nobody was going to make me turn my back on them. (Nobody wanted me to, they said, but I associated one thing with another, in a possibly illogical way.) I liked my new companions very much, but could never desert the old. It did not take long to discern that the motives behind higher education, or some of them, were divisive. You were there to get on. Of course, this was a very congenial target for some. Ghastly little getters-on are born as well as made. I saw no reason for getting on: saw none then, and see none now. I was born contented with my lot. My parents urged me to '*do better*'—'We want you to *do better* than we've done—ah, a sight better,' dad would say, shaking his head over my dreadfully disappointing school reports. 'Ah, lad, if only I'd had your chances.'

Impossible to explain to the dear man that I thought he'd got it made in a marvellously complete way. If only I could do half as well as he had done, he who left school at thirteen, I'd be more than satisfied. I did try to explain this to him, but it was no go. How could I explain to the man I so loved and admired that I really had no intention ever of getting on —that, in fact, I had half made up my mind to go on the bum as soon as I left school? I couldn't bring myself to disappoint him by actually telling him, but such was my intention, and often I've wished I'd stuck to it. Surrounded by the very poor, many of whom were my close friends; already well aware of the divisions, the great gulf between the affluence of the few and the grinding poverty of most; personally wounded by the assault on human dignity involved in the struggle to scratch a living, and utterly indifferent to the trappings of social life—I was already what nowadays we might call a drop-out. It didn't last very long; I caught up, or got caught-up, and went with the wave. But from ten to fourteen or fifteen, I was disaffected. It showed in my work, in my school reports, and in my truancies, which became quite famous in our small world.

They really were quite effective truancies. I got it off to an art. It involved telling lies, I'm afraid. I overcame the habit of telling down-right lies when I was a young man, and can say I have lived quite honestly since, but as a boy I was an unscrupulous liar on occasion. I would not lie to my friends, of course, but teachers and even parents did not rank as friends, alas. Love and friendship were separate. When I found out how easy it was simply to skip hated school, skipping it became a comfortable habit. I took a day off whenever the fancy took me, turning up later bland-eyed and innocent, with some febrile excuse at the ready. It is very easy to be a crook. After some practice, I set out on more ambitious truancies, two of which became mildly historic.

One truancy, which lasted many weeks, I spent as an unpaid worker for Messrs Harrison's, the colliery owners, who ran Harrison's Main and Harrison's Sinking, at Wyrley. Off one morning on my bike, with the undone homework nestling in my satchel, I ambled down the green and muddy lanes I loved so well, intent on a bit of fishing in one of the local canals. Fate took me down a dirt road which, at one point, crossed a narrow miniature railway cutting. I paused on the bridge to watch the trains of coal tubs, hauled up and down between the Main and the Sinking on an endless cable running over pulleys. Here below, nestling up by the rudimentary bridge, I spied a little hut with a roof of corrugated iron, on which turves were laid snugly. It had a chimney whence smoke rose straight in the late autumn air. Inside, sitting on a bench made of a rough plank laid on two oil drums, was a young man with a candid friendly eye. We exchanged greetings, and at his invitation I clambered down the embankment. So I became a toiler, unpaid, for Messrs Harrison's.

This young man, Ben, had an extremely simple job, which attracted me greatly. It was his uncomplicated task to go out with an iron bar, when a train of tubs approached, and if they were going uphill, to tighten the clamp which fixed them to the cable; if they were going downhill, to slack off the clamp, so that they would outrun the steady pace of the endless cable and reach the bottom the faster. Just my drop! I soon took over from Ben, who expressed himself well satisfied with the arrangement. My presence gave him leisure to sit by the fire and grill bits of streaky bacon and the occasional sausage, and make toast and tea. I raided the larder circumspectly and contributed my quota, and I also spent my dinner money on little luxuries like tea and sugar and crumpets (which we called pikelets). We lived like lords. Ben must have known that I was playing the wag, but it did not affect him one way or another. I suppose he must have been slightly simple—his job would indicate it. Well, I was simple too. We both had the cunning of the simple, which includes the cunning of saying nothing about subjects which are likely to arouse ill-feeling. Ben was a married man and he told me about various subjects on which nobody had yet enlightened me. Apart from sport and gardening, his favourite subject was sex, which he called rommin' (ramming). I dare say that throws some light on his calibre as a lover. I was a bit perplexed by this usage, until one day all was made clear when an acquaintance of his stopped on the parapet to have a chat, conducted, at that distance, in shouts. One exchange was enlightening.

'Sin owd Airbut lately, Ben?'

'No. Ay sid im fer wiks. 'Ow's 'e gerrin on?'

'Oi 'ear they've lost one. Pleurisy, Oi think they said.'

'O ar? Worra shame. See, 'ow many 'ave they got?'

'Lemme see. Was it nineteen or twenty? Oi think it was twenty, with the twins.'

'Bin some rommin' there, ay?'

'Ar.'

The life with Ben suited me so well, I might have gone on for ever, but unfortunately I miscalculated the date of term's ending, and my report, which I should have carried home in person, arrived by post one horrible morning. My father walked into the attic, where I slept, with it in his hand, looking like the wrath of God; of which, indeed, he proceeded to give a very fair imitation. What a dreadful Christmas! A marked man now! But within a term I was off again, driven out by sheer boredom, the awful boredom of algebra, French, the O.T.C., and getting on.

This time, with a friend whom I suborned, we lived for a while in a hut in a wood, and when discovered, made a false floor a few feet down an old mine shaft, a floor of young tree boles on which we reclined, smoking foul huge pipes, under the rotting lid which was intended to seal off the disused shaft. I suppose we might have died, easily. But before death could claim us, a fearsome old hag with whom we had exchanged insults informed on us, and the game was up. Fearful retribution followed, which I didn't really mind, could not resent. It was growing-up time, anyway; the sap was stirring. I have never played truant for a moment, since. The froth and stir of revolt was weakening, I'd had my fling. I was actually getting a bit interested in learning for its own sweet sake. Suddenly I began to do rather well—not brilliantly, but quite well. I still had no ambitions, at least, no ambitions to which I dared own; but life was almost all of a piece again, after those fretful years, I got on well with almost everybody, work was not only fairly easy but actually interesting. At fourteen or fifteen, I settled down. So far as I ever should.

Chapter Seven

The year 1926 meant long trousers, the General Strike, and the fight between Jack Dempsey and Gene Tunney. I mean the first fight, when Jack, having lost the furious edge of aggression, lost his title fair and square to a man who had trained harder. I became fourteen in 1926. Fourteen was the recognised age of growing up. It was the age at which you left school (unless you were lucky, like me, and receiving the Higher Education) and started work. If you were old enough to work, and wear long trousers, you were old enough to get girls into trouble, and girls were old enough to be got. Fourteen was a very magical age.

After fourteen you were ashamed to be still at school, still wearing a schoolboy's cap, still dependent and juvenile. I very much wished to leave school at fourteen and start work, and begged to be allowed to do so. But my parents knew better. I fancied a job at the factory, or alternatively at the fairground: anything which would leave the evenings free, for fishing and fornication. Though this latter was still in the imaginative–speculative stage. One heard strange tales.

Two boys at school claimed to have had it. One, a pale and unlikely candidate for the distinction (as I thought then, but I know better now) told us in the greatest detail how he was seduced into the bed of a much older cousin who lived at their house. According to him, he had it nearly every night. The other was a burly and reprehensible boy, of fine physique and with a great extrovert enjoyment of life, who said, simply, 'It's like dipping it in a can of worms.' I believed *him*.

The first mini-skirt craze occurred in this golden year, though the name had not been invented and the skirts were not so short. But they were short enough. They were shorter than they had ever been, or ever would be again till 1966. The knee was revealed, and sometimes an inch or so above. But the knee, anyway—the fateful hinge, the hinge of fate. At that time girls wore garters, and sometimes the flash of their garters was to be seen, and was exciting. This mode was infinitely more sexy and enticing, more teasing and provocative, than the mini-skirt, which is relatively pure. Sex is an obstacle race; there is no fun in it if it is all too easy and straightforward. There must be a touch of mystery. The fashionable erogenic zone at this time was not so much the bosom as the leg, especially the bit of thigh just above the knee. It still left a good deal to be explored, even when you could see the knee for free.

We had a young history master, just down from Cambridge, who discussed with us the attractiveness or otherwise of the knee. 'A woman's knees are her ugliest part,' he argued. Then he recollected himself and changed the subject. But few agreed with him. Oxford bags were ugly, too: we were all wearing them, to the open contempt and derision of working-class boys, who remained narrow for years to come.

When you were out chasing the girls they would sometimes break into a run, showing their garters and even, occasionally, the gathered or ruched hems of their directoire knickers, made of 'artificial silk'. French knickers, wide-legged, were in, but, like cami-knickers, were still considered a bit fast. It was held that they actually invited the groping hand, or even the insinuating member. I suppose they did, too: it cannot be denied that they facilitated research. The nicest girls did not wear them. French knickers were not only fast, but accident-prone. Yet all girls wore decorative garters, some with rosettes. Sometimes you could see them through the skirts of respectable maidens when they were sitting down. They could only have been worn for reasons of enticement and provocation, for the stockings were kept up by suspenders. It was a distracting time to be fourteen.

Ages later I first heard the soldiers' maxim; 'If they're big enough, they're old enough'. At the time, one knew that at fourteen they were old enough, never mind how big they were. High winds, girls on bicycles, hot summer days when they stood against the light wearing thin dresses. ... Frankly, one lived in an almost uninterrupted daydream of fishing and fornication and fast motorbikes. No wonder school work took a low place in the list of attractive propositions.

But the carnal dream was not the only aspect of the love life. Not by a long chalk. Love may be a purely biological urge, as one hears said by various know-alls and prissy pundits. But it was always hopelessly mixed up with romantic feelings. In retrospect it is possible to disentangle the two strands, to identify the instinctual drive; but at the time one was often, indeed *most* often, only very hazily aware of the animal urge, and not too gladly aware at that. 'Love' was a transporting emotion, deeply affected by literature, and by no means synonymous with sex. Dirty talk among dirty-minded little boys was one aspect of awakening. I never have enjoyed schoolboy smut, never remembered a dirty joke for five minutes; later in life the endlessly repetitive smut of adolescent adults was, and remained, a fearful bore. I was deeply in thrall to sex: too deeply, perhaps, to enjoy feeble-minded jokes about it. I never saw it as a joke. It has its ludicrous aspect, God knows; but is not funny, except perhaps in a cosmic sense, the biggest joke played on us by the creator. But it was no laughing matter to the boy who rarely thought of anything else.

One hardly confessed even to oneself that there was a relation between the animal drive and the wildly romantic, almost masochistic emotion of love, which frequently involved notions of self-sacrifice and almost never included fantasies of copulation. There was a big deep gulf between one's falling in love with actual known girls, girls with names and addresses, and one's fantasy dreams of masterful, oriental domination of much older women, often strangers. The sexual fantasies of puberty frequently included harem dreams of extremely complex and precise organisational detail. The 'truth' might be that one was a shy schoolboy who could not organise a picnic or a pair of shoe laces that stayed tied; one's pushbike was a wreck with rattling mudguards and squeaky chain. Ah yes, but all the organisational power and imaginative resource were pouring into a potentate fantasy which had its exquisitely valid geography and logistics, an administration of surpassing precision. In this vast harem, which was sometimes located in an underground system of tunnels and chambers carved out of the belly of a mountain, sometimes in a remote Welsh castle bristling with one's heavily armed eunuch friends (how surprised they would have been to find themselves cast for castration) there was assembled a choice seraglio of utterly respectable women, some well known to us in real life, some ravished from the public palimpsest—actresses, though few, heroines of the news pages, various members of the aristocracy selected not because of their rank but because their rank got their pictures into the papers. To this floating population were always being added nameless beauties glimpsed fleetingly in the streets, from the bike or car; these perhaps were one's favourites, the unknown and unknowable, often young matrons seen shopping, glimpsed getting in or out of cars, passed briefly on pavements, a whiff of perfume, the turn of a head.

The inhabitants of the seraglio had only two things in common: that they were respectable and that they never by any chance wore dresses. Respectable is a shorthand word, which will be understood as such; it indicates that they were not loose women. In those far-off days harlots alone looked like harlots. One had no interest in them, had indeed never seen one, for sure. It embarrasses me sometimes today to see innocent little girls, and matrons for that matter, made up like whores. There is nothing less alluring than a siren with painted face. The whole point of my fantasy harem was that all the women kidnapped to serve it were, not necessarily chaste, but at any rate wholesome. It is a little strange, in retrospect, how general and diffused was the actual sexual core of the dream, how 'clean' and ordinary. One knew practically nothing, of course, of the art of love. One was far from prurient, by no means coarse. When it 'came down to brass tacks', very little sexual intercourse took place in the fantasy: one was fully occupied in the endless organisational difficulties. It had to be made plausible in the mind. Vast reserves of what I must for want of a better phrase call intellectual energy went into the dramaturgy: to make this little lot plausible, even to me, was almost a full-time dream-job. The erotic essence of it all was not very interesting, I imagine. It was more a case of looking than touching, and sleep usually intervened before coitus with the night's selected bedfellow took place.

The seraglio fantasy recurred throughout the early stages of adolescence, well into the teens. In real life things were different. True, I was for ever in and out of love, but never out for long. The force that drove me towards the real-life little girls was doubtless of the same stem as the force that energised the seraglio fantasy, all part of the same natural drive. But it issued as a very different thing, hardly to be reconciled with the other. On the one hand, one desired various desirable girls: on the other hand, one loved various innocent maidens with a love that seemed wholly pure, being romantic and largely illusory and without any sexual component. The two drives never fused into one homogeneous passion—at least, they never did in this period of wild and confused awakening. I first fell in love with a little girl when I was five: others followed at regular intervals. There were desert periods, of course, when one was out of love. They were quite frequent, when I was wholly absorbed in hero-worship, adventure, and the simple supreme joy of being an anarch with a secret life of absolute dissent and singularity—the life lived in the woods, in the hut by the stream. But love was never far away. It could be kindled by a glance.

The General Strike split the school, in a mild way. Some of the older boys went off, against orders, as volunteers to keep the services running. Some of us knew the other side of the picture only too well. I had known the colliers all my life; lived next door to a whole row of them, been the mate and fishing friend, the confidant and hunting companion, the honorary and actual nephew, and perhaps in a tiny way the benefactor, of too many of them. I remember seeing in 1922 a procession of ragged miners pass our house, on strike and bound for the Slang, a piece of waste land where there was to be a massed meeting. They carried their pick axes. Rumour had it that one of them had put his pick through the head of one of the owners' men; we easily believed it, and indeed it might well have been true.

Why should he not? Life was outright war between them. I heard A. J. Cook, the miners' leader (or agitator, as some called him: he was of course both) speak with his wild unearthly eloquence on the Slang. I remembered him, and them, when I was writing my first radical pieces for *The Adelphi*, when it was edited by John Middleton Murry and Sir Richard Rees.

The patience, endurance and stoicism of the colliers were almost incredible. They were men of oak. Some of them, deeply religious, were also deeply conservative. They may have wished their own lot to be improved a bit—it could not conceivably have been worse—but they did not question the way things were. Not fundamentally, that is. These were men who accepted that life was hard, and chancy: did not expect, would almost have resented as a reflection on their manhood, any radical softening of their lot. I imbibed this attitude from them so completely that I have never expected or wished to 'get on', never asked for a rise, almost always understood that the worst would very likely happen. It hasn't stopped me being intermittently cheerful, as it did not stop them. It is an acceptance not without dignity. Of course, I have been almost infinitely luckier than them: but the basic outlook is the same—don't expect anything much of life, don't stoop to beg, expect the worst and put a good front on it.

Uncle Tom Westwood, another honorary uncle, was perhaps the prime exemplar of this philosophy. Though doubtless it is not an explicitly reasoned philosophy, but simply an attitude. Like Joe and Grandfather Haycock, Uncle Tom was a checkweighman. He lived in a pale pink semi-detached house, with a bay window, one of a pair, at Great Wyrley. For many years Tom and Fanny Westwood were our parents' dearest friends, though I do not know precisely how they met. Wesleyanism, no doubt, played a part. Tom and Fanny were gentle, quiet, long-suffering, upright, and devout. What sort of picture do those few adjectives offer? The wrong one, I'll be bound. For they were anything but stuffy, or priggish: nowhere did we enjoy ourselves more than at Croxdene, the respectable, scrupulously clean little house on the Walsall Road. Apart from other visits, and our annual holidays which we always took together, Christmas was the great occasion which united us in a celebration which we nippers thought of as timeless and indestructible.

There is one thing which comparative poverty does for you, that cannot be counterfeited by untold wealth. It preserves and enhances the sense of occasion. If you have only one meal a day, you make the most of it. If you eat meat only once a week, you look forward to it. If *Christmas comes but once a year*, then *when it comes it brings good cheer*. In my childhood there were no moveable feasts and there was no satiety. And no refrigeration. The custom of the annual holiday was still confined to the slightly better-off—a week, perhaps, at the sea. Poor working people could not look forward even to that, though as the Twenties changed into the Thirties, of course, more and more of them did manage the few days at the sea. But for one and all, save only the most desperately poor, Christmas counted. For the majority around our parts, Christmas and Bloxwich Wake were the highlights of a spartan year. Some, like us, added a third great occasion, the trip to Rhyl or Llandudno. But we were the lucky ones.

Christmas was a whole season. It began immediately after Bloxwich Wake; and that took place on the third Saturday in August, though, to be sure, it continued on the Monday and the Tuesday. Up to the Wake, it was summer, even high summer. After the Wake, after that sad day when you saw the roundabouts being dismantled and the glittering minaret of the helter-skelter coming down, you had to face autumn, and beyond autumn, winter. And the best support you had in facing them was the certainty of Christmas coming. We began to take it seriously when it was twelve weeks ahead. That was when the countdown began, kept up to date (no lack of volunteers) on a chart on the wall.

There were several interesting events on the way to Christmas—my birthday, for one, which conveniently coincided with Trafalgar Day; and Bonfire Night, of course; and conkers. All these happy occasions, like baked potatoes, the return of the herring, and pike, helped to keep us simmering; but the really definitive events which occurred with a splendid inevitability, to punctuate the sodden trudge from the Wake to Christmas, were four in number. The making of the mincemeat, the making of the puddings, the making of the cake, and the making of the decorations. Inescapably, these were preceded by the ordering of the ingredients, and this was an event in itself, like the ordering of the cards.

There was always some mousey party who made a little pin money by acting as agent for a Christmas card publisher. Memory refuses to recall a single face, but some plain body would always arrive, by discreetly-canvassed appointment, in late summer or early autumn, with a great thick album of cards. Choosing the cards was a family event, and served to illustrate, even at that early age, the divergences between us as critics in the aesthetic field. Tradition fought innovation to the death. We were incorrigibly sentimental, of course, and a card had to have the heart of the matter in it—or, come to think, it had *not* to have the heart of the matter, but the Dickensian superstructure. We were all fervid Dickensians; Christmas was a Dingley Dell, Christmas Carol festival, or it was nothing. So we eschewed religious cards, turned over the Nativity, the Star Over Bethlehem, the Child in the Crib—somehow those reminders of the central message slightly embarrassed us, religious though we were. But a card had to have snow, robins, holly, a four-in-hand stage coach, a great fire of logs in an inglenook, red-faced fat men in knee breeches toasting one another in punch—that sort of sentimentality. There was often quite a battle, but in the end, of course, mother chose the cards. Since we were in the money, relatively speaking, the chosen card had to be over-printed with our parents' name and our address. A printed card was a status symbol, I'm afraid.

Mother was a champion retail shopper, indefatigably enthusiastic. From her father she inherited this trait of shopping in the smallest quantities possible—partly, I think, to please as many shopkeepers as possible by spreading her custom around; partly for the sheer pleasure of shopping, which should be made the most of. Many a time we ate a dinner bought from three competing butcher's shops. Father despaired of curing mother of this habit, and he did right to despair. The Christmas goodies, though, were bought mainly from Cousin Arthur. He again was more like an uncle than a cousin. He was one of mother's innumerable nephews, and after the War he went into partnership in a provision merchant's store in Walsall. Nothing so common as a grocer's: a provision merchant's. Very posh in its little way, with plateglass windows and counter-fronts and display cabinets, but I missed the atmosphere of the old-fashioned grocer, where everything possible was in bulk—cheeses to be cut into, mounds of butter to be sliced and patted into one-pounds by butter patters, each with its own distinctive pattern.

When I was a boy you could go into a grocer's and try a bit of various cheeses, even a bit of butter. Hams and flitches of bacon hung waiting to be cut, to your specified thickness. Tea and sugar, rice and sago, tapioca and dried fruits, waited in lovely great bins to be served out, poured into blue paper bags at your express order, dexterously wrapped and twisted, anything from an ounce to a couple of pounds. That was a grocer's, and it had the grocer's characteristic smell. The provision merchant was a cut above the grocer, or thought he was. He was also a step on the way to today's vast impersonal stores where everything possible is removed as far as it conceivably may be from its natural state, everything ready cut, ready weighed, ready wrapped. Chits of girls buying cuts of meat, unrecognisable, in plastic bags—not knowing what part of which sort of beast it came from, not knowing even what cut it is, not knowing or caring one thing about the breeding, feeding, curing of the beast, not wanting to know, not wanting there to be any connection between the necessity of eating and the often bloody necessity of growing food. A sterilised shopping for a sterilised society, utterly out of touch and glad to be out of touch with the realities of the natural life and the realities of food production. We deserve all the devitalised rubbish we get.

Cousin Arthur, a big burly pink man with wavy golden hair and glinting glasses, called every Monday evening for his order. But the order which mattered was the Christmas order, given and taken some time in the wet and windy equinoctial days. Soliciting custom and delivering, Cousin Arthur, though a full participating partner in the business, drove a Dunelt motorbike with a box sidecar. As soon as I heard it tutting and pishing, in the manner of two-strokes, into the yard, I was off out, never mind the homework or the weather. Cousin Arthur came in through the kitchen door, slapping his gauntlet gloves and crying 'God save the King, Aunt Lucy, it's perishing.' He wore a two-piece Sidcot suit of fawn twill over his shop suit, and gauntlet gloves, but strangely enough, he always wore a bowler hat. 'Hello, Arthur, you do look cold,' mother would say. 'Sit yourself down in the grand-father chair and have a cup of tea with a drop of whisky in it.' 'God save the King, Aunt Lucy, I think I will,' said Arthur.

Arthur did not actually like my riding his boxcar combination, perhaps, but he always pretended that it did no harm. 'God save the King, Aunt Lucy, the lad won't come to no harm,' he said. But that was before I developed the knack of actually starting it up. Thereafter I used to drive it round and round the yard, in tight circles on full right lock. Cousin Arthur got a little bit edgy then. But nothing untoward happened and he began to relax. After a few Monday evenings on full right lock, though, I naturally fancied a change and switched over to full left lock. A sidecar combination is a tricky thing to drive, until you know how, especially when you turn left, against the third wheel. The box sidecar rose in the air as I opened the throttle a bit after a few sedate circles. Feeling it rise, I lost control, over-corrected to the right, and wedged the outfit firmly in the narrow passage between the coffin shed and one of the outside lavatories. All firmly built of brick. The noise brought Cousin Arthur out at a smart trot, followed by the entire clan. But his self-control was admirable. 'God save the King, Aunt Lucy, he's buggered it up,' was all he said.

It was not the only motorbike I practised on. Fortunately for my peace of mind, if for no-one else's, several friends of the family had motorbikes, and while young I spent much time sitting on them, pretending great rides. As soon as I had the minimal physical strength to start the engines, I rode them. First of all sedately round the garden and the builder's yard, later on the open road. One or two of the mediums who visited us on Sundays came by motorbike, and they will never know my indebtedness to them. Unless the spirit friends told them, of course. I wanted a motorbike more than anything on earth. It was just about the only *thing* I did want. I could manage without practically anything else, but I wanted a motorbike and a fishing rod. They were joint necessities for the kind of life I had in mind.

It was during Cousin Arthur's visit to solicit the Christmas order that we heard again those thrilling words muscatels, almonds, raisins, tangerines, crystallised fruits. These words meant Christmas. It would have been unthinkable to eat those goodies at any other time of year. Doubtless we could have afforded them, and doubtless we could have obtained them had we really tried. But they were never proffered, or wanted, at any other time. It was the same with the one bottle of cowslip wine, one bottle of raisin wine, which we ordered for Christmas. Those innocuous drinks, supplemented in later years by a bottle of ginger wine, were the only concessions we made to the alcoholic basis of the Dickensian Christmas, which otherwise we followed as loyally as we could. They were for drinking the toasts in on Christmas night, and drinking mother's health at a minute after midnight, when her birthday began.

Strange as it may seem, whisky, used purely for medicinal purposes, was a feature of the store cupboard all through this period. Grown-ups were encouraged, and some needed little encouragement, to take a drop in their tea, to keep the cold out. Somehow this did not count. For quite a long time, on actual doctors' orders, mother had a bottle of stout with her cold dinner on Monday, washing day, and there was always this drop of whisky to go in favoured cups of tea. Otherwise our tee-totalitarianism was pretty total. We never had beer in the house, never drank wine, never stocked gin, never entered pubs. When we were all grown up the rule was relaxed, and sherry and brandy were stocked and quite freely drunk, in a mild way. Our later years were quite normal, compared with the early ones, which were more interesting because more cranky, I suppose. Though God knows we never really quite ceased to be cranky. I sometimes wonder who does.

Apart from Cousin Arthur's goodies, vast quantities of stuff were fetched from up The Street for the making of the mincemeat, the puddings and the cake, and these were communal activities in the sense that we all gave a hand in the blending and stirring, though mother actually did the cooking. One sacred day was set aside for boiling the Christmas puddings, of which we made a round dozen, and on another golden day the first of many batches of mince pies were baked. Thereafter everyone who called, be it to visit or merely to leave something at the back door, such as the milk, was regaled with a mince pie, and we knew we were really getting near the great day of days. Heaven knows how many mince pies mother made, but I do know my little mates cottoned on to the realities of the situation at an early age, and made calls on various desperately ingenious pretexts.

'Please, Missiz Wiggin, can we get yer a load of coal in?'

'Please, Missiz, me mom says can I chop yer some firewood?'

'Please, Missiz, me dad says would yer like 'im to come and pluck yer some fowl?'

None went unrewarded. Actually 'getting the coal in' was my job, and it stayed my job until long after I had gone up to Oxford. In those days a load of coal—a ton—cost little more than a pound, dumped in the road outside your house from a horse and cart. You had to get it in before dark, if possible, otherwise the rare wayfarer on bike or car might run into it, and come blustering round talking of compensation, or a punch up the ear'ole. Not to mention the crafty perishers who would be strolling innocently past with a barrow or pushcart, and helping themselves. I reckon I must have shifted a few hundred tons in my time—lovely best brights straight from one of the local pits. One thing nobody ever seemed to go short of in our parts was coal. During the General Strike, when the miners were missing their allowance, we all swarmed out on to the great tips, scratching for coal, of which there was a fair amount to be had. I was forbidden to go but I went.

Loyalties were always divided like that, right down the line. Though definitely against God, I took my Christianity seriously. I wasn't even aware of any paradox here, didn't see the contradictions inherent in the attitude, if you could call it an attitude, when it was really only a surge of undisciplined emotion. I thought God was a rotter, to allow so much suffering, but on the other hand I thought Jesus was on the right lines when he stuck up for the poor and damned the rich, because that was how I felt myself. What I'd seen of the rich, I didn't much care for. This was unfair of me, since they hadn't done me the slightest harm, indeed had been uniformly polite to a little boy. I really hadn't a thing against the rich, but was intermittently very much upset by the condition of the poor. I was far from sure what money-changers were, but on the whole glad that Jesus, showing practically the only touch of spirit recorded of Him, had whipped them out of the Temple. If He had done a lot more scourging and whipping and upsetting of tables, and a bit less preaching the turning of the other cheek, He would have made a bigger hit with us lads. Most boys had no time for Jesus; he was a namby-pamby wan figure, as represented to us in chapel and Sunday school: not a sportsman. *'Gentle Jesus, meek and mild'*. Turning the other cheek ran counter to every instinct. However, the weight of instruction, from infancy, was heavy on us, we never spoke out our private thoughts very clearly, though you could make a guess at what they were. And as a man who was on the side of the poor against the rich, of course Jesus was very much in the groove.

Most of us were definitely on the side of the poor, since we were poor. I am speaking now in general terms about the district as I knew it, about the poor whom I knew. As one of the rich, among the poor, I was naturally suspect and had to make my position unequivocally clear. As one of the poor, among the rich, I naturally spoke even more precisely of their untenable position vis-à-vis salvation. I convinced myself at a very early age of the righteousness of poverty and the wickedness of wealth. It is difficult to grow completely out of a conviction that sets like concrete so early in life. In the last fifty years I have known quite a few really rich people, a great number of quite well to do people, and a steadily diminishing number of poor people. This is perhaps as good a time as any to mention, in passing, though it is of no importance, that I now realise the truth to be elsewhere.

There are mean skrimshanking bastards in every class or 'socio-economic' stratum; mean poor people as well as mean rich people, rather nice and very nasty types everywhere along the scale from rags to riches. 'Some they's bastids, some they's ain't, that's the score' (Kerouac's negro). However, it remains clear to me that Jesus had got it about right when he observed that the rich man would have a bit of trouble entering the kingdom of heaven, approximately on the scale of a camel trying to squeeze through the eye of a needle. Life confirms that. Getting rich really isn't worth the bother, and on the whole I find money the most boring subject there is, so boring that I cannot be bothered even to fill in a pools coupon. Of course, there are many for whom this does not hold true. I know quite a few people whose hobby, whose vocation, whose obsession is the acquisition of money. They are not the nicest among us, but do they care? Do they hell.

A couple of weeks before Christmas we made the paper chains. I'm sure this family custom has died out. We went up to Wheeler's, the stationers, in The Street, and bought sheets of tissue paper, red, blue, green and yellow. We cut them into strips about an inch and a half wide and then we made them into chains using a paste of flour and water. The decorations were stored on tops of wardrobes, under beds, etcetera, until the putting up day, which was about two days before Christmas. Holly and mistletoe were hung at the same time, and the tree arrived the day before Christmas Eve, decorated by my sisters, who were rightly considered to have a better eye for the aesthetics of the situation than me. Occasionally the paste dried out prematurely and a chain would flutter down, causing unease—awful premonitions of Twelfth Night, when all had to come down and the whole delirious season of magic and goodwill was over.

On Christmas Eve we were invariably slightly sick with joy and anticipation. For the grown-ups it was a plain working day, in those days, unless of course it fell on a Sunday, and shops stayed open quite late. However, at length the time came when we little 'uns were packed off to bed, there to lie listening to the magical sounds from downstairs. We believed in Santa Claus even though we knew perfectly well that it was daddy who crept up the stairs and put the presents by our beds. This comfortable faculty for holding simultaneously, and holding with some passion, mutually contradictory and irreconcilable views, never left some of us. This fondness for myth makes for a happy life, on the whole, until the moment arrives, as it surely will, when you have to stand on one belief or the other. Then a certain amount of confusion ensues. Wars begin this way.

The Wiggins, who were great givers of gifts, at the appropriate times, had an engaging custom of visiting one another on Christmas Eve. This meant some careful timing, for at almost any moment there were Wiggins of one branch on the way to visit Wiggins of another branch. However, it all got sorted out, in the miraculous way things do, or did. Our lot would leave quite early, dad on his rounds to every other Wiggin household, bearing gifts and goodwill expressions. Then at intervals throughout the evening we upstairs would hear one or other of our uncles arriving. The warm confident Wiggin voices, trained to public expression of goodwill, rang richly through the house like gongs. Tea, we knew, was being brewed continually—none of them ever took any stronger stimulant, nor needed it—and now and again we would catch the faint clang of the oven door as mother, who had been on her feet since dawn, baked yet another batch of mince pies. We had a kitchen range, of course, the tall and splendidly comfortable black sort with a central fire flanked by ovens. Doubtless housewives everywhere were only too glad to see the back of it, but the going of the range meant something to a kitchen: it was never quite the same again. With its central narrow fire, flanked by ovens and hobs, and hooks above on a spit, and a frontal grill at which pikelets and toast could be toasted and bacon and bangers and tomatoes and mushrooms cooked in a Dutch oven, all spitting and flaring, it was a homely and laborious affair, but when newly blackleaded and spruced up and stoked with good small coal, it gave a massive air of solid comfort to any kitchen.

When eventually ours was torn out and replaced by a very modern thing which boasted a proper 'sitting-room' open fire, though it still had an oven set in a neat tiled surround, I had to admit that progress was really rather wonderful. For *that*, too, made a very cosy kitchen, and still quite useful and workmanlike, and needing infinitely less labour. The kitchen was always my favourite room. I really can't get on with the modern super American kitchen, I just feel lost in it. The kitchen was the heart of the home. There was a scrubbed white deal table on knobby legs, sometimes covered with the standard red chenille tasselled cloth, a windsor or grandfather chair, several dining chairs of a plain kind, a one-armed sofa or chaise longue covered with American cloth, a big dresser, and rag rugs lovely on the red brick floor which was scrubbed and mopped every day, by mistress or maid.

The resident maid was an institution. We always had one—just one, a 'general'—until maids died out, about I suppose 1927 or thereabouts. Perhaps they didn't die out quite so soon as that, perhaps it was merely thought unwise to keep a resident maid after I became adolescent, and slightly sex-mad. I don't know. I do know that when, in later years, it occurred to me that we always used to have a maid sleeping in the attic, I was momentarily rather sad about all those missed opportunities. The fact is that maids tended to get into trouble. Not our maids particularly; maids in general. I recollect an occasion or two when there were tears in the kitchen, a large motherly woman sitting there drinking a cup of tea with a drop of whisky in it (for shock) and telling our mother the sad story of how her daughter had gone and got herself into trouble. I was always hustled out of the way, of course, but my sisters told me the score.

Well, it was never my doing, I can honestly say that. For one thing, apart from lack of opportunity, I never fancied any of them. Mistresses chose the plainest maids they could find, for obvious reasons. I think mother was a good mistress, since she hadn't much idea of class, one way or another, she was really a nice classless person even though she urged me, as a duty, to 'get on'. She couldn't have brought herself to be uppish to anyone. I don't mean that she was exactly saintly—she could be real 'ticklish', as the saying went. Hard to please. But she wouldn't know how to speak to anyone *superiorly*: they were all sisters, even if sisters sometimes fell out. She spoke to the maid exactly as she spoke to us or to anyone else. There is a great deal of comfort and reassurement in this sort of attitude. She might be out of temper, but if she was, everyone felt it equally. Whereas my father could put on a touch of the old sergeant-major, if he had to, and equally could adjust respectfully upwards, though he was never servile. I don't think people really mind being told what to do—most of 'em need to be told, having only the foggiest idea themselves. But it all depends on the tone of voice in which they are told. Few of us really want to be truly independent, which means entirely dependent on our own judgment for every move of our lives, every decision great and small. But human dignity is easily outraged, and what outrages it fastest and most irrevocably is tone of voice. Mother had only one tone of voice, for the maid, for her beloved son, for everybody. She was all of a piece.

Christmas lost much of its savour the day we were allowed to sit up late and receive our gifts downstairs. Feeling the mystery drain away, one of us wept. That was intuitive weeping, those were premonitory tears.

First thing on Christmas morning, feeling that already the best was over, the element of mystery exhausted, but determined to sustain the illusion as long as we could, we ate an enormous breakfast of bacon and eggs and tomatoes, ill fitted to prepare us for the gorging that was to follow, while music was played on the gramophone. Dad always got up first, on Sundays and Christmas Day, and played favourite records. The house quivered with tremendous sounds. Our taste was impeccable. Vast orchestral music, top-flight solo singers, boomed and blitzed away. It never meant anything very much to me, but everyone else loved it. I was then limited to an emotive tune, with an emotive lyric: they could and did stir me deeply, but formal music merely started me off on a daydream. My loss. I came to love and appreciate good music with some depth to it rather late in life.

Then the regular chores, delightfully congenial. For years we cooked our own turkey, and then, for years more, we took it out to one of the local bakers to be roasted. This was my job as soon as I was old enough to have a driving licence. Once we brought the wrong one home, or so mother insisted: she said the labels had been switched. She may have been right, at that, but nobody else cared a hoot. One turkey was as good as another and anyway who wanted a row on Christmas Day? Mother did, for one. To mother, circumstances never altered cases. She had a stubborn streak, though she could be as easy-going as you liked. On this occasion she dug her heels in. There was nothing for it but back to the baker's. Naturally he denied all guilt, but his manner, I must say, was far from easy. Anyway, even if a mistake had been made, the other turkey, which we claimed as ours, had been delivered and was doubtless now being eaten. Nothing for it but to return with the disputed and now cooling bird. Mother was beside herself with rage at the thought that she had been swindled, though no-one else could see where the swindle lay. That was Christmas under a cloud, if you like. But it was the exception.

The great event of the morning was fetching the Westwoods, Tom and Fanny and young Bert, from Wyrley for dinner. I travelled with my father in the open Tin Lizzie or Model T Ford, year after year, sitting up beside him, with the wind whistling in through the split and shaking side-curtains of opaque yellowed celluloid, the hood flapping in the gale of our progress at 20 m.p.h. When I could drive and the Fords had been succeeded by Standard tourers, also with flapping hoods and opaque sidescreens, I did the trip by myself, a sacred trust and my favourite obligation. Sometimes it was foggy, sometimes it rained, sometimes it snowed. We were never beaten. When we decanted our frozen living cargo into the Oaks, with loud yells of greeting and heart-felt wishes freely expressed, for we had no inhibitions about loving-kindness though several about love, then you might say Time had been beaten back into his lair again, the ritual re-established triumphantly. O that warm feeling that come what may, despite the disasters of the year, Christmas was an indestructible commemoration that brought us all together again, the best of friends, armoured by loving-kindness against the cold winds of reality and the creeping disease of change.

That was really the high point of the festival, for the long day of satiety and parlour games was a gradual let-down, even to children, desperately though we strove to sustain the illusion that time had stopped and everything was magical. But we had our devices. It was traditional that at tea time Uncle Tom should rise and recite his annual report in verse on the familial developments of the year. Occasionally he pretended that he had lost the poem, or had had no inspiration this year; in the end he always obliged, drawing from his inside coat pocket a double sheet of foolscap which he had covered, in his meticulous flowing copperplate hand, with rhyming couplets.

I suppose it was doggerel, but that sounds a harsh word for such a labour of love. He must have worked on it for weeks beforehand, bringing in graceful and witty references to the exploits of the year, great moments at Rhyl and on the way to Rhyl, our minor peccadilloes in so far as they were public property, and mentionable, our aspirations in so far as they were admitted and laudable. How I wish that one of his poems of celebration had been preserved. They were a living part of a folk art that was dying on its feet: Uncle Tom one of the last of the amateur rhymsters. I called it doggerel, but in justice must add that Uncle Tom never missed a trick. He could turn a felicitous phrase with the best of them, and only the iron necessity of producing rhymes made his graceful verses sometimes stilted.

Tom was a remarkable man in an age of iron men. Cursed, like me, with a weak stomach, chronically bilious, nearly stone deaf, hammered by a series of accidents in the pit and permanently short of money, yet he was one of the blithest men, in a quiet way, that I have known. His faith in Jesus armed him against disaster, I suppose; though he never spoke of it. But it was not just a case of belief. He never preached. His character was one hundred per cent pure gold.

And so was Aunt Fanny's: they were made for one another. When they were married they went to this little house and there they lived out the remainder of their long lives. Not only did it not occur to them to envy those who had more; they positively gave thanks, in every action of their stoical and meek and tranquil and generous lives, for their good fortune in being preserved from worse, far worse. As I have said, no-one ever heard them preach: their religion was integrated into their lives, it was not (unlike ours) something to talk about. They were very likely the *best* people I have ever known; at any rate, it is impossible to imagine anyone living sweeter, purer lives, entirely without self-seeking or guilt or malice or deceit. Naturally of sound character and pre-disposed to goodness and humility, they were brought up, trained, to accept the moral framework of the Christian life.

And what did they get as their reward? Nothing but a succession of blows which would have soured the vast majority. Ill-health, lack of means; the only rewards of virtue, as far as one could see, were further blows. They retained their sweet-natured stoicism to the end. When I think of Uncle Tom and Aunt Fanny, and I often do, I always feel in a way diminished—blindingly aware of my imperfections compared with them. Yet, in another way, I feel furious and outraged, on their behalf, on behalf of anyone who accepts the given Christian moral structure in its entirety, and lives bravely by its rules. Does the inner peace of integrity atone for the indifference or spite of cruel Fate? Who can say? Not I. I do not possess it.

Well, we spread it out until midnight struck on the grandfather clock and mother's birthday had begun. Then after the toasts, fulsome and trite as they were, but blindingly sincere, it was all bustle. We had to drive the Westwoods home, and next morning it all started up again when we visited them for Boxing Day, which meant another succession of vast indigestible meals, almost certain biliousness for me and Uncle Tom, and just possibly a tantrum or two as satiety and fatigue combined to spoil the spirit of Christmas. But it was always thrilling to be in the house where oil lamps burned and the toilet was an earth closet down the blue-brick yard. Uncle Tom and Aunt Fanny were so kind, so tolerant, so fond of a joke, so serene. You felt that the whole gentle and kindly spirit of Christmas was within them.

When we arrived at Croxdene we drove the Model T round the back and drained the radiator. At midnight—not a minute earlier: that would be to admit defeat—we issued forth with kettles of boiling water to refill it, and dad and Uncle Tom swung the starting handle to get it going. Then it was the slow doddle home, chuntering along sleepily in the frozen air, with the yellow lamps throwing vague shimmering pools of mysterious and ambiguous light on fresh snow or black glittering tarmac. We never saw a soul on the road. Dad put the Ford away in its shed while we filled hot water bottles and wrapped old strips of blanket round bricks that had been heating all day in the oven of the range. Then to bed, with the certainty that tomorrow we should find the world as it was when last we left it before the intoxication set in; its ordinary blear-eyed self. The festival was over, and though nobody would ever admit it, it had gone on too long.

Chapter Eight

Total cynicism set in somewhere between fourteen and fifteen; or so I thought at the time. I misjudged the personal situation, as usual. Perhaps I am a manic-depressive, as it is called now, in the jargon of half-digested psychological crap that passes from hand to hand among the drools, a greasy currency indeed. Perhaps it was simply a melancholy spell of unusual duration. It is impossible to diagnose in retrospect with any certainty. Frustration may well have played a part, though I doubt it, for life was singularly gay at the time, with motorbikes and girls coming into the orbit.

But it is a curious fact that as I hardened off a little towards school and the adult world, taking it more easily in my stride (or slouch) and not letting it worry me so much, there developed at the same time a scepticism which suddenly saw right through *everything*. Alas, it was variable, intermittent, impermanent, and the old romanticism re-asserted itself from time to time, disastrously. But basically, intellectually, I had become a non-believer. I disbelieved in God, parsons, spiritualism, patriotism, capitalism, and the public school spirit. This was excellent so far as it went, and should have meant a happy life ahead. Alas, inconsistency has always been my *forte*, and although I disbelieved in so much, I was still absurdly subject to crushes and pashes of a personal kind, and at the same time was a slave to the printed word.

Thus, although I had seen through everything, I was still ready to fall for any *person* who was nice to me, and congenial, and I was also ridiculously prone to accept what I saw in print, between the covers of books, provided it was well written. Thus, though all schoolmasters were by definition untrustworthy, unctuous serfs of the system, yet *some* schoolmasters, those who happened to be friendly towards me, were credible, shining, lovable. Thus, while the family unit was clearly a relic of a barbarous and infantile tribal past, yet one's own parents, simply by being loved and lovable, might not be distressed. (They *were* distressed, frequently, but by inadvertence and the mere whirl of thoughtless youth: all such cross-purposes were sincerely, even bitterly, regretted.)

What I am trying to say, and making a right old mess of it, is that my intellectual life, which was OK so far as it went, was quite divorced from my emotional life, which was also OK so far as it went. I was and possibly still am a lover, one who falls for people and even, I must admit it, for things; atmospheres, states of mind and being, romantic abstractions, names, colours, sounds and symbols. This makes for an extremely satisfactory emotional life, intense and awfully complicated, but rich and steaming. Whereas intellectually, though always ready to talk myself into anything, I was and still am basically quite clear-sighted. Ready to talk myself out of anything. I know that life is a preposterous joke, which can turn into a very bad joke indeed if one is not careful, or lucky, or both. But intellectual clarity was not allied to strength of character or stubborn egotism. I was always willing to go to work on preposterous hypotheses, perhaps because they had a certain poetic appeal, more likely because they already appealed to someone with whom I was temporarily in love. A poetic 'frame of reference' was a basic necessity.

After some very dreary school years enlivened by frequent truancies and daydreaming, I woke up academically, in a mild way, when I was about fifteen, and began to do fairly well—in the top three, as a rule, of the fifth form. It must be said that it was not a very good form. I was in Vc. Va was for classical students, Vb for those who studied physics and chemistry, Vc for the dregs who might just possibly crawl through the barbed wire fence of the Oxford School Certificate in such utterly bogus subjects as English, literature, art, history, geography, French. Well, geography is not bogus, and French has to be learned. But English, art, even history, really do offer a temptation to second-rate minds. It is too easy to pick up the tricks of the trade, to learn to 'derive' one author from another, to parade the sham symbols. I could do it as well as the next second-rater.

However, there remained mathematics, a severe obstacle. I could do the arithmetic, with ease, and the geometry with some distaste for its aridity; but algebra, for some reason, I never cottoned on to, though now I can see that it has a certain formal charm, even elegance. But I was always far too personal and emotional a lad to recognise the formal charms of so abstract a science; and I certainly was never taught well. So although I showed up well in term, and people began to say I was a late developer (no-one knew *how* late) and likely to make good after all, when it came to O levels, as they are called today, I only just made it, without distinction. (What we actually took was the School Leaving Certificate of the Oxford and Cambridge Joint Board. It was known briefly as School Cert, or 'the Oxford'.)

Having got through School Cert with my modest but adequate score of five 'credits', I was all set to leave school and get stuck into journalism. For some weird reason I *wanted* to be a journalist. I found drama in the papers. It was also the only job I could really see myself doing, assuming that I was not to be allowed to go into the factory or the forest. And I was not. My father may have had certain shortcomings as a business man, but he was quite shrewd enough to see that there was no future for me in the family firm. He himself was a self-appointed renegade who had left the family firm; even when he went back into it, he was not the top man, and never would be. Furthermore, my cousins were virtually all senior to me. And seniority, in a family firm, is virtually as implacable and unchangeable as in the Army or the Church or the civil service. If I went in as the junior member of my generation, I should remain the junior member, for life. This was clear even to me. Not that I really cared a hoot about seniority; I had no material ambitions beyond owning a motorbike. But I don't suppose the family firm wanted me, anyway. What had I to offer? A few poems and letters and stories published in the local rag—whom would that impress? The gift of the gab: not very viable in basic industry, though indispensable in the higher board room reaches, of course. Not practical, not biddable, a known truant and outspoken revolutionary: hardly board room material, then as now. So this mild and unfervid ambition quietly died. After all, I only wanted to wear the fawn twill overall and mess about at Bro'duss's: I didn't really have anything to offer. I should just have slopped about, contentedly, dreamily filling in the time between breakfast and dinner, dinner and tea.

Mark you, if it had been offered, it would have been accepted. I doubt if I should have lasted long, even in a family firm: my outrageous talent for saying the wrong thing at the wrong time would have nobbled me. I was so agin the capitalist system, it would have been a joke. Fraternising with the workers would have been more my line. I know I should have blown my top at the first crisis in labour relations, siding with the chaps against the bosses. But there it was. The question never arose. And I know that my father was right. Anyway, journalism seemed very much more like my cup of tea.

Journalism was also the only visible escape route from teaching. Teaching was something that had to be avoided at all costs. I loathed the notion. In those distant days—I don't know how it is now, but have my suspicions—in those days teaching was the big get-out from the economic stresses of the system. To thousands of lower middle and working class boys and girls, it was what clerkly orders had been to earlier generations of status seekers and go-getters and general cringes. It was a way of life miraculously freed from economic insecurity, the scourge of all our parents' lives. It also confered status.

There were several of these ill-paid but secure occupations: the police, the railways, the minor local civil service, and, glittering above them all, teaching. True, there was also the army, but that was for desperate cases. Professional soldiers in the ranks were slaves, treated like animals, not even well fed. We knew that. It was true, too. (Professional officers did not come from our stratum of society.) But the main idea was to get a secure job which was not subject to the fearful buffetings of the economic system. It was difficult to get on the almost hereditary railways, and exceedingly ill paid if you did, though eminently secure. No boy of spirit wanted to be a policeman. The minor local civil service, again, was not easy to get into, and very ill paid, and generally unattractive. But teaching, with its huge holidays, modestly bearable pay (elementary teachers started at round about £4 a week, secondary teachers at about £6) plus its very real status then in a community prone to take education's claims for granted—this was all highly desirable. Except to me. I didn't give a damn for security and had only one really fervent wish—to get away from school and never come back. But scores of my little mates were set on being teachers, to teach other generations of miserable little getters-on to be teachers. It was a treadmill, a vicious circle. I had no wish to set foot on it.

However, like most boys, and quite understandably, I still had virtually no freedom of choice. My parents took the majority view, that teaching was unexceptionably attractive, indeed a form of state insurance or dole for the idle. Not that they put it quite in that way. To anyone who had actually had to claw his way through the economic jungle to a mildly comfortable and prestigious position, it did indeed look very like a case of being paid to be idle. Several members of the family, many friends and friends of friends, were already launched in the teaching profession. It was taken for granted that I should follow them. My strong plea to be allowed to leave school and try to get a job on a local paper, as a cub reporter, met with unusually implacable opposition. And I did not really greatly care—I knew that somehow, miraculously, I would get out of teaching and into print, and the layabout in me did not seriously revolt at the prospect of two years in the Sixth form. The Sixth was different: one was treated more like a man, school as such was over, adulthood had begun. It wasn't so bad. So I soldiered on with equanimity, biding my time.

VIc was a genial collection of layabouts, I must say. I felt at home with them, though they numbered no heroes among them, with the possible exception of Bowie Roberts, who fulfilled the usual requirements, being blond, brave, brachycephalous, and athletic. But Bowie's cynicism was of an unusually well developed order, and discouraged hero worship. He was most congenial company. His elder brother was in his day one of the conventional school heroes, top boy in this and that and a major Influence For Good. Actually he was a bit of a bore. No-one could say that of Bowie. I remember once the window of the prefects' room upstairs was flung open, during break, and a senior prefect called down.

'Roberts, I'm going to tan your kid brother. Do you mind?'

'Certainly not,' said Roberts Senior with prompt correctitude. 'I'm sure he deserves it.'

How, I wondered, how the hell could he know that Bowie deserved it? He didn't know *anything* about the incident. But that's the bloody police class, I thought, they all stick together. The facts of the case don't concern them.

A couple or three years later I was a member of the police class myself. For some reason which I shall never understand, never did and never shall, I was made a prefect. When my appointment was announced, one first-morning-of-term in assembly, I was stunned. And I wasn't the only one. Perhaps it was believed that a little mild authority would bring me to a recollection of my better self? However that may be, I was a prefect for my last two years, and although on occasion I offered the badge back to the headmaster, even told him what he could do with it, it was never accepted. I arrested no-one, handed out no penalties. I accepted the segregation of the snug prefects' room during break, and that was about all. I have no talent for bossing people around, though of course I know they like it; or many of them do. The drill-pig mentality is odious. I developed a fine 'word-of-command' during the war, when I was a sergeant in the Royal Air Force, and can still on occasion reproduce it, for fun. It's amazing how well it goes down, with some of the sheep. Arrogance can get away with anything.

But the military attitude was without appeal. I resigned from the O.T.C. on principle when I was in the fifth form, after reading *Death of a Hero*, by Richard Aldington. They tried to persuade me to soldier on by offering me a second stripe, but I was not to be had. It was wonderful to be free from all the debilitating bullshit of parades, not to mention the squalor of field days, and those wretched puttees and itching khaki. Bowie and I spent the parade periods reading French literature, happy in the knowledge that we were marked men, undesirables, unreliable. All of a sudden we had cottoned on to 'meaningful' modern literature: Aldington, D. H. Lawrence, Siegfried Sassoon, Edmund Blunden, Wilfrid Owen, Robert Graves. It actually meant something. I had also discovered Thoreau, Walt Whitman, Whittier, and was wrestling with Tolstoy, Turgenev and Dostoyevsky. Now I began to develop a taste for French and Russian literature which has never left me. It was right and natural to be a rebel. The O.T.C. was the first casualty. Thus I just missed taking Certificate 'A', which might have got me a commission when war came, as the masters never ceased to remind us. But *ta la fada*.

A great fierce eccentric headmaster, E. N. Marshall, was still in charge when I joined the school, but he retired, or died, and was succeeded though not exactly replaced by a succession of grey men who made no appeal. Marshall would stroll down from the Headmaster's House to the post box on the corner in his pyjamas. You could see why boys revered him. He was a character. The Second Master was Crop Thomas, who should have got the succession; but safe men vote for safe men, mediocrity calls to mediocrity; he was passed over though by far the most characterful master in the school. He was a fiery Welshman, though not all that Welsh Nationalist; brother to Parry Thomas who was killed trying to break the world speed record on Pendine Sands in a chain-driven Leyland car. The chain broke and decapitated him. Crop was a sort of poet, and he had won the Military Cross in Flanders, which was enough to be going on with. He was a very fierce-looking man, saturnine, with close-cropped hair and piercing eyes and a rasping voice which we liked to imitate. One of his poems, published privately by W. H. Smith's at Walsall, began

> There's an old cracked bell
> In a broken tree,
> And it tolls the knell
> For its swinging free ...

Not much of a poet, as you see. But Crop was both loved and admired by several generations of boys. If he wasn't much of a poet, at any rate he loved and understood the nature of poetry, and passed it on. He taught me the truth about the hexameter.

With the hexameter rises the fountain's silvery column

He introduced us to A. H. Clough, a great hexametrist, and also to

Gerard Manley Hopkins, who had a hypnotic effect, worse than Swinburne. In those days we didn't need drugs, we had poetry, which has a more lasting effect. Crop may not have been a great poet himself, but he knew the difference between poetry and its imitations. He was the first expert to read my stuff, and his reactions were true, and typical. I remember one day he called me out, during a history lesson. He had a sheaf of my rubbish on his desk. He stared glumly down at it, then he peered at me as if he had never seen me before and was none too pleased to see me now.

'This ain't poetry, Wiggin,' he snarled. He really did snarl.

'What is it then, sir?'

'Don't be impertinent, boy,' Crop roared. Then he was silent for a long time, staring sadly at my verses.

'If you want to set your feet on the path that leads to Helicon, boy, you must learn humility,' he growled. He really did growl. '*Humility,* boy, you snivelling child.'

'Well, sir, you aren't humble, and you're a poet.'

Crop was so pleased he gave me a terrible blow on the ear. Form Vc roared its appreciation.

'Silence, you snivelling snotty-nosed louts,' Crop roared in a great voice. 'Westwood, stand up, if your frame will support you, and tell us all you know about the great battle of Espagnols-sur-Mer.'

There was an appreciative guffaw. Crop always pronounced Espagnols-sur-Mer exactly as it is written, in English. He was the despair of the French masters. I don't think he cared greatly for the French Masters, or even for the French, like some others who had fought on the Western Front. Several to my certain knowledge came home with more respect for the Germans than for our gallant Allies, frog 'em all.

Westwood heaved his feeble frame upright and began to drone out the little he knew about the great battle of Espagnols-sur-Mer. Crop did not listen. Nobody listened. Willis who sat behind drove a sharp pencil forcefully up Westwood's backside, producing a strangled squeak, and Cashmore, who read Blake and hit ferocious sixes, thoughtfully arranged three drawing pins on his seat.

Crop shuffled despairingly through my sheaf of wretched verses and handed them back without looking at me. Then he took out of his desk a copy of *The Path To Helicon.*

'Study it, wretched boy, and pray for humility,' he growled hopelessly. His Welsh eyes glowed in his dark face. Then he grinned and drove a short left jab to my ribs. I rode it.

I went back to my place. On the way I had to step over Bowie Roberts's foot, which he stuck out a fraction too soon. I backheeled smartly and got his ankle bone.

'Christ!' hissed Bowie.

I removed a drawing pin from my seat and sat down. Bowie murmured, 'What did the bastard say?'

'Humility is a poet's first duty.'

'What does *he* know about poetry?' Bowie began to chant quietly, in a reasonable imitation of Crop's cracked snarl.

> There's an old cracked bell
> In a broken tree,
> And it tolls the knell
> For its swinging free ...

But he *did* know, and I knew that he knew. I respected that man.

It was the news of Parry Thomas's death which really set us off on one of those truancies. Hardy and I had a conference when the news reached us. We discussed it while riding home, sweating it out on our bikes up the cobblestones of Pratt's Bridge. The consensus of opinion was that we should play the wag for a couple of days in order to attend his funeral, which was to take place at Pendine Sands.

'Owe it to the old school, really, Wiggy,' Hardy panted, standing on the pedals. He was a great one for the old school though he didn't spend very much more time there than I did. But Hardy was not only impressionable in the ways in which I was impressionable, but also in some ways in which I was decidedly not. He could never resist a bit of mass propaganda especially if it tended, as paradoxically it often did, to make him feel exclusive. This was the big difference between us, who were otherwise closer than brothers. Hardy was eminently a clubbable boy.

'Bugger the old school,' I replied.

'Yes, but Wiggy, apart from the old school, we owe it to the memory of a gallant sportsman.'

Hardy really did talk like that. Unlike me, he adored *Stalky & Co.* He was thrilled to bits when we learned that our headmaster had been invited to attend the Headmasters' Conference. That made the grammar school a 'minor public school', according to Hardy. It was worth an extra two inches in height to him. Anyway, by the time we reached Blakenhall Lane, where our ways parted, we had come to a provisional agreement to play the wag anyway, in order to commemorate a gallant sportsman, but we left it open whether we should actually cycle to Pendine or just go fishing. Pendine was about 170 miles away and on the day of the funeral it was raining and we had one-and-a-penny between us. So we played the wag instead.

They decided to send me to Dudley Training College, which was the nearest local institution for turning out elementary school teachers, and a right bloody bog-'ole as the saying went. I shouldn't be the first of the family to go there. The prospect held no charms. When I went there for the interview, and met the mob of creeps collected for the same purpose, I realised that it really wasn't on. I should have to run away. Talk about dim. God knows modesty has always been my main fault, but even I couldn't stomach that bunch of bums. However, before I actually got the rucksack packed and chose my route to freedom, the family underwent a curious change of mind, or heart. I never understood what was behind it, and I do not understand it now. It certainly wasn't on account of anything I said: I was keeping exceptionally quiet. They decided that I should go to Oxford. No Wiggin had been to Oxford or Cambridge. My cousin Harold, Enoch's lad, or one of them, had gone on from Queen Mary's to Birmingham University, where he did very well, becoming an industrial chemist or physicist (I wouldn't rightly tell the difference) with the Valor Oil Company. Harold was not only brainy, but cheerful and characterful. But they couldn't have been thinking I should ever make an industrial what's-it. No, perhaps it was simply the fact that various local lads of low degree had been winning scholarships and exhibitions to Oxford. That might have something to do with it. It's a real mystery to me, now as then.

Anyway, my father solemnly announced, one day, that he would pay for me to go to Oxford for one year. If by the end of that year I had won enough awards to support myself, well and good. If not, I should have to come down.

I accepted this surprising edict with the same calm fatalism with which I accepted most events. Fair enough. I was so idle, so lacking in schematic decisiveness, that I tended to accept almost anything as an act of Fate. If I had really had any clear-cut plan for my future, I would certainly have acted upon it—as I did, more than once, later on, when the decisions were my own. But apart from an overpowering feeling that I was going to end up a journalist, come what may, I had no immediate plans—nor a ha'penny to bless myself with. The prospect of one year at Oxford (I did not see any likelihood of it becoming three) was neither attractive nor repulsive. I had several friends already up or ready to go up, and didn't see what harm another year of idleness could do. So I said yes, dad, thank you very much, I'll try it.

Meanwhile I had a couple of terms of pupil teaching to get through, and one term back in the Sixth Form, utterly wasted, of course. I had got my A levels—or, as we said then, had passed the Higher School Certificate examination—with consummate ease. I didn't actually do all that brilliantly, but I realised that I could have done, if I'd tried. It was quite simple, and only the fact that I hadn't read the set books held me back from doing well. Even as it was, I didn't do badly. I had the feeling now that my mind was average if not a bit better than average, and knew that only laziness, or distaste, or both, would hold me back. That was all I wanted to know. It has ever remained true. I have only a second-rate mind, at best, but even that is better than I used to fear. But my intuitions are sharp. I am a good guesser. In particular, I always know what people are really thinking, never mind what they say. If I can see my own shortcomings clearly, I can also see theirs. I know when I'm being phoney, and when I'm not the only one.

I did my stint as a pupil teacher at Leamore Junior. What a waste of time that was. I dare say the pupil teacher was a bit of a nuisance to the regular professionals, though some creeps, of course, were probably useful dogsbodies. But I didn't take to it, really. I was perfectly willing, at the beginning, but had a nasty shock right away. It being a blithe September morning, I turned up wearing an open-necked shirt. It made sense. But I was immediately told off, very pompously as I thought, and warned to wear a tie. This gave me an immediate poor impression of the good sense of the headmaster and staff, which further events failed to correct. So it was a bloody uniform job, was it? I knuckled under—didn't have any option—but although I wore a tie, it was a red tie. And that was symbolical. Of course I wasn't a Communist in the sense of being a Party member—had hardly heard of them, to tell the truth—but I flaunted my red tie as a challenge. It went down very ill. At the end of my stint the headmaster, an oily bird, told me that he had given me a report that would 'get me into heaven'. But he was a liar. He didn't give me a good report, and he was within his rights in not doing so. For although I can expound something which I understand and enjoy, I was not cut out for the dreary routine of teaching little boys and girls up to eleven years old, the same thing day after day. There were one or two embarrassing moments when I actually did not know the facts I was supposed to pass on—Scripture, for instance. The gaps in my knowledge amaze me to this day, and would depress me if I let them.

But apart from those incidents, which were unimportant, I was so bored by the curriculum and the drear buildings and the fixed pattern of the hours: life went grey. I was thinking only about girls and motorbikes and fishing and poetry, the wild romance of life. Teaching, or rather being a teacher, which is a different thing, struck me as extremely wearisome. I did not detest the children. Some of them I loved. It was jolly to take the boys out for cross-country runs after school hours, to referee soccer matches against neighbouring schools, to arbitrate in their private disputes, to listen to their dreams and troubles. I enjoyed all that. But even those congenial extra-mural activities were not without social friction.

I introduced the paperchase to the school. It involved pounding across various farmers' fields, with the hares (two in number) scattering torn-up newspaper, and the field spread out at a great distance behind them. Complaints poured in from far and wide. Farmers, private citizens, and finally the police, assailed the headmaster with bitter grumbles about paper littering their gardens and fields and hedges, kids trampling and scrambling over their blessed turf. Parents complained furiously about worn-out shoes and torn clothes. Of course there was no rational answer. But we all felt quite bitter about it. I told the headmaster that so far as I was concerned extra-mural activities were at an end, and they were, too, except those in which I indulged myself, which didn't bear talking about. The incidents reinforced my growing feeling that the bourgeoisie (of which I was born a member) were a lot of stuffy bastards, entirely without faith, hope, or charity. On such trivial grounds are considerable edifices of ideology built. We believe what is congenial to us.

I was paid £1 a week, or to be exact, £4 a month. I gave my mother £3 out of my monthly screw, kept £1 for myself. Both parties were well satisfied with the arrangement. Five bob a week seemed good pocket money at the time. A lot of grown men, with families, managed on less. At that time the dole for a single man was seventeen shillings a week or thereabouts. I knew several men who had never worked since leaving school. Teaching was cushy, all right. But unbearable. I didn't expect much, I was fully prepared, mentally I mean, for the bundle and the billycan, but not for the treadmill of a sufficiency-routine. Music lessons at the grammar school were such torture to me that it was soon accepted that I should be a passenger, not asked to participate, indeed asked *not* to participate, but one song which we sang every term I did learn, and it became one of my favourites. It was the one which goes

> Give to me the life I love,
> Let the lave go by me,
> All I ask is the heaven above,
> And the highway nigh me . . .

This I took literally. I sang it with the fervour of one who really believed its grotesque statements. 'Bread I dip in the river' was a lot to swallow, admittedly: I didn't really fancy dry bread dipped in the river. But with that rider, I approved the whole *schema*. How could *I* expect to make a comfortable living, when so many good men and true couldn't make ends meet? I knew my defects of character better than anyone. True, I didn't actually believe in God; nevertheless, a rudimentary but burning notion of justice (very religious, had I but realised it) made me see the unlikelihood, nay, the gross impropriety, of a worthless daydreamer like me making a living when solid characters with good morals and diligent natures failed. It had not yet been borne in on me that there is no such thing as Auden's imaginary 'justice, the contribution of our star'.

My elder sister had a young man whom we called Rock. His name was Horace, but he hated that. Originally we called him Rock because he sang 'Rock of ages, cleft for me' with such fervour and joy: the name stuck because his qualities of character were so rocklike, though he was gentleness incarnate. He was a darling man, one of the sweetest characters I ever knew: I revere and love his memory, for he died, alas, 'before his time'. Rock had fought as a boy in the Great War: literally, a boy, out there in No Man's Land. After the war, during which he got his first taste of alcoholic liquor, he worked with his brother Ted in the family firm, which consisted of a cycle shop and ironmonger's, combined with an oil round. Rock ran the oil round, trundling through the villages around Rushall and Pelsall with an old horse and cart, selling paraffin or as we called it lamp-oil to the cottages and terrace houses and scattered little small holdings which were still, in that year of grace, un-electrified. It wasn't much of a living. One day sitting in the grandfather chair in the kitchen at The Oaks, when we were talking about the general roughness of the times (it would be 1926, the year of the General Strike) Rock said something which stuck in my little mind like a burr.

'I managed on ten bob last week,' he said.

There was a silence and everybody was thinking different-shaded thoughts. Some were embarrassed for poor Rock, some pitied him, at least one (I can vouch for this personally) notched another black mark up against God, the hypocritical old bastard. Yet Rock believed in God. When I had recovered from the first shock—a shock not lessened by the memory that I had just a few minutes before touched Rock for a tanner, as a contribution to the funds of the Bloxwich Junior Engineers, a firm I had set up for the purposes of extortion and incidentally of making a motorbike—we went out together for our training run. We frequently trained by lapping our bottom lawn a fantastic number of times. On the way down I said

'I don't believe in God, Rock.'

'Why not, Sam?'

'If He was any good He wouldn't let people have such a rough time.' (This was as near as I could get, out of delicacy, to mentioning the financial straits to which he had just confessed.)

'We can't all be rich, Sam. Anyway, there's far more important things than money, lad. Money doesn't matter.'

'No, I know it doesn't. But it does seem the wrong people have it.'

'Ar, now that's a different matter. You're right there. Some people have the gift of making money. Some people put other things first.'

'You put other things first, don't you, Rock?'

'Ar, I do, Sam. And I hope you will.'

'Oh, I will, I will. I don't like money.'

'I don't like the mentality of bloodsuckers.'

There was another phrase to stick like a burr. 'The mentality of bloodsuckers.' I hadn't heard about usury yet, but it was coming.

'Still, Sam, you don't want to say things like that about God. It isn't God's fault. It's the fault of people. God made a world of infinite beauty and wonder. It's people who mess it up. Now come on, forty laps at a jogtrot, then we'll have a bit of wrestling.'

At the back of my mind, a doubt suppressed. I was a sharp little hand at a syllogism, even then. Sharper than now, perhaps. 'God made the world . . . people mess it up.' But if God made the world, he also made the people . . .

However, I kept my little mouth shut, this time. Rock had suffered enough. If he wanted me to believe in God, I'd try.

Needless to say, Rock never did very well, in a material sense. He was not cut out for material success. He remained, to the end of his life, the old Rock who came back from the Western Front, a boy who had seen too much, with a taste for beer but no head for liquor, a belief in the fundamental goodness of mankind, a distaste for the great carve-up of commercial life, an innate sweetness that disappointment never wholly soured, though of course he grew quieter as he grew older. You either grow quieter and more reserved, or outspokenly bitter. Or, if you're lucky, you never see it, still less see through it; you grow pompous and smug and actually believe your own lies, actually value your bleeding trophies and empty honours at the world's valuation. The worst company in the world is the company of old men, whether illusioned still or disillusioned. If they've seen through it they've nothing to utter but bitterness, and if they haven't, what bores they are, chuntering on about their ghastly little successes, preening themselves like old sleek cocks, their vile predatory little eyes glittering with self-satisfaction and self-praise. Vast bores of saloon bar, club, and home, men who drive women mad with despair. All through my adult life as a journalist I was meeting them, those ghastly old men so unctuous with success and satisfaction.

Saloon bar and club were still far away. It was later—but as soon as I was old enough—that Rock and I used to sneak into the public bar and have a pint of mild; often only half a pint. I suppose I might easily have become an alcoholic at eighteen. I first got the taste of fermented liquor in a curious, risible way. A number of local families made wine, though we of course as bounden teetotallers did not. At the Orl we became very friendly with a family called Selvey: might easily have become related to them in a big way, for Mr and Mrs Selvey had two lovely girls and a fine strapping son. It was just the quirk of fate that we didn't become related. I was in love at various times with both Hilda and Florence, sometimes both at the same moment, and one of my sisters was much liked by Bill. But there it is: we all might so easily have married someone else, and might perhaps have become different people thereby. Rock and I used to visit the Selveys often, for every sound reason of true friendship and for the additional reason that Mrs Selvey made as potent a brew of wine as anyone for miles around. For a long time I was aware of this only academically, intellectually: and a fat lot of use that sort of knowledge is. But one day Mrs Selvey gave my mother a bottle of mangold wine and a bottle of parsnip. I was fifteen at the time, a hardened smoker, but still virgin to booze. It was a Wednesday. On Wednesday we were supposed to spend the afternoon playing compulsory games, but of course the very idea of compulsory games struck me as absurd, as indeed it is, and I cut them whenever I could.

On this particular heaven-sent Wednesday I cycled home to find the house quiet and empty. My dinner was waiting for me in the oven, and on the kitchen table stood these two bottles labelled mangold and parsnip. To me, they were plainly 'pop'—our universal name for soft drinks. I did not associate them with alcohol, of which I had an inbred though purely academic dread. I drank a tumbler of the one, then a tumbler of the other. They were delicious. I sank into a semi-coma of delightful happiness. It became a matter of over-riding importance to get the levels in the two bottles exactly adjusted, exactly the same height. This meant drinking a drop out of one then a drop out of the other. By the time I had got the levels level I had drunk the better part of half of each.

I rose and went up to my attic room, conscious of unearthly power. I seemed to float up the steep stairs. I lay down on the bed—the oldest in the house, with brass knobs—to snatch a nap before starting my swot. There the family found me at half-past five. I felt a little odd, but still very happy. Everyone was ashamed, for it was obvious to them that I was still slightly drunk. It was a thing we had never had happen in the family before, at least in my generation and the one ahead of it. I fancy there was a bit of drunkenness hidden away somewhere in the archives, something that no-one ever spoke about, a dark and un-acknowledged secret in the familial memory. That would help to explain the horror and dread of drink which permeated my father's generation and was passed on to mine, though not with utter success, as you see.

This nasty incident opened my eyes to the delights and possibilities of booze. I realised that it was the gateway to nirvana—the only one, so far as I knew. Of course it was a long time before another sip passed my lips, but in a quiet way I was definitely intrigued, and when I passed the open door of a pub, the reek of ale no longer sickened me, but made me feel vaguely and tremulously excited. It was some time before I could go in and order half a pint of twopenny mild, but there was always Mrs Selvey ... Rock and I, genuine friends of the family long before this, often visited them, sitting in the glorious snug kitchen, scrubbed and shining, with a big fire banked and roaring in the range grate, the classic scrubbed deal table with its red chenille cloth, the one-ended sofa (we never heard the term 'chaise longue') trimmed with shiny black American cloth, the grandfather chair, the rag rugs on the gleaming red tiles of the floor.

It was undiluted heaven to be there, even before the wine began to enter our lives, chatting about the economic ills of the world, which were all too obvious, about sport and nature and spiritualism, and singing the good old songs. We even sang hymns, and there was nothing sanctimonious about that: they were simply songs, and among the best songs extant. Many the happy Saturday night! The Selveys were robust folk, in build and mind and heart. A little later on in life, as I say, wine entered into the ceremony, generously dispensed, and then we had to make a discreet entrance when we got home again for supper. I was suspect for egging Rock on, he being known to have a weakness in that direction, and he was suspect for egging me on, ditto. This helped to throw us more closely together still. One night we felt it necessary to climb a lamp-post in Bell Lane. The news of it reached home before we did—pitch dark as it was, in mid-winter. Talk about prying eyes. Of course everything was 'all for your own good, lad'—including spying and informing. It was becoming clear to me that religiosity and a certain meanness of spirit too often went hand in hand. I broke away from the Orl and all other forms of religious activity about this time, and never felt anything but a sense of liberation. Of course I remained interested in religion, in fact I've spent half my life thinking and wondering and worrying about it, though I worry no more.

One of the old girls who loved to inform on me resided in a house owned by my mother. Mother had laboriously purchased, over the years, a terrace of five houses in Broad Lane and two semi-detached just off Stafford Road. 'Get your money in bricks-and-mortar', they all said, sagely, wagging their miserable old turnip-tops. I doubt if mother made a farthing out of her 'property', but its ownership was a very portentous thing. The rents were a few shillings a week, round about five bob when I was a boy. I was always made to collect them, during school holidays, and this was a chore I loathed. Not that the tenants weren't decent to me: they were decency itself: but I felt their straits and stringency so keenly. Sometimes they couldn't pay anything, sometimes they could only pay part. I duly entered it all up in the rent book, and reported home on my shortcomings as a taskmaster.

Mother, who was as soft as butter when face to face with the sufferings of people worse-off than herself, could be as bold as brass when the suffering was out of sight, at a distance. She upbraided me for *my* softness, urged me to take a tougher line. I know she was out-of-pocket on the wretched houses most of the time. Quite often one of the women would ask me to ask my mother to provide wallpaper—they would provide the labour, of course. This always threw ma into a tantrum, but she usually obliged. However, the whole operation had the worst possible effect on the natural and ever-deepening ambivalence of my social outlook.

I was against the capitalist classes as a matter of course, close friend and playmate of the poor. Yet here I was acting as the agent of the landlord, by definition a capitalist. Since I loved my mother and what's more could see perfectly clearly how little of a grasping ogre she was, and since I rather tended to love the tenants too, and could see how little they got out of life, I was properly messed-about by this chore. I hated it but there was no way out.

Long before the end of my schooldays I had seen the light. Suddenly it struck me that all this textbook theorising about capital and labour was a lot of boloney. People were people, children of environment and heredity and above all playthings of blind chance. It was put to me so often that *I* was lucky in the matter of my birth—suddenly it struck me that, equally, *they* were unlucky in the matter of theirs. Luck worked both ways; all ways. I could easily have been one of them. Can you really eliminate luck by taking thought? From this moment, seeing both sides—which was ever my rotten luck—and what's more *knowing* both sides—which was ever my great good fortune—from this moment I struck a certain fatalistic balance. I could see that some capitalists were kind and humane, some poor victims richly deserved to be poor victims. See it with my own two close-set eyes. I remained on the side of kindness and decency, but no longer believed that legislation would make much difference.

This saved me from a great deal of self-deception, and the other kind, when I got to the age of revolt. I was rarely able to persuade myself that common action was called for, or likely to do much good. My natural unclubbability was strengthened. I never feel that ganging up helped anything. What matters is what is inside you. The only person you should convert is yourself.

Yet I had my clubbable moments. I must try not to distort the record. Wildly gregarious in fact, I founded the Bloxwich Radio Club in 1923, the Bloxwich Junior Engineers some time later, and tried to found a magazine before I was out of my teens. All ended in chaos: I have little organisational talent and no administrative talent whatever, cannot boss people about, can only lead those who wish to be led, cannot even bother to persuade people whom I don't personally care for. These are severe limitations on the would-be leader of men. I have never believed in the leadership principle: it involves humbug. Some people are naturally bossy and interfering, some are not bossy. Of the not-bossy, which is the larger segment of mankind, I think some are willing to be bossed, some refuse to be. I am a refuser. The Bloxwich Radio Club was a happy little social organisation with an ostensible technical aim. It might seem a modest aim: we simply hoped to build a wireless set that worked. In 1923, this was quite an ambition. The only working wireless in Bloxwich was constructed by Frank Yarnall, who lived in one of the top cottages at Mount Pleasant, where now stands a block of skyscraper flats. Frank was a serious young man who actually got Manchester on the earphones at a time when most people couldn't even claim to get Birmingham (5IT). Naturally, none of us up there could get London (2LO) but we felt we weren't missing much. The B.R.C. met in our summer arbour. This was a hexagonal structure with slatted mahogany seats all round the inside walls. It was sturdily built, with a roughcast roof and a small flagpole atop that. The windows were of stained glass, possibly a job lot from some disused chapel. Bear in mind that it was built by Saml. Wootton, Bldr & Contractr, Funerals Furnished. The vague religious light which filtered in through those windows, plus the old home atmosphere, may have had something to do with the fact that our meetings began and ended with prayer. All or almost all the members were children of fervent spiritualists: the Radio Club was a sort of annexe of the Lyceum (spiritualist Sunday School). Several of us were at that time in training to become some sort of public orator; oratory was all around us. We were rotten with rhetoric. So it seemed natural to begin and end with prayer. We were serious little boys; at times.

We never did get a set made, not one worth calling a set. The main force of the club was social, of course—we escaped into it. Little work was done on the wireless, partly because I kept on changing the plan for a more ambitious one, with valves and a loudspeaker. The secondary aim of the society was to raise money, which was kept in a black japanned cash box loaned by dad from his office. Ingenious were the schemes devised for raising cash, but often enough it came down to a straight touch of highway robbery. Adult friends came to dread the sight of us. When the club broke up we had upwards of six shillings in the black tin box. We shared it out when we disbanded—of course, we weren't actually disbanding anywhere, we were just admitting that the prayers and meetings and indeed the whole business of wireless had become a bore. It worked out at more than a shilling each, though I'm afraid there were hard words when I suggested that I should hold the lot against another scheme that was burning in my mind. In fact words came to blows, as they so often do, and the B.R.C. really *did* disband, with a touch of huffiness. But I think we were all relieved. Who wanted to listen to the wireless, anyway? It soon became commonplace, soon enough everybody had heard the magical sounds squeezing through the earphones. They didn't stay magical very long. Then it was valves and loudspeakers and the tedium of a commonplace miracle. The only programme I recall from all those years was Tyrone Guthrie's play, *The Flowers Are Not For You To Pick,* which made us shiver with delight.

The theme of the Bloxwich Junior Engineers, which followed a bit later, was vastly more exciting and ambitious. We hoped to build a motorbike from various relics, including a cycle frame long past its best and a tiny gas engine which my father had made, or had made, at the factory. Needless to say, it came to nothing, if you can call the total destruction of both bike and engine nothing. But it was something vaunting and conspiratorial to be going on with, while waiting for the blessed age of fourteen, the lowest legal age, in those days, at which one could ride a motorbike. My father promised me, when I was about six, that I should have a motorbike when I was fourteen. He may have forgotten those idle words, but I never did. That promise glowed in my mind, through fair days and foul, the one fixed star in an otherwise uncertain future. I was besotted about motorbikes from infancy. At the age of three, at Broduss's, I had clambered aboard Cousin Norman's Triumph and brought it crashing down on top of me. In a manner of speaking I am covered by fading scars, almost all of them from motorbikes; the latest sustained only about yesterday, when I was well into my fifties. I have been more or less compelled to promise never to ride one again, but left to my own devices I would ride nothing else.

As my fourteenth birthday approached I began to badger the old man severely to redeem his ancient promise and give me a motorbike. I may say I was appalled to discover that he seemed to have forgotten his promise. What could this be—cracks in the edifice, the first glimpse of feet of clay? Poor old dear, he was simply a bit hard-up, and of course I hadn't given much evidence of a strong sense of responsibility, I daresay he expected me to do myself untold damage. I had come off my pushbike so often, my knees were patterned with scars like lace. Fast cornering was the thing, you see; leaning it inwards like Jimmy Guthrie or Stanley Woods. When you went a bit too far and the machine slid out from under you, you were quite likely to do a few yards in the grit and granite chippings on your kneecap. Mine were a sight. I had also caused a certain amount of damage to the motorbikes of various good friends. Altogether I don't blame dad for trying to back-pedal on his promise, didn't even blame him then. But he hadn't much hope.

For months before my fourteenth birthday I had had the old ear permanently to the ground. I knew of every reputed 'bargain' for miles around. Over midday dinner one Saturday (beefsteak, sausages and mash; the Saturday tradition) I worked on dad incessantly to allow me simply to 'go and have a look' at a bike which was for sale at a little garage at Wyrley, near Tom and Fanny's. It was offered by yet another of the Halls in our life: this one was known as Drummer. He was a tough and taciturn old chap; of course when I say 'old' I mean that he was quite a bit younger than I am now. But he was middle-aged, which is pretty horrible. Dad finally relaxed enough to give me permission to 'have a look at it', and I was off like a shot. Much to everyone's surprise, I returned with the bike, turning in through the old red-painted gates of the yard on something black and spidery that went *tut* and *pish* and wobbled somewhat. By riding it home on the public roads I had contravened some few laws: neither it nor I was licensed. I had also gone far beyond the terms of the unformulated agreement.

However, we hadn't had a motorbike in the family since father's 'Big Six' New Hudson with a wickerwork sidecar, and frankly he was as intrigued as I was. He had a little ride on it, up The Sandbank, and found no particular fault, which makes me wonder if he was really looking for one. There was very little he could do, really, except give his dubious permission and fork out six quid. He did this cheerfully enough, bless him, and after swearing a few oaths which a saint would have been pushed to keep, I became for the first time owner of my own private transport. Between such a one and one who depends on public transport there is fixed a gulf unbridgeable, deeper than that between Christian and pagan, black and white, Tory and Red. No-one who has ever so briefly enjoyed the boom of owning his own private transport wants to go back to being dependent on public transport.

This is one of the central facts of our age, vastly more important in its effects than any ideology. I have darned near ruined myself trying to keep on the 'right' side of the gulf, and so have millions of others. There is no vice more extravagant than motoring. It is cheaper to take to booze or gambling, or to pursue women. Few indeed, I come to believe, of those who run motorcars, can really afford to. One way and another it puts several hundred pounds a year on to your expenses, and saves you nothing, nett. It is the great vice of our times. It is anti-social, it has ruined the countryside and made the towns uninhabitable. Motoring brings out the worst in everyone. The coming of the car has blown the gaff on human nature. We don't need wars while we have cars.

But, of course, none of this has the least effect on the addict. We never count the cost. Fundamentally we do what we want to do, we do what gives us pleasure: even though the pleasure is a self-inflicted wound. I was lucky in that I knew motoring when it was an occupation of enthusiasts, and the open road was actually open. Motoring was delightful up to about the early 1950s, when the mob began to swarm out on to the roads. Of course all those ghastly creeps have exactly the same right to be on the roads as everyone else, including me. That's democracy. I believe in democracy. But I don't humbug myself about its results.

Perhaps democracy, too, is a self-inflicted wound.

It certainly isn't a pleasure.

It is a pleasure to believe in it, as it is a pleasure to believe in any other spiritual or mystical communion. It reduces the sense of loneliness and insignificance and ... yes ... sin. But the pleasure of believing in it and the pain of experiencing it are different things. Or perhaps they are the two sides of the same thing.

The reality is the price you pay for the ideal, or dream.

Life without dreams would be insupportable.

The motorbike was an instrument of the dream. I did not in fact get so very much farther afield than I had done on the pushbike, on which we covered huge mileages, but how different it was! With an engine purring, warm, between your calves, levers to manipulate, the smell of petrol and oil, the looks it drew from girls and boys ... The sudden bound into another world, a grown-up world of freedom, danger, and wide gestures. No cowboy galloping down the main street of Dodge City and braking to a halt, dusty, wearing chaps and guns, bringing with him intimations of wide-open spaces and mortality and high adventure, no such folk hero has it over the boy on his first motorbike braking to a halt outside a coffee stall. The dream ingredients within are exactly the same.

When you grow too old to enjoy this, when the motorbike becomes a dirty, noisy, dangerous thing that right-thinking citizens deplore, then you are past it, you are indeed growing old.

You can get on with your French literature. You've had it. You are an onlooker, no longer a contributor to the drama, and few will miss you when you depart.

All life's eagerly awaited peaks are transient and orgasmic. It was not too long before the essential thrill of owning a motorbike, any motorbike, wore off. Not the thrill of motor cycling, but the thrill of that particular first bike, in its original form. Then set in the period of improving, modifying, messing about. Very bad for the bike, I must say. I have always had ingenious ideas about machines, but not too much talent for putting them into practice. I'm not greatly gifted as a craftsman, though I think it's largely a question of temperament. I'm too impetuous, lack patience, want to see it all done and finished with in one fell swoop. This is why I shall never make a gardener, though heaven knows I enjoy a garden, and have tried hard. I can mow and trim a lawn, or weed a bed, or prune a rose bush, with the next man. But I walk away from it as from a finished task, expecting it to stay finished.

My friends in the motor-cycling world had better bikes than mine. With one of them I used to go racing on the public roads. How disgusting that sounds now. But the roads were empty then: you could cruise for miles, looking for a foe worthy of your mettle. The Norton Model 18, with me on the pillion clutching Frank's waist, blurred in the wind, bloodshot and gritty . . . We used to patrol the Watling Street looking for likely lads on Velocettes and Sunbeams and A.J.S.'s. Then for the ten-mile blind, flat-out, crouched low and howling along, the big single-cylinder engine beating out its raucous song, the wind upon us. Winners or losers, we felt transfigured, rode home sturdily, like twin centaurs, leaning as one when the bike leaned on the cruel bends.

I have been involved in thirteen accidents *as a passenger*. Few people can have been driven nonchalantly into more immovable objects by more sublimely confident idiots. No wonder I grew into a touchy and querulous passenger, never entirely happy that the man in charge was quite all there. The safest driver I ever travelled with was my father, who held firmly to the ideal chauffeur's dogma—'the passenger should never be made aware of any sudden change in the vehicle's direction or velocity'. He was as steady as a rock. In his entire long life on the roads he slightly and unavoidably injured one dog. And it really was the dog's fault. This mishap grieved him for weeks, if not longer.

Personally, I drive ever with the dog and cat in mind, going absurdly slowly where some people would swoop blithely on. I don't want to run over a dog or cat darting out of a gateway. I suppose I wouldn't really like to run over a person, either, but it isn't people I'm thinking of, to tell the truth. Properly brought up in this respect if no other, I have always been fairly cautious in built-up areas, despite all those blinds in the open country. Of course, there *was* some open country then. The thrill of speed is basic to our times. I enjoyed it as much as anyone. It wears off a bit as you get older, and more scarey.

But even then, the thrill of speed was definitely only one, perhaps minor, factor in the enjoyment of motoring, or motor-cycling. Just pottering slowly, just sitting on the bike at the kerb, feeling it warm and all potential between your thighs—this almost sexual feeling was the essence; this, not the raving blinds. Possession of a motorbike was, to a lad, very much what possession of a horse must have been in other times. It was a symbol and it was also a freedom. Ridiculous as it may sound, you felt that your motorbike conferred something like knightly status. It made you free of a footloose and dangerous world. It enlarged your liberty and your potential. It was the one and only *thing*, the one possession, that tied me to the world of algebra and wages, the respectable world of getting on. I could do without almost anything else.

Chapter Nine

I could certainly have done without Oxford. When it was all over and I was let loose on the working world, my father, in a burst of pride, had some visiting cards printed for me, as a surprise gift. They read, so pompously, MAURICE S. WIGGIN, B.A. (OXON.). They gave him immense pleasure, the dear man, but even at the time I was ashamed to use them. What did it all amount to? I had some sort of degree, useful in, say, the teaching profession, but probably nowhere else. Not being a determined little creep of a go-getter, or even a commonsense citizen, I had failed to make 'useful friends'. I made friends, certainly, but not useful ones. Is there such a thing as a 'useful friend'? Well, of course there *is*: I know it now. But the few useful friends I've managed to make have been useful by accident. I mean I made friends with them because I liked them: their usefulness, though real, though I acknowledge it all the time, was a bonus. They were simply friends who happened to turn out useful. I hope I've been useful to them. I don't mind being used, much, but I hate to use people. Oxford was crammed with people using other people and/or being used by them.

I don't know how it is now, but in 1931 Oxford was precisely the environment I least needed. At eighteen I was ripe and ready to drop out of the race; what is now called the rat race, though the term had not then been invented. There were no beatniks then; it had not occurred to anyone that going around looking like a lousy gorilla was somehow a sign of superior spirituality. Or perhaps it had—Christ and his apostles were not only beatniks, but looked it. But the young were not then a significant consumer group, therefore little or no attention was focused on them. They were the poorest of all the poor in England, and since they had no money to spend, no vast cabal of cynical exploiters flattered them and made them self-conscious by unctuous publicity.

The young wore what they could get: there were no fashions for them, they merely followed their elders. Thus our clothing was quite ordinary, though a tendency to wear roll-neck sweaters marked out the undergraduate, if anything did. Hair was just hair: poets tended to let it grow a bit, as poets seem always to have done; and what poets did, poetasters did also. But there were more close crops than longhairs, even among the more aesthetically inclined. Naturally there were dandies, as there have always been, but their dandyism, at any rate in dress, would look a bit stuffy on a stockbroker today.

I think it was, historically, a very dull time even for Oxford, which is one of the dullest places in England. The extravagances of the Twenties had been replaced by the cautious conformity of the Thirties. The fearful economic situation of Britain probably had something to do with it. When I went up the great swindle of 1931 had just been perpetrated: that blowhard Ramsay MacDonald had done his despicable deal with the really insufferable Tories, the Liberal party was ruined, the Means Test was in operation, unemployment was fearful, trade at a low ebb, the war had receded leaving nothing but a litter of ruined men and a great vacuum where the best had been.

Were there any great causes? I don't think so. The more liberal and compassionate grew bitter and radical as the plight of the poor grew ever more desperate; but what could they do? Hitler had not yet arisen to make an obvious target. I think many of us felt then, as we feel now in 1968 when Harold Wilson is Prime Minister, that England had sunk so low, public affairs were so dismal, public men so odious and small, that it really wasn't worth taking public affairs, or anything, seriously. If success, ultimate success, meant being a creep like Ramsay MacDonald, or a bullfrog like Baldwin, or something utterly repellent like John Simon, then plainly success was absolutely not worth pursuing. One was not only helpless (which is a normal condition) but also hopeless. If this was what 'getting on' meant, then plainly it was a positive sin, or vice, to get on. Suddenly and for the first time in many years, I felt attracted to Christ. I began to love him as a supremely lovable failure. I love him still, for the same reason.

I don't mean that I became religious, or even that I got a touch of religiosity. Not at all. This was my least religious period. Uncle Joe Simpson Hall had given me an introduction—the only one I carried up to Oxford—to the leading Methodist parson in the area. I am sincerely sorry that I have forgotten his name; forgot it about 1934. He was a nice scrubbed scoutmasterly man who with his wife gave At Homes in a big old manse somewhere on the Cornmarket. I attended one of these ghastly evenings, which began with prayer and ended with coffee, and found the atmosphere unbreathable. I had only gone to please Uncle

Sim, and did not go again. But I did strike up an acquaintanceship with the Franciscan friars who lived in the new Friary on the Iffley Road; some attended lectures at St Catherine's. I was very much taken by the rigours of their life; it appealed deeply to the masochist in me, the element which has landed me periodically in hair-shirt penances which are always succeeded by wild outbursts of extravagance. For the first time I considered the attractions of the monkish life. Would a monastery be the answer? There was obviously much to be said for it. Calm and quiet, the element of self-denial which appealed so deeply, the routine of early rising, getting up in the middle of the night for a service, the little cell with its austere furnishings and hard pallet to lie on, the sparse food taken standing up at scrubbed tables, the apparent democracy, the absence of the getting-on spirit, of the drive of ambition. . . All very attractive: and a consoling sense of Larger Purpose, too.

Many a time I was to consider this prospect, not very seriously, of course, since I had no religion, but as an aesthetic proposition. It has a certain dubious charm. But . . . what did one do about sex? I knew too well that a life without womankind would never do for me. I broached the subject to a Balliol friend, a man even keener on sex than me, if that were possible, while walking to Dorchester and back for our health's sake. What on earth did the monks and friars do about it? He suggested that they found their relief in masturbation. Thinking of those pink-cheeked, clear-eyed young Franciscans, I could not quite see them doing it. But that may have been naïf of me. Anyway they certainly managed without the solace of sex, and I knew I could never do that.

So tea at the Friary remained the full scope of my experience of the monastic life. But I greatly enjoyed tea at the Friary; an hour's asceticism was plenty, then out into the Iffley Road, with the wintry lights coming on, girls cycling home from work, all the pullulating richness (as it seemed then) of the sensual life. Ah, there's nothing like contrasts for enjoyment.

I went up to St Catherine's, because it was cheapest. It used to be called the Non-Collegiate Society, a plain name for a plain fact. But the weakness for euphemism, though not such a leading factor in British life then as it has since become, was strongly at work, and they began to call it St Catherine's Society some years before I joined. It is now St Catherine's College. But there was no real college then. We spent the whole of our time—three years or four, as the case might be—in digs, licensed by the authorities but still digs. Naturally we St Catherine's chaps sought out the cheapest.

My first lodgings were in Walton Street, a little to the north of Worcester College. My father drove me up in the old Standard tourer, I showed him round a bit, and made the most of the old central buildings which we had next door to the Examination Schools—after all, he had to see something which looked a bit like a college—and then he dropped me off at the digs ('my rooms'). He looked a bit puzzled, dear man. After all, the ancient university ethos isn't very markedly apparent in Walton Street, which is a slum. As he was going out of the sitting room door he turned and awkwardly kissed me on the cheek. I was too flummoxed to return his embrace. I watched him drive away, back to the Black Country and its grinding strains and stresses. He had left me three quid to pay my first week's digs and board. I had a sitting room, bedroom, full board and 'attendance' for £2 17s. 6d. a week. The extra half-crown was my pocket money. Thereafter my parents sent me a registered letter once a week containing three pound notes and half a crown. And of course they paid the college bills, for tuition and so on, and bought my books. That was the economic basis of my first year at Oxford.

I should perhaps point out that three pounds a week was more than most families had to live on. You can judge the temper of the times from that central fact—£2 17s. 6d. for two rooms, firing and lighting, full board and 'attendance'. On that price my landlady made a profit sufficiently attractive and important to her to justify all she had to put up with. And, of course, she had to keep the rooms free during those long holidays; at least, nominally. When people back home learned what I was paying, they were aghast.

'Profiteering old cow.'

'She must 'a' sin yer comin'.'

''er'll be retirin' in another couple o' years.'

Back home a single man could get digs and full board (though not, perhaps, a private sitting room) for thirty bob a week, or less. But back home, whole families were eking out their existences on thirty bob a week.

You have to bear these things in mind.

Well, there I was, completely adrift. To me, that weekly registered letter represented real sacrifice. It was more than twice as much as my mother got from her rents of seven houses. It was a real sum of money, a good week's wages for many skilled craftsmen. It hurt me to take it; on the other hand, I was surrounded at Oxford by evidences of another world, a world of wealth, where £3 a week meant nothing. To my old friends at Bloxwich, I was a pampered playboy living on the fat of the land, sucking in enormous sums of money weekly, one of destiny's darlings, a parasite. In the ambience of Oxford, I was one of the poorest of the poor. I didn't know which way to turn.

I hated my dependence, I hated taking money that could ill be spared, I loathed the implication that I was a pampered playboy, I was sickened by the gulf that opened between me and my old friends of the working class. To be conscious at the same time of grinding poverty was quite a strain. Yet my poverty was real, in the circumstances. Living at Oxford on five bob a week, it's not easy.

So here I was, torn by the first tremendous dichotomy. Though I suppose I'd seen it coming. I suppose the answers were obvious, had I had the wit to see them. One answer would be, to get stuck into my work, press on, *get on*, rise out of the slough of economic stress and latch on to the prosperous professional classes. That was the obvious course, that was what it was all in aid of. 'Make the most of your advantages'. The other alternative would have been to jack it all in, make a clean breast of it—'I cannot take your money, I do not want to *get on*' —and vanish into the underworld of honest poverty which so attracted me. I did neither. True, I didn't see those alternatives so clearly then as I have seen them since, though they were implicit in all my thought. But I didn't possess the character, as they call it: meaning that I took the line of least resistance, let it all wash over me.

I didn't expect it to last, anyway. To me that first year was highly provisional. I fully expected to be sent down, or rather to have to go down, when at the end of the year I had failed to get a scholarship or exhibition. I had not then heard the old French adage, '*Le provisoire dure longtemps*'. And I should not have believed in it even if I had. Youth is a time when one does not believe in the enduring qualities of the provisional. It seems that one can always change things, and for the better, by dramatic and radical action.

Not that I proposed any particularly dramatic and radical action. In so far as I thought of the future at all, I saw myself dreaming through a year of sensuous experience, then vanishing into some sort of unspecified limbo; cub reporter, garret-starving poet, tramp, hermit, shepherd's mate, fisherman. Even then, I had no faith whatever in social action of any kind. I knew that all corporate action is ineffectual. I was a *fainéant* with a vengeance. It was perfectly clear to me then, and it still is, that when two or three are gathered together you've got a talking shop, and that's all you've got. The loudest or most strenuous or cunning talker will get his way, and it will very likely be the wrong way. The quietest may very well possess the best solution, but no-one will listen to him.

Yak-yak-bloody-well-yak. I despised all politicians, and I still don't exactly revere them. There are no political solutions, only political compromises and disasters. Life is a shag-bag of compromises. The only soul you may possibly save is your own; and that's unlikely. I had had enough of public speaking, oratory, rhetoric, man management, to last me a lifetime. Gasbags, windbags, go-getters, crawlers, creepers, suckers-up, committee men, aspirants for office, toadies, climbers of every description, every known sort of official—perish them all. That was my attitude. 'Those who can, do; those who can't, teach.' Or if they don't teach, they orate, manage, administer. 'Those who know, don't say; those who say, don't know'. I had all this crystallised in the old heart, a rock or jewel of negative certitude, the only faith I ever had, the one indestructible item of faith, or non-faith. I have no belief in action, only in being. There were very few people to whom I could confess it. I doubt if I even confessed it to myself. It is very difficult to admit to yourself that the whole social and 'official' structure of life is a fallacy and farce. Still, I knew that it was. It was mitigated, this rigour of disbelief, by the purely personal and irrational capacity for love. This was what made an otherwise completely barmy and meaningless existence not only tolerable, but rich, joyful, exciting. In private personal relationship I found the answer to every problem, the assertion and justification of all idealism. The giving and accepting of love seemed to me then the full reach of living. I'm still very far from sure that this was mistaken. Life teaches that even love can humiliate, but what else is so well worth humiliation?

Some of my reading supported this approach, some was curiously at variance with it. But consistency was never a strong point. I was naturally attracted to rebellious, hopeless and unworldly idealists, but at the same time I was somewhat in thrall, for mainly stylistic reasons, to the Catholic apologists, notably Chesterton and Belloc. I heard them both speak, but was too shy to speak to them. At this time I regarded Chesterton as the more brilliant, but later Belloc came to be seen, even by me, as a superior man, if not a superior writer. When I read Richard Aldington's cry, 'O, who will deliver us from the Roman Catholic bores!' I was astounded and dismayed, for though Aldington was at that time some sort of hero to me, I simply could not see that Chesterton and Belloc were bores. I cannot see it now. They are both far better writers than Aldington ever could be.

When it came to writing my essays for the exhibition which was to keep me up at Oxford, I relied on Chesterton to an extent which surprises me now. My essays were (I'm sure) pure pastiches of Chesterton. It so happened that the examiners shared my enthusiasm. They must have. For they awarded me the exhibition. I suppose the truth is, so far as one can get at the truth, that the Chesterbelloc kept me from going too far the other way. I was trying to enjoy D. H. Lawrence, and in fact I shared many of his views, I was more a Lawrentian than a Chestertonian. But, you see, the grim fact is that Lawrence was not nearly such a good *writer* as Chesterton. He may have known better, his ideas may have been better, but he did not write so well. I have some respect for D. H. Lawrence as a prophet, a revolutionary on the scale of Blake, and very little respect for Chesterton or even for Belloc: I see them now as a couple of gigantic self-deceivers, escapists on a cosmic scale. But this does not alter the fact that as writers they were full of genius. They had the gift and the mastery of *words*, and Lawrence, for all his genius of perception, did not. So I struggled on with Lawrence, wanting to see the genius others saw in his writing, and strongly in sympathy with some of his views; but it was hard sleddin'. Whereas the the Chesterbelloc had me in thrall almost as soon as they opened their mouths, though their views on social organisation were far removed from mine.

However, there was a big and growing gulf between what was read and written, and what was felt and done. I was feeling the strain of the two worlds too acutely to settle down very seriously at my books. Mail from home—not just from the family: I mean mail from friends—unsettled me every time I got it. It spoke of the realities as I knew them: severe stresses borne with patience, injustice met with dignified bewilderment, a scheme of material getting-by (never mind getting-on) which had nothing in common with the world of books and lectures. Too modest to rate my personal fate higher than theirs, too sceptical to believe in any scheme of amelioration or revolution, too contemptuous of the plain-though-veiled objectives of the getting-on society, too idle to be really happy about myself ... I went through some hard dark nights of the soul during those halcyon Oxford days. But no-one would have suspected it, I fancy.

There was plenty of surface gaiety, though needless to say I never fell for the factitious excitements, the bullfrog self-importance and puerile hysterics of university club life. I looked in at the Union a time or two, and saw clearly that this was for posturing go-getters and vain creeps of the kind I could never stomach. The innumerable clubs and societies meant little or nothing: one always discovered—one always does discover—that club life is for its enthusiasts a substitute for real life, a hiding-away, a wistful and unhealthy quasi-organisation of the unorganisable. I was a member of a few, but never attended any of them more than once, and cannot even remember their names, save only the October Club; brief membership whereof was the nearest I ever came to membership of the Communist Party. Oxford served to confirm me in the belief, one of the few beliefs I might be said to have held, that membership of any organisation smaller than the human race was an aberration. I never fancied segregation, always suspected self-elected élites.

I see now that these prejudices were naïve.

But I do not wish to cook the book.

All descriptions are abstractions; infinitely simpler than the simplest processes which they seek to describe. Nothing is so homogeneous as it is made to sound. At the time when all these vague but really rather painful decisions, or non-decisions, were being formulated, life was going on, as it does, and there was a great deal of youthful high-spirited fun mixed up with the sombre philosophising. When I was elected to the Shute Exhibition in Modern History, life picked up quite sharply, since I also won a School Leaving Exhibition and a Borough Major Scholarship at the same time. This meant £40 plus £30 plus £50 per annum, an impressive total of £120 a year, or forty pounds a term. It was hardly enough, of course, but it seemed suddenly like wealth. For the first time in my life, I had a bank account. My father took me into the bank at Bloxwich, introduced me with touching pride to the old manager, and we paid in my first cheques. I was issued with a cheque book, on which I could draw at the rate of £3 a day. Naturally, no-one intended that I should draw £3 *every* day: that was the maximum I might draw on any one day. It was very nearly fatal. To be able to saunter into the bank, on the corner of the High and the Cornmarket, and draw £3 on demand—this was heady stuff, and my head, as you may have gathered, was none too strong. I'm ashamed to confess that I was overdrawn in my very first term as a monied man. Of course there was a terrible shindy. The old man and the bank manager separately and collectively gave me a good talking-to, dad settled my little debt (it was trifling—I hadn't suddenly developed expensive tastes, merely frittered the stuff away on booze and tobacco and a very few clothes) and I promised to mend my ways. I suppose I must have done, too, for there was only that one big blow-up, and my debts when I finally came down were tiny.

Oxford was a very bad place in which to be poor, and an even worse place in which to be just bearably solvent. Those seductive shops, beckoning you inside to buy wholly unnecessary clothes and things—

and the credit so freely offered, so gentlemanly and insidious ... I don't wonder that lots of lads took the wrong turning. Credit buying is a rotten bad thing, the tool of usury. I've bought several cars, in fact a lot of cars, on hire-purchase, but, that apart, strangely enough I've never used credit, even when my credit has been good and the offer tempting. If you can't afford to put the money down, do without: a good sound motto, and simple common sense. I never had any too much common sense, but in this respect if no other I am a model to all growing lads. Nor did I ever form a wistful attachment to exotic stuff like wine and cigars and rare tobaccos and foods—which have ruined the lives of so many impressionable undergraduates. Exotic cars, yes— that's a separate and singular chapter: the inborn Wiggin taste for *good* engineering has been a terrible burden to me, financially and in other ways, though on the other hand it has given me a great deal of transient pleasure.

But aside from cars, I have rarely been tempted by expensive *things*. Cars were quite enough. I never gave a damn about clothes, never wanted a splendid house or fine furniture, never fell for objets d'art, never seriously worried about fine food and wine and smokes (though I had my fleeting moments of epicureanism). I began on Woodbines and Gold Flakes, I end up rolling my own. I began on Erinmore and Tom Long, I end up on Tom Long. My suits come off the peg and my underwear from Marks & Spencer. I still like fish and chips, bacon and egg, sausage and mash, bread and butter, plain sharp Cheddar cheese. In the intervening years I have sampled a great wide selection of the world's *cuisine*, both *haute* and very *basse*, and thoroughly enjoyed it, and enjoy it still. But the point is, I can take it or leave it alone. My tastes are almost irreducibly simple, and plain, but by no means Puritan: I enjoy everything I have.

This Achilles heel of mine, the love of motors, first showed itself while I was still up at Oxford, plodding through my last year in a sort of happy dream punctuated by moments of nightmare. I was lodging with a jolly nice stick named Harry Walford, way up out of town just off the Iffley Road. His missis was no raving beauty, but she could cook, she was motherly and indulgent; and Harry was an outstanding man in several ways. He was a toiler at the bloody Morris car factory, that ghastly eyesore up Cowley way, and that being the case, he was naturally out of work as often as in. He spoke of the economic system in a manner with which I was very familiar. But although Harry's economic troubles were merely yet another factor which helped to confirm me in my contempt for the politicians and the goddam slave-driving capitalists, it should not be thought that all our time was spent in discussion of the political and economic structure. Hardly.

Harry had been a sergeant-major in the Great War, he was a sensationally handsome blond viking sort of man with wonderful twinkling blue eyes, he had an explosive temper but an affectionate and forgiving heart. Although he was from a different part of the forest, I recognised Harry as, in my life, a Smith. He did not exactly represent, it's not the right word, rather he expressed the style and temper of the Smith myth. He was the sort of man I tended to latch on to, given the chance; he was the incarnation of those qualities which I found admirable, and the fact that he was not bookish, that his solid stores of knowledge—knowledge of how life was lived and how it might be lived—came directly from experience and his uncluttered apprehension of the realities, including the social ones, this was a fact much in his favour. I was continually comparing Harry with the dons, the savants. He came out of the comparison very well.

There was just one don with whom I got on very well indeed. He was a plump and big Welsh parson (Anglican, of course) who was chief tutor at Saint Catherine's and who taught modern history. He was, in fact, my tutor. His name was the Rev. Trevor Davies, M.A. We did not spend any great amount of time together, but there was this instant rapport. Trevor was the only Oxford don I ever bothered to go back to see, though, to be sure, I waited twenty years before I went back to see even him. I could tell that he liked me, and I liked him. Without him I would not have had a friend in the governing classes at Oxford. The Dean was a dry and almost absurdly donnish Scot with a face like a withered lemon, a miserable fault-finding Puritanical pedant in my eyes, waspish, thoroughly uncongenial, with a voice like Fyfe Robertson and a strong distaste for my apparently careless approach to life, which concealed such agonising cares. He would have had me out if he had found a good excuse, I did not doubt. The Master (then called the Censor) was a hearty bald churchman whose approach to life was very much unlike my own, and not very uncongenial. He was a bit of a wit in his way. He used to have us to breakfast or tea or some such ghastly meal, once a term or thereabouts, and though his wife was gentle and really nice and strove to make the nervous and disaffected feel at home, I never quite did. I listened to the constant flow of donnish wit, the hearty-avuncular rattle of professional platitude and pious persiflage, and my heart sank. I recognised with one half of me that this was presumably *it*, the authentic stuff, donnish repartee in the Master's drawing room, just the job, just the thing to talk about back in Walsall;

but with the other half I recognised, all too clearly, if misguidedly, that it was also the authentic boloney. This was the professional patter: I wanted the heart of the matter. I was too young, naïf and silly to realise, then, that the professional patter *is* the heart of the matter. ('The medium *is* the message.') It struck chill into my innocent and tender heart. The conviction hardened that I was not cut out for success in the world. How could I be? I did not make the necessary responses. I chose the wrong friends. My 'values' were hopelessly unsmart, uncommercial, unsuccessful.

They still are.

Most Saturday nights Harry and I had a quiet booze-up in the kitchen, after his family had been chased upstairs. I was back where I belonged, or believed I belonged, which is near enough the same thing. We got through some very peculiar drink. I was beginning to experiment in a perfectly ordinary undergraduate way. We alternated glasses of beer with weird concoctions: liqueurs, mainly, the more exotic the better. Of course, even with my talent for cashing £3 cheques, I couldn't really afford anything of the sort, and though we liked a spot of Green Chartreuse and Benedictine and Cointreau and that sort of thing, we often had to settle for a cheap bottle of some vile sweet ready-made 'cocktail' with a name like Silver Lady or White Nymph.

I shall never forget those Saturday nights. Sitting either side the kitchen fire, smoking ourselves silly and growing quietly maudlin, we talked, or rather Harry talked, about women and war. Those were our only subjects, or at any rate they were Harry's only subjects, and whatever else I gained or failed to gain from my undergraduate days, I can honestly say that I emerged with a considerable knowledge, if only at secondhand, of women and war. Round about midnight Harry would be sufficiently well-oiled to open up with the real McCoy, and with a touch of awe I would realise that I was eavesdropping (it always seems like eavesdropping when you listen to a man much older than yourself in such circumstances) on the genuine as opposed to the formalised and fictional story of human life. Of course I was getting drunk, too, and my memories are hazy now: but I know that I received what I had never received from my own father or any of my academic instructors, a total view of the passion of human existence.

It was not a squalid view, let me say quickly: Harry, despite his hard times, remained a full romantic. Though he could be reasonably bawdy, in private, he still believed in the validity of certain concepts and standards of behaviour. Of course, being a man of his generation and upbringing, he accepted the masculine double standard of morality, unconsciously; yet he had cast-iron notions of honour, dignity, and courage, he was compassionate in his way, and despite the terror and risk and sometimes the degradation of the wartime which had moulded him as a young man, he managed to invest his stories with a lurid glamour even while he stubbornly refused to glamourise them. This is no paradox. Harry told the truth, of that I have no particle of doubt, but to Harry, the terrible truth remained, even through his scepticism and rough distaste for tarting a story up, something rather splendid to have lived through. And here I think he had something. It is best to tell the truth, better still to acknowledge it to your secret self: but still, since we have to face it, we might as well face it, grim though it be, with a touch of panache.

Strange Indian Summer of boyhood, strange Spring of manhood . . . a dappled chiaroscuro of cross-purposes and conflicting urges. I had a number of jolly friends, some close; one real close friend, from whom, alas, I was to part, years later, in sorrow. But I loved him dearly then; the memory is still green. My spiritual home was Balliol, where my best friends were. My really 'Oxford' type of memories are mainly of Balliol, which I haunted, since my friends were Balliol men; sitting on the grass, near the buttery, drinking Balliol beer and eating Balliol bread and cheese, dining in Hall, soaked in the Balliol ethos as much as an outsider could be . . .

My tutor predicted for me a First, in writing: which speaks well for the essay style I had at my disposal then, for I knew, though he it seems did not, that my knowledge of the set books was not so sound as it should have been. The real stumbling block was constitutional documents. In those days we 'historians' were faced with the hurdle of a fat grim book called *Stubbs' Charters*. I could never get into it. But it was a must, a compulsory subject. If you could not get through on Stubbs, you could not qualify for a First or even a Second. I could not get through on Stubbs, but this my dear tutor did not know. So easy-going was the prevailing system that I was never examined in Stubbs at any point during my three-year course. I literally knew almost nothing about Stubbs and his ghastly dull Charters—yet no-one knew how little I knew. A strange situation, since remedied, I do not doubt. When it came to the push I sat through Final Schools, wearing my subfusc in a heatwave, and I think I may have done quite well in various subjects, for I could not have failed to absorb something: I was quite interested, in a mild way, and even then thought I understood something of the real springs of history. At the *viva voce* the examiners seemed slightly puzzled, though of course they were not so puzzled as me. But with my total inability to read, much less remember, the awful Stubbs, I could not be allowed a First or even a Second. I got a Third.

I doubt if I should have read Stubbs even if I had not fallen in a big way for the motoring mania during my last year. Harry and a friend owned jointly a rather repulsive old Morris Oxford bullnose touring car, dated 1921, painted in what was euphemistically called French Grey. Nowadays it would be worth its weight in brass, to us barmy aficionados of the vintage cult. In 1933, it was simply a very regrettably obsolete car, a figure of fun. Harry and his mate, in and out of work, could not possibly afford to run it. Neither could I, of course, but when did that little deterrent deter? Harry delicately offered me the heap of junk for £2. I was particularly hard-up at the time, but I went into partnership with the close friend aforementioned, a sweet-natured exhibitioner from the Forest of Dean. Jo chipped in with £1, and by the time we had rustled up some sort of rudimentary insurance, and the minimal tax, and filled the tank with petrol, we were flat broke.

This did not prevent us from instantly setting out for London, a place vaguely believed to be interesting. We used to visit London on Saturdays, quite frequently, using the cheap train which cost, if I remember rightly, five bob. With a packet of 20 Gold Flake and another of 20 Players, and a few beers alternated by Green Chartreuse and Grand Marnier and Calvados, we would pass a cheerful evening around Piccadilly Circus, returning by midnight on the Flying Fornicator, which we frequently caught as it was drawing out of Paddington. But to be driving down to London in our own car was another thing again. I do seriously put it forward as a credible proposition that this was a turning-point in my life. I don't know about Jo's and would not wish to inculpate him.

Motoring today is among the most dismal ordeals which people can wish upon themselves. But in those halcyon days of which I speak there was little traffic, the roads were free and fine, and it was possible to enjoy the sensation of motoring for its own sake and without any reference to utility or transportation. Like other things in the island, fishing for one, the pleasure has been ruined because everybody can indulge in it. This is a small island and there are far too many people in it. In 1933 it seemed relatively empty.

I have written about my motormania (I have owned 36 cars at the time of writing) in a book called *My Life On Wheels*, published by John Baker, which is still in print.

In 1933, motoring at Oxford was hedged around with medieval-style restrictions. One was not permitted to keep a motor car anywhere except in a garage licensed by the University authorities. One was not permitted to drive more than 50 miles from Carfax. One had to have a green side lamp rigged up, so that it was permanently alight when the side lights were switched on—this, to enable the Proctors and their bulldogs to spot one. The whole complex of regulations struck Jo and me as quite absurd. We kept the old car in a shed owned by a friend of Harry's. This put us at his mercy, of course, but I have always preferred the wild chances of personal relationships to the stifling certitudes of official ones. This man was an ex-bearing scraper at Rolls-Royce, which is another way of saying that he belonged to the aristocracy of fitters. He used to sit on the running board supervising operations while Jo and I greased the ancient car. This was an operation which involved unscrewing some thirty beautifully made brass cups, filling them with grease, and screwing them down again, on exceedingly fine threads. Such workmanship, on a mass-produced car! But of course it all took time: time which might have been spent in better, or at least other, ways.

Doddling quietly down the Henley road towards London—a road we used to walk at least once a week, taking the twenty-mile stroll to Dorchester and back in our stride—I became conscious of a small, sad certainty. There have not been so many certainties in my life that I am likely to forget one. I realised that only two things, of grossly unequal value, were likely to make me an industrious citizen with his nose to the treadmill. One factor was love, which in my case inevitably led to marriage. The other was motoring. I wanted to be married and 'do the right thing', in the sense of setting up some sort of home. I also, very much, wanted to own a vehicle of my own. I was really a bit potty about motors. I regret this now, vividly, but there it was. I was still in thrall to the drop-out writers: Lawrence to some extent, Whitman of course; Dostoyevsky, Turgenev and Tolstoy were strong influences. I was very much in thrall to the Tolstoyan dream. Gogol and Gorki, the Stevenson of *Travels With A Donkey*; the example of Gauguin; and, lately, T. S. Eliot and Yeats—these were all influences pushing me out of the centripetal swing. They may sound a mixed bunch, they *are* a mixed bunch: but so am I. They all thrust in the same general direction, the direction of footloose freedom. The 'system' stank; all systems stank. Even then I felt, obscurely, that any one system was pretty well bound to be replaced by another system, since people were quite obviously systematic, lovers of routine and order and administration. I paid no great attention to the political side of life.

My father was elected a socialist councillor about this time: Jo and I sent him a congratulatory telegram which read Hoob Luddy Ray. To get that through the Post Office system seemed to us a genial jest. But my father's conversion to socialism (he had been a lifelong Liberal, like all the Wiggins, or almost all) though obviously a step in the right direction, was not nearly drastic and dramatic enough for me. I was disaffected not only by the rottenness of the lives of the helpless poor, as he was, but by the entire human scheme of arbitrary relationships, getting-on, bossiness, organisation. I never took to communism because it was so obviously just another system—better, perhaps, in the sense that it put or purported to put the interests of the toiling masses rather higher in the list of desirable priorities, but still an authoritarian system of government. I was a pure anarchist. I knew perfectly well that anarchy was unworkable and wholly impossible. I never preached it (or anything else). But anarchy *for me*—that was the goal. I envisaged nothing more than a shack in the woods, a spartan life of bread and cheese. I was not at all sure how the bread and cheese were to be obtained. But somehow, perhaps. I was not going to ask anything of anybody. I did not want *them* to be anarchists, or anything else: I merely wanted them to be themselves, and prayed that I would be allowed to be myself, living like a hermit and giving nobody any trouble, scraping some sort of exiguous living as a writer, chopping my own firewood, living as a recluse by some sacred spring of holy water in the Welsh hills. A pretty vague outlook.

Now into this unformulated dream, which was little more than a hazy image of unimaginable freedom, came three factors which decisively shaped the life I lacked the iron will to shape for myself. One of them was this utterly contradictory love of motors. One was love of a woman. The third was journalism. For I had already begun to be a journalist.

Chapter Ten

The dichotomy persisted even when it came to the craft. The first things I had printed were verses and letters, in the local papers. Then I managed to get some poems and stories and polemical pieces into *The Adelphi*, at the time when it was edited by John Middleton Murry with the assistance of Sir Richard Rees. 'Mr Murry likes your poems, and so do I,' said the first letter from Rees. The sun swung through a giddy arc and came uncertainly to rest again; the glum pavements trembled under my feet. I was sick with joy. Strangely enough, I did not follow up this lead. I went to London on a five-shilling cheap day excursion from Birmingham, during one early Oxford vacation, and walked miles until I found the office of *The Adelphi*, somewhere near Carlyle's old home, I think it was, off the Chelsea Embankment. I trudged up dusty stairs and knocked on the door, but no-one answered. I had no appointment—though I had been vaguely, kindly, beckoned to 'call in any time and have a talk'. Of all life's vitally important missed chances, I fancy this was the most serious. I walked back to Paddington and went home without seeing Richard Rees or Middleton Murry. One can never be sure, but I like to think that a talk with either of them might have set my life on a different course. Of course it might not, too. But this is one of my very few dreams of what might have been.

A Birmingham paper, the *Evening Despatch*, began to pay readers for letters, at the rate of three-ha'pence a line; the minimum (and often maximum) fee was half-a-crown. I got into the habit of writing sharp comments on local affairs. This sort of journalism is fatally easy. It really is fatal, too—when money and prestige are involved, you soon fake emotions you do not feel, especially the emotion of righteous indignation. I was in fact a sort of embryo leader writer. I was editor-ialising. So soon! Facile, glib, and easy. I suppose I persuaded myself, as all the writers of righteous letters do, that I really felt some concern about the subjects which I wrote with such feeling. The sight of your name in print is a powerful drug. You can form an addiction overnight.

Then suddenly I became unpaid Oxford University Correspondent, on the subject of motor sport, to *Sporting Life*. I do not really remember how it came about, but I know that Tommy Wisdom, the famous sporting motorist and journalist on Odhams, encouraged me to send him little accounts of the goings-on of the Oxford University Motor Club, if indeed that was its name. I hung around Reggie Tongue, a rich undergraduate who ran the Club and raced an Aston Martin, and sent off my little stories, and what's more they appeared. For some reason I never told my tutor.

So there we were. Theoretically I was off to the woods any minute now, but in fact (1) I had fallen in love and was burning to marry, (2) I had formed this attachment for motors, and (3) I had well and truly got the smell of printer's ink in my nostrils. Everything was wildly contradictory: the mixed impulses were enough to drive you mad. Actually I wanted only to be a poet, as now I want only to be a poet, as I have truly always wanted only to be a poet. But poets are elected, by holy grace. I had never met anyone who actually enjoyed any poem I had written, though of course I knew several who *said* they enjoyed them. But enjoyment cannot be counterfeited. I did not then know the truth of the matter, which may be summed up in a short poem of which I am fond:

> Write only for yourself.
> Whisper in your own ear.
> You may if you are lucky
> Have eavesdroppers.

I know now that that is true; it is the only advice a writer should be given. But at the time I was anxious to please. Being anxious to please has always been a failing. It is only an extension of that natural Celtic courtesy which made my father anxious to say what he thought his hearers might like to hear. I have more or less grown out of it now, have grown indifferent to censure and impervious to abuse. This is another way of saying that my manners have worsened. But it gives me a fugitive and failing hope that one day, in the time that remains, I may write something worth the trouble—of writing and of reading.

André Gide, in his *Journal* (1914), writes:

> The secret of almost all my weakness is that
> frightful modesty of which I cannot cure myself.
>
> I can never persuade myself that I have a
> right to anything.

I might have written those words myself. Unlike Gide, I have never had a private income. Had I not had to earn my living, like most people, I might have devoted my whole life to the manufacture of a poem. I can imagine nothing more rewarding; though of course a waste of time for anyone without the natural gift. But having to scrape a living, I made the mistake of living by my pen. In the only way which seemed to be opening out to me, in newspapers.

My parents still cherished (against all the evidence) some vague and fitful hope that I might become a respectable member of the teaching profession. But when the news of my Third came home, that hope, which never had much weight behind it, vanished. I had, in any case, made up my mind to try to break into journalism. People break into journalism in many different ways. There is no universal jemmy. A great many readers who write nice letters to me really want my job, though some are astute enough not actually to say so, outright. For the benefit of all aspirants, I will indicate how I broke in. The method does not necessarily hold good for anyone else. But I may say it is easy to break in. The portals are not well guarded. The hall of fame is full of misfits who slipped in because there was no-one on watch to turn them away.

I dare say I should have got in anyway, for I was determined as rarely in my indeterminate life, which has not been conspicuous for acts of decision. Sooner or later, somewhere or other, I should have found my place. I was wholly resolved. But how it *actually* happened is a story which pleasantly illustrates the part which chance plays in human affairs.

I had sent in to the Birmingham *Evening Despatch* a leader-page article (not that I had yet heard the term leader-page) which I headed *No Compromise!* It was a powerful plea for something or other, I forget just what; on the whole, I think it indicated a keenness to get stuck into the business of living free and footloose without too much materialism. I heard not a word from the Editor, but within a couple of days it appeared in full, under the interesting headline, *I Have 2s. and I Am Going To LIVE!* My name was there at the end of it, in ten point black capitals, an eighth of an inch tall. They seemed huge.

I was pleased, but the family did not quite know whether to laugh or cry. The bit about the two shillings did not go down any too well, though it was true at the time of writing, like practically every other statement I ever made. *True at the time of writing:* it should be engraved on my headstone. Reading this fairly passionate plea for an adventurous and unmaterialistic approach to life, my dear old dad could hardly have cherished any very warm hope that I should ever become a Director of Education. (For that is what he had in mind: he had actually made some sort of not unsuccessful overture to the then Director of Education in Walsall, V. J. Moore, hoping to get me into his office as a trainee or p.a. or something like that.) It was becoming plain to all that journalism or at any rate some form of writing was likely to be my line.

Now occurred one of those really weird little chances which make you believe in luck, blind fate, or even pre-destination. I was leaning on the counter of a jeweller's shop in Bloxwich High Street—I put in a lot of time leaning on the counters of shop-keeping friends, and in fact I still do: they have always been most indulgent—and naturally my notorious article, which had made quite a little stir in the village, came up. I confided in dear old Henderson, the jeweller and watchmaker, that I really fancied breaking into journalism, and he came out with the extraordinary remark that his wife was distantly related to the circulation manager of this very same *Evening Despatch* which had printed my article. You might think that a very flimsy sign or portent, but to me it was an omen vouchsafed directly from on high. It was nothing of the sort of course, but I believed that it was. So it had the same effect. Two or three times in my life I have felt this certainty that a sign has been given, and have gone ahead firmly, confidently, in some vast venture, filled with inner certitude that nothing could go wrong. It never occurred to me that the sign might be the work of the devil.

Within an hour of hearing this extraordinary news from Mr Henderson I was telephoning T. J. Taylor of the Birmingham *Evening Despatch*. Maybe he was circulation manager for the entire little group, in addition to the evening paper—there was a morning daily, the *Birmingham Gazette*, a Sunday paper, the *Sunday Mercury*, an early morning horse-racing rag called the *Sporting Buff*, and a profitable Saturday afternoon football rag called the *Sports Argus*. The whole outfit was owned by Westminster Press Provincial Newspapers Ltd., meanest firm I ever worked for. It used to be called the Starmer Group. Behind that vainglorious and bombastic titular façade lurked the puritan or at least Quakerish Cadbury cocoa moguls. Once you have worked for Quakers you get a bit of understanding for Catholics. And, perhaps, *vice versa*.

As I say, T. J. Taylor was circulation manager, whether of the evening paper only or of the group I cannot remember, and do not much care. Nowadays I would not put a lot of faith in a tenuous introduction to a circulation manager, for circulation managers are by no means editors' best friends; but ignorance is bliss, and I must have spoken fairly eloquently on the telephone, and Mr Taylor invited me to call on him. I arranged to do this next day. The family were off then on the annual pilgrimage to Rhyl, but this time I was not going with them. Family life had reached a moment of irreversible change. Things would never be quite the same again, after my Third. I can laugh now, but at the time it did not seem a very good joke. The results of Final Schools were published in full in the more sober newspapers of the time. Our local sober newspaper was the *Birmingham Post*, and that is probably the one I bought, on the appropriate morning, from the little shop next door to Tanky Reynolds's fish shop in The Street, after what I must confess was a slightly disturbed night. As I had expected, I found myself with a Third, and on the whole I was a little relieved that it was not a Fourth, or even just a Pass degree, for I saw that my best Balliol friend had got a Fourth, and he was a lively lad indeed, who did well later in the contraceptive industry.

When I walked in and with a false show of satisfaction announced that I had won 'a Third Class Honours Degree', sounding the capital letter initials and altogether making the most of it, the atmosphere was very bad. Mother was in quite a temper, though father put on a good front. I don't suppose mother had any too precise a notion of what was involved in winning a First, but she knew quite well the difference between first, second and third. She also knew, for I had to admit it there and then, that another Bloxwich boy, Raymond Baldwin, had got a First, and that seemed to make my performance a slight on the family which, I was given clearly to understand, would take a lot of living down. How was mother to show her face up The Street? I couldn't say. The fact that I was the first Wiggin to get an Oxford degree of any kind was irrelevant and immaterial. As mother might have put it, I was also the first to get a Third.

Father with his kindly talent for diplomacy did what he could to make me feel a bit less of a pariah, but it was an uncomfortable day in the old home, and I realised that nothing would ever be quite the same again. I was really quite sad, inside, for I had to acknowledge to myself, if to no-one else, that I might have done better. Some if not most of my Oxford contemporaries were plodders, trudging round the treadmill. Of course there were brilliant souls, as there always are, but I never counted myself among them, and certainly never aspired to academic brilliance. The multitude were careerists of a grisly sort, settling so young for safety, opting so willingly out of life's lovely wildness in favour of the secondhand life of the minor professions: nature's dominies, superior and pretentious clerks. I never thought that what we were offered in the way of academic instruction had the slightest relevance to living in the real world that sloshed and bashed, like a racing tide crested with scum and wrack, around the walls of the university enclave. Anyway, the resolve to be a reporter was by now quite old. It had been aired a few times, but always had to be shelved, or hidden.

'Don't talk to *me* about reporters! I don't want any son of mine to be a reporter. Drunken, cadging sort of fellows.'

'How d'you know that, mum?'

'Doctor Gilchrist told me. He knows a reporter. Always cadging for whisky at the Golf club, Doctor Gilchrist says. Not a penny to his name. Doctor Gilchrist says he doesn't think there are any prospects in being a reporter.'

'I don't want any prospects, ma. I want some fun.'

'Fun! All you think about is fun. Your dad and I want you to do a bit better than we've done. You're getting a good education. Why don't you want to be a teacher, son?'

'I don't like teachers, dear.'

'Well, I don't know what your dad will say. I really don't. After all we've done for you. Don't you want to pay us back a bit for all we've done for you?'

'Sure, mum.'

Mother dashes a duster up and down the keyboard of the upright piano. She always takes it out of the piano when she gets steam up. When mother fetches a duster and starts on the piano it's a sign.

'Mother.'

'Yes?' *Doh ray me far soh lah te doh.*

'If I leave school this term and start work on a newspaper, I could pay you back a lot sooner.'

'We don't *want* you to pay us back. We want you to do a bit better than we've done.'

'But you just said you *did* want me to pay you back.'

Mother bites her lip to kill the smile. *Doh te lah soh far me ray doh.* The white cat Pure comes running in to join in a duet.

'Well, we'll see what your dad says. I don't think he'll let you. He's set his heart on you going to college. You could be Director of Education if you set your mind to it, like Mr Moore. Wouldn't you like that?'

'I should hate it. I've had enough education. I mean, dear, I'm grateful to you and dad for all you've done for me, honestly I am, but

I've had enough of school. Bill Pemberton, he's going to be a reporter on the Walsall Times . . .'

'Now let's hear no more about it. Your dad will decide. I don't expect for a moment he'll let you. Now you can get me a bit of coal in.'

> *Jesus lover of my soul*
> *Let me to Thy bosom fly,*
> *While the nearer waters roll,*
> *While the tempest still is high*

Dear mother. Never listens to an argument, never lets logic interfere with the warm impulses of her heart. Singing around the house, a girl's voice still, a bird's heart. Capricious, unpredictable, generous, tactless, stubborn, unreasonable and lovable mother.

'Sam!'

'Yes, mother. What is it?' Father attacks his poached egg as if it were an enemy.

'I've been telling him what Doctor Gilchrist said about that reporter.'

'I should think so, and all. What in the name of faith do you want to get mixed up in that lot for, son?'

'He says he wants to have some *fun*. I told him, I said, never mind about fun, he ought to be thinking about paying us back a bit for all we've done for him.'

'Now, mother!' Dad holds up his knife like a baton. He has finished savaging his egg. He chops it into a hundred pieces and mixes them up, yolk and white, on his toast, like a painter's palette. Then he drenches the lot with pepper and salt. To this day I follow his routine in every detail when I eat a poached egg. There can be no other right way.

'Now, mother! Don't ever let me hear you say that again. We don't *want* paying back. It's our duty and privilege to give the lad the best chance we can, and we're proud to do it. Nobody's *thinking* of being paid back. What're you smiling at, our mother? What I can't fathom is why he wants to throw up the chance of a lifetime and get mixed up with *that* ragtime lot. I tell you, my lad, I wish *I'd* had your chance. My goodness, wouldn't I just have jumped at it! Ar, with both hands. Your old dad had to leave school at twelve.'

'I know, dad, and look at you now.'

'What d'you mean, look at me now?'

'I mean, if I turned out half as well as you've done, I should be very proud. If you can do what you've done . . .'

'Don't be silly! We want you to do *better* than we've done—ar, a sight better. That's all your mother and I are worrying about. Now why can't you settle down like all the other lads and make the most of your chances?'

'Have you seen 'the other lads', dad?'

''Course I've seen them. What do you mean? What's to stop you turning out as well as the Holyman brothers? Their father a farm worker, and all his family going to Oxford. I should think he's very proud of *his* family. And *we* want to be proud of *you*.'

'Well, I want you to be, really, I suppose. Only . . . Well, I just like the idea of being a reporter best, see? I don't want to waste any more time.'

'Nor you shan't! You'll get up those stairs as soon as you've finished your tea and get down to your studying. I tell you! I won't have it! We're going to see that you make the most of your education. Now don't let's hear any more about it.'

God give me strength. God give me patience. Up the bloody stairs, into the bloody attic. Over to the little table by the window under the eaves. *A Short History of the English People*, by John Richard Green. Plug John Richard Green. *England and the British Empire, Vol. III, 1698–1802.* Same to you, Innes. Plug Innes twice. Oh, well! Better open something. Open an exercise book, too. And let your longing look saunter over the sun-drenched park. There are girls in the park, strolling in their second-best or weekday wear, utterly delectable and desirable. Strolling coquettishly within hail of boys, free boys, poor boys, working boys with wages. Out of sight, out of the park, out of temptation, the Holyman brothers are swotting, Raymond Baldwin is swotting, Luke Freeman is swotting, Hardy is swotting; you are swotting. Quickly the resentment simmers down, and passes, as you begin to write, with an occasional truant eye on the trance-like scene in the evening park. The shadows deepen and lengthen over the grass, in the enclave of trees and bushes there is an occasional flash of colour, and wisps of crude laughter float on the dreamy air. Within you mixed motives wrangle, quite amicably, and as darkness approaches you heed the park less and less and the stir of writing sidles like alcohol into your blood.

'Wiggin.'

'Sir.'

'This is quite a good essay you have written On The Characteristics of the Augustan Age. Quite good.'

'Thank you, sir.' Little does he know how your house was divided. The magnetic pull of the park . . . Can he ever have felt it?

'Wait a minute, I haven't finished. Impetuosity, Wiggin, impetuosity is your failing. Perhaps I should say, *one* of your failings. One of the more conspicuous of a number of conspicuous failings. H'm.'

The Sixth Form laughs dutifully. Anything for a laugh. Anything for a break from the boredom of history as she is taught, history with no visible relationship to the history of the times we are *living* in; dead history. I enjoy it with them. What's wrong with being impetuous? I haven't yet learned. Perhaps I never shall.

'In fact, Wiggin, it might be said that your essay is one long exclamation mark. Yes, one long exclamation mark. You appear to have read and absorbed something of your subject, and you appear to hold strong opinions about it. Perhaps unreasonably strong. But I am not quarrelling with your opinions. The virtue of history is that it guides us to the formation of opinions. No. What I am complaining about is the immoderate vehemence with which you express those opinions. May I counsel you—not that I imagine my counsel will be heeded—may I counsel you to cultivate moderation of language, if not of thought? You write well, for a boy—very well, for a boy. But the adjudicator reading your answers in an examination does not want to be assaulted by a verbal ... how shall I put it? ... a verbal assault-and-battery. Vehemence militates against academic success, Wiggin.'

'Yes, sir. But I don't want academic success, sir. I'm going to be a reporter.'

'Good heavens! Well, I suppose there is something to be said for your decision. Yes, Perhaps the Press would be the best solution. The Yellow Press, I presume?'

Laugh, my hearties. I'm laughing with you. None of us here can know how the circle will come full round, twice. First I shall have the laugh on you, later you will have the laugh on me. Thank heaven the future is sealed off.

Meanwhile, you're beaten by sheer weight of numbers. Let it simmer. Let it ride. Sooner or later you are going to be a newspaperman. A reporter. A story-teller. Strangely enough you have no urge to invent. You are fascinated by the actual world around you: everything, good and evil, adventurous and homely, bright and drab. You are intoxicated by its quiddity and variety. Everything has its own native taste, its *ownness*, its singularity, its absolute private integrity of simply being. You want to rub your nose into as many aspects as you can of the life that fascinates and repels and haunts you: you enjoy the ugly, the dour, the stark, the clanging and the resonant, the rough and the impure, just as you enjoy the beautiful, the serene, the gay, the calm, the innocent.

You have not yet developed the critical faculty, except in so far as you are an intransigent critic of tyranny and humbug. You enjoy, savour, relish, roll round the tongue the experience in its pure essence of closeness, openness, valour, prudence, cosiness, windsweptness, You find beauty in the Black Country, the seaboard, the Welsh hills, the deep crooked valleys of the March, the chiaroscuro of the Potteries and the ample shimmering plains. You are a full romantic.

Fish aren't biting. It is cool on the canal bank, the wind rustles the reeds, a shirr and shimmer of wavelets like shot silk whisk the surface of the water. Your red-tipped float will never dip again. You know it. There is not a fish for a mile either way, from Fishley to Essington not a scale nor a fin. You can take your eyes off the float.

'Bloody cold, Hardy.'

'Bloody cold. Bloody hungry.'

'Hardy.'

'What?'

'Want to get warm?'

'How?'

'Pump your front tyre up. It's flat.'

'Oh, God and little fishes! That tube's *perished*, you know. The whole bloody bike's perished, come to that. I'm sick of bloody old bikes. When I leave college, Wiggy, you know what I'm going to get? Straight away, with my first month's pay?'

'A new bike.'

'A new bike? A new *bike*! Wiggy, I'm going to put down the deposit on a T.T. Replica Norton. A T.T. Replica, Wiggy, old boy. Nothing less.'

'And how much is your first month's pay going to come to, may I ask? A T.T. Replica costs eighty quid.'

'Well, perhaps I shall borrow the deposit from the old man. He won't mind, once I'm teaching. How about you? Any progress with the family about being a reporter?'

'Never discuss it now. No use. Looks as if they mean to send me to college. But take it from me, Hardy boy—the moment I'm off the chain I'm straight into a newspaper office. One teacher's enough in any family.'

'One! We've got three already in ours, as you well know. Still, I don't really care, one way or another. Long hols—that's my idea. Plenty of time for tuning the T.T. Replica.'

'Hardy, you're drooling.'

*

Whether Hardy's motives for entering the teaching profession were average or exceptional, any reader is free to judge for himself. I know what I think! I never knew what anybody else's motives were for entering the world of newspapers, and nowadays cannot imagine why anyone does. But now is now and then was extremely then.

So far as I know, you need the same qualifications to get a job on a newspaper now as you needed in 1934: luck, confidence, and a ready tongue. There are no recognised professional standards, as there are for lawyers and doctors and engineers, and although this grieves a good many people including many good people—not to mention the host of busybodies who like to poke their noses into everybody else's business—it is inherent in the nature of things that there never will be. For journalism is a matter of flair and opportunism. There are schools of journalism, of which I know nothing either for or against, but there are no degrees, and I doubt if any editor or proprietor would be very much impressed by them if they existed. The whole thing is a wild gamble, like the stage or practically anything you care to name, and, like almost every other occupation, the business is crowded with hopeless misfits, most of whom never suspect even in extreme old age that they have taken the wrong turning.

There are still, I think, two ways of entering the newspaper business on the editorial side. (Nowadays there are several other sides: the business has suddenly blown up with vast layers of chaps doing weird and wonderful things called market research, promotion, and so on: I know nothing about these activities and wish to know nothing. I belong to the pre-computer age when an editor followed his hunches.) On the editorial side, you can start straight from school, on a local paper, and work your way up. Or you can talk your way in, and/or write your way in, on a loftier level, a good deal later in life. Whichever way you take, you will be despised, if only secretly, by almost everyone who took the other way. Newspapermen who started by fetching cups of tea are forever telling anybody who will listen that the only way to become a good newspaperman is to start by fetching cups of tea. Ex-university boys tell each other that most of the newspapermen who started by fetching cups of tea should still be fetching them. There is something to be said for both points of view.

I both wrote and talked my way in, as you have gathered. When that article appeared, 'I Have 2s. and I am Going To *LIVE*', the family tacitly threw their hand in. Obviously I was set on it, and, more surprisingly, I could obviously make a copper or two out of it. I was paid 22s. 6d. for that piece, at the prevailing rate of three-ha'pence a line.

Easy money! That surely was the thought in many heads. Including, I must say, mine. To be paid for doing what you most enjoy doing, that really is something. So I was left at home, this time, when the family left for Rhyl. Within an hour of seeing the back of the family Austin disappearing down Stafford Road I was in a telephone kiosk in Birmingham haranguing poor T. J. Taylor, to whom Mr Henderson's wife was a cousin three times removed, or whatever it may have been. Once safely in his office I poured out my soul, or at least my ambitions (practically the same thing, wouldn't you say?) with a distinct lack of reserve. He was a big, plump, pink faced man with silver hair, who smiled faintly. He took me seriously enough, at any rate, to escort me to the office of the Managing Editor, and there he left me, with a smile I could not quite fathom. He was a big-hearted man whose memory is green with me.

I was slightly taken aback to find that the Managing Editor did not actually remember my article off-hand. He insisted on reading it there and then, on the files, and he read it terribly slowly and with a fixed expression of gloom. From that moment to this, I have always detested having to stand by while editors read my copy, and will go to considerable lengths to avoid the situation. But in the fullness of time he, too, gave birth to a strangulated smile, and after a few searching questions which I answered with more candour than good sense prescribed, he told me, as one conferring an unheard-of bonus, that I might work as a general reporter for a month, without pay, if I really cared to, and after that they would *see*. I left his office in a daze of joy. I'm not sure I didn't walk out backwards, as from Royalty.

This was the moment of liberation and fulfilment. Doubtless if by some unimaginable stroke of fortune I could now kiss the profession goodbye and retire to the hills with my gramophone and books and records, never again to write a line for pay, I should experience the moment of liberation all over again. It's quite possible. But in between that moment of leaving T. T. Stanley's office with his generous permission to work myself silly for a month for nothing, and this moment, though there have been two or three other occasions of significant enfranchisement, there has been nothing quite so orgasmic and intoxicating. I was 'in'. From the autumn of 1934 to the spring of 1939 I hurried to that office eagerly, every day. I gave myself to the practice of journalism with a fervour, an enthusiasm, and a sense of responsibility, which I had never brought to anything else and which, to tell the truth, nobody who knew me had any reason to suspect were in me. I am one of nature's love fanciers and have loved a lot of things (and people) in my life, but nothing more wholly and passionately than that first job.

This joyous approach might have been severely modified—indeed, I might easily have chucked the whole business, early on—had anybody else been my boss in place of the man who actually was. The Editor of the *Evening Despatch* was a character named Harold Benoit, whose like I have not met again. Ben had a tremendous zest for the business, and the knack of communicating his zest. By far the most important factor—he gave me a free hand. He had courage and magnanimity. He took a broad view of the prospects and he was sure of himself. He knew what he knew, and he knew what he did not know. He knew his own limitations and he recognised the qualities of other people. He knew how to encourage and when to give a free rein to enthusiasm. This was vital in our relationship. Newspapermen quite often think of themselves as artists, or at least as artists *manqués*; and although such a claim is doubtless absurd, still they must be allowed the tatters of artistic temperament if they are to do their best and most joyous work, and I think they tend to feel frustration rather more easily and more keenly than do bank clerks and butchers. And I dare say it is important that they should.

My beginnings could hardly have been humbler. I did the routine jobs on 'the diary', under the direction of a rather depressed and depressing character named Harry Boote, who was known as the Chief Reporter: an honest and exact term, now passing into oblivion in favour of the more glamorous and meaningless title, 'News Editor'. (As rat catchers are Rodent Officers and dustmen Disposal Operatives, or whatever the canting euphemism may be.) In his big diary Harry Boote kept notes of forthcoming events, which were duly 'covered', assuming there was anyone to spare to cover them, when they came off. There were also daily routine calls—fire stations, police stations and courts, hospitals, stock exchange, and doubtless others which I have forgotten. I did my stint at these chores, and reported the magistrates' courts, and enjoyed myself enormously. This was Life. I covered fires and accidents, cats up trees and dogs down shafts, golden weddings, art shows, beauty contests, amateur dramatics, motor car and motor cycle trials and races, minor football games, retirements and presentations, and virtually every job that turns up for a local newspaper. I say I enjoyed it all, and I did, more or less, but even so early I recognised that there was one aspect of newspaper work in which I was unlikely to shine, and that was the business of going up to a perfect stranger and asking him personal questions. I was too shy for that, and it seemed so odd. I was never one for sticking my foot in the door. If instantly there was struck up a harmonious rapport, then I might do very well, get a really sympathetic interview: but if it began on the wrong foot, with suspicion and resentment, there it ended. So that was one vital aspect of newspaper work—the tough reporting which boils down to haunting people who don't want any part of you—at which I was plainly going to fail. But of course it was only one aspect: there are many sides to the work.

Feature articles, written voluntarily out of one's own head and (at least nominally) in one's own time, were remunerated at that very handsome rate of three-ha'pence a line, and during my month's trial at no salary I lived well. At the end of the four weeks I was taken on the staff at a salary of £2 a week, the Managing Editor pointing out that it was open to me to supplement that admittedly meagre salary by writing feature articles and paragraphs for the column of local gossip called Despatch Man's Diary. I did this to the tune of about £10 a week for three or four weeks, and felt that the Lord had indeed vouchsafed a sign to his servant. The family could not believe their eyes. I was then smartly given a rise, the accounting side having cottoned on to the situation. My new salary was £4 5s. or £4 10s. a week—and I was firmly told that in future I should *not* be paid extra for features, gossip paragraphs, and so on.

So the wild dream of wealth faded fast, but it had always seemed far too good to last, I had really been waiting for the blow. At any rate, I was established, so soon, as one of the world's paid workers, a fact on which no-one had been able to count with any certitude. And I had already bought Whitney, my Austin Seven Chummy tourer, named after Whitney Straight, the current hero of Shelsley Walsh and other motor racing venues. It cost me £15 and of course I was paying for it at the rate of £1 a week. During the whole of my working youth it was an understood thing that you were always in hock for your car to the tune of £1 a week. Once my obligation rose to 30s. a week, and then I was really worried. My new salary hardly covered my expenses, in the life I had begun to lead, but I felt no resentment. I could never bring myself to feel very strongly that I had a right to be paid for doing something which I so much enjoyed doing. The glamour of the trade had me in thrall and that was almost enough to live on by itself.

After this period of routine chores Ben noticed me and sent me wandering around the midlands (which we always printed The Midlands) to write a vast number of uninhibited pieces about factories and places and people, all of which defied sub-editing, for there was really nothing you could do with them except either print them entire or leave them out altogether. I am sure they were very rum and rhapsodical pieces, but they were written with passion, gaiety, and a certain undamaged perceptiveness which may have come as something fresh in that solidly professional atmosphere.

They were, of course, the first fruits of a spoiled child. I know that. They were the product of a young writer who had never *had* to earn his living in any of the deadening and destroying ways known only too well to the mass of mankind. It is one thing to drive a lorry in vacations, as I had often done. It is one thing to knock-on tubs of coal, unpaid, for Messrs Harrison's collieries, while playing truant, and to join in the communal chore of picking coal off the tips during strike and shut-down. It is one thing to love your poor friends and admire their stoicism. But it is quite another thing to creep day after day into some ghastly office where everybody hates everybody else.

My stuff went down quite well because I literally did not know what I was talking about. I enjoyed my experiences because they came fresh and did not endure. The freshness came out in the writing. I had my sensibilities, my sensitive little soul, I had a good vocabulary and a feeling for words, and I had this morning glory of innocence, which is indistinguishable from illusion. I was of course not ignorant of meanness and envy and falseness, but I was ignorant of *ennui*, I knew nothing of the drabness of the drab. I knew starkness and ugliness very well, but they are not the same thing as mere drabness, and in certain circumstances they can be enjoyed. I combined a fondness for adventure and eccentricity with a lively love of homeliness, a keen delight in the poetry of everyday things. In short, I was a full romantic; and such is a boon to a newspaper, for a short time, until the romanticism has been beaten out of him. (Not by the newspaper, but by time and life.)

Have no fear that I intend to inflict any of those old articles on you. Even I cannot re-read them. Some years ago I went through a few thousand of them, my wife's hoarding of years, and burned the lot without a pang. They were not written by me, but by a bright-eyed young rhapsodiser who saw almost everything, even the process of welding motor car bodies, with the eye of wonder. But they must have made their little mark, for within nine months of entering the business I was promoted Literary Editor of the *Evening Despatch*.

Literary Editor is a highly misleading term, though one of which I am fond. Originally it denoted (and on newspapers of quality, like *The Sunday Times*, it still denotes) an assistant editor whose particular responsibility is the literary pages. On the literary pages were printed such things as book reviews, criticism (not exactly the same thing, I'm told), reviews and news of music, drama, films, ballet, and essays. In short, nearly literature, and sometimes quite. Lord Northcliffe put an end to all that nonsense when he introduced into journalism the sound business principle of playing down to the meanest intelligence. By the time I entered journalism, if there was one thing a popular newspaper avoided more successfully than another it was the taint of literature. The literary pages had become 'feature' pages, and the literary editor, though sometimes he was the last to realise it, had become the features editor. I was features editor in fact.

A features editor is a popular man. Whatever he says is witty and profound. He receives countless invitations to drink and dine. People are even willing to lend him money. He receives free first-night tickets and copies of new books. He gets a fine assortment of Christmas cards, many from people he does not recall having met. If he stops being a features editor and becomes a writer on his own account, exchanging the state of buyer for that of seller, he finds himself mysteriously less crowded, less witty, less well-beloved. A curious phenomenon which I have several times had the pleasure of experiencing. Since those halcyon days of 1934–9, I have been features editor of several national newspapers, apart from other executive appointments of an even more resounding and glamorous sort; and I have given them all up, voluntarily, perhaps foolishly, in favour of various writing jobs. So I have had plenty of opportunity to observe the behaviour of writers *vis-à-vis* executives. Now that I am permanently on the writing side, and quite certain never again to become an executive, I am able to adjust my own behaviour towards the executives who have a say in shaping my life and work. I am open to correction, but I fancy they would confirm, rising as one man to the vote, that I never insult them by a too ingratiating servility.

The fact that I knew nothing about the job discouraged neither Ben nor me. It was no sinecure. The *Evening Despatch* was a full-size newspaper (not a tabloid, that is to say) with anything from 14 to 24 pages daily. My ration of feature pages was about one-third of the paper. So each day I was solely responsible for anything from four to eight nice big pages. I had no help, and wanted none. I was the entire features department: my own copy-taster, ideas man, sub-editor, re-write man, headline writer, caption writer, typographer, layout man, picture editor, and often writer as well. Nowadays I see large staffs of London weekly papers growing ulcers like mushrooms in the effort to produce a smaller acreage of feature pages than I used to produce single-handed every day. But, of course, what they produce is better. It ought to be.

However, I enjoyed it best when I was on my own. Empire-building is popular with executives everywhere, not just in the civil service. I have had some experience of it. When I became features editor of the London *Evening Standard*, after the war, I didn't even have a secretary. When I opted out of the job, two years later, in order to write a column called My Court Casebook, the features department was a flourishing or at least a growing concern with people dashing about all over the place. But at Birmingham, for the first two or three years, I was entirely on my own, and as an individualist first and last, I had the happiest time of my entire working life, and on the whole I wish to God I'd never left the place.

The key to my happiness here was the independence which Ben allowed me. But another factor of almost equal importance was that I found the composing room immensely congenial. The composing room (known loosely as 'the printers' ') is the nearest thing in journalism to a factory. I felt instantly at home amid the light *swish* and *chink* of the Linotype machines, and the faint acrid smells of ink and hot metal and warm papier-mâché, the men with black hands, the presses, and the long cast-iron work-benches that are still called stones, on which the pages are physically composed. It was a factory *plus*: a factory plus words, plus drama, plus the special excitements peculiar to journalism. I could not have been pitch-forked into a milieu which suited me better. Perhaps I ought never to have left it.

Printers, in my experience, are invariably an obliging if a grumbling race of men, manly and friendly and patient to a degree. Not all of them, perhaps, are deeply interested in the art of display, but there are always some who have retained their interest in the art despite long association with arrogant editorial men who could not be trusted to address an envelope attractively. At Birmingham there were several first-rate men. I was on excellent terms with them all. I was living the life I loved, making something in a remarkable sort of factory. They probably recognised that I had my heart in the job and appreciated the difference between a page that is flung together and a page that is *composed*, and they taught me first the basic grammar of print, the rudiments, and thereafter quietly egged me on to ever more reckless ventures. We dragged into the light of day cases of type that had not had the dust off them since the Great War, or thereabouts, and although I daresay we mixed them indiscriminately at first, in the sheer joy of discovery, order soon emerged, and our pages took on character, vitality and energy, and ultimately a quite high gloss finish, such as I have never been able to achieve since on any of the various newspapers which have employed me. Nothing that I have done for money, in all my working life, has given me more sheer joy than designing those feature pages and seeing them through 'the printers'.

My working day took on a pattern which would kill me now. I arrived at 8 a.m. and went straight down into the composing room, to supervise the making-up of the feature pages which I had prepared the evening previously. I was 'on the stone', working in co-operation with the stone-hands who actually put the type and picture-blocks into the steel frames of the pages, for about four hours. With a batch of galley proofs in my hand, I cut when cuts were needed, wrote bits extra when they were wanted to fill a column, checked captions against pictures, and conducted an affectionate running battle with the chief stone-hand, a gnarled and sceptical character named Walter Ensor, who made marvellous home-brewed wine, and with the overseer, Wally Stevens, to whom I fear I caused more anguish than should be caused by one human being to another. All in a good cause.

The last feature pages were due 'away' about noon. Our first edition appeared about half-past. The news and sports pages changed all through the day. We published about six editions in quiet times and more in times of crisis or delirium, which, in the Thirties, were not rare. But the feature pages usually stayed put all day as originally published, and once the first edition had gone to bed I was normally free to start all over again, getting the next day's pages ready. Ben told me what advertisements my pages had to carry, and I measured them in. The rest was mine. Absolutely mine. Nothing in my working life, before or since, has given me more pure joy than I used to feel when I contemplated all those big, bare, inviting pages.

I cannot draw or paint. Careful, lip-licking drawings of twigs and catkins and wild flowers, at the Nashnul, were about my limit. But I found that I had the happy knack of being able to 'visualise'—I had some sort of notion what the finished job might look like, when printed. I absorbed everything laid down by Eric Gill and Stanley Morison, but the fertilising influence was John Rayner, who was then Day Assistant Editor of the *Daily Express*. He put through something very like a single-handed revolution in newspaper design, in the early Thirties. He, too, had a boss who gave him his head, Arthur Christiansen. The *Daily Express* may have been mad, editorially, but it looked very fine to me; at least the feature pages did. Rayner was an erudite young man who combined excellent taste in aesthetic matters with courage and originality. I was his disciple, albeit at a distance and unknown to him. I don't mean that I slavishly copied the *Daily Express* of that time, but it was certainly my model. When the time came for me to move on he accepted me on the *Daily Express* without a second thought, as his assistant. My *Evening Despatch* pages used to be reproduced in the *World's Press News*, our trade magazine, as examples of go-ahead stuff coming out in the provinces. With-it Wiggin!

So I designed the pages, subbed the copy, wrote the headlines, dug out the pictures, got the illustrations drawn, and altogether had a rather full day. At the peak of this happy time I discovered an artist named Ronald Neibour, known professionally and personally as Neb. His pocket cartoons delighted a generation of readers of the *Daily Mail* and the *London Evening News*. Neb had come to us from the *Oxford Mail*, and I discovered him sitting sadly at a desk in the library, gazing glumly out over the vile prospect of Birmingham when he was not being utterly wasted in the soul-destroying occupation of re-touching bad photographs. No-one in the building had realised that he could draw, though it was his drawings that had got him a job; no-one had cottoned on to the fact that this great big shy man with a stammer and a look of amiable dejection, like a St Bernard that has lost the cask, had a delicious sense of humour and almost infinite potentialities. I wish to boast of the fact that I set him to drawing tremendously. Our friendship is one that has survived the tensions of growing into middle age. His work added gaiety to our pages, and gaiety we were always in search of, for, if you remember, those were tightish times and the outlook was not good.

It was not all plain sailing. Neb, like others, sometimes found my demands extortionate. Sometimes I had to thump him into a proper sense of the urgency of the situation, with short chopping left hooks and right jabs to the ribs. When sufficiently aroused, he would shamble into action like some great bear, and chase me out of the library and down the corridor and into the *Gentlemen*; where, if cornered, I would have to take a heavy swing or two. Boote took a dim view of these running battles, but his discomfort did not discommode us. Life was active and gay. I had no great taste for a decorous atmosphere. We got results, after a fashion, even if we had to thump them out of one another. Sometimes, on particularly good creative days, we got home black and blue. I do not know of any other office which used this system for increasing productivity.

I must confess that the only thing I really cared about passionately was the look of the pages, and the headlines. The actual content, the text, mattered to me less. I had no money to spend, and although there was no great lack of bright ideas about, mine and other people's, it was not too easy to get them carried out. I could buy articles from agencies which employed young hopefuls to churn them out, but at fifteen shillings a time, they were hardly brilliant. My main source was the reporters, who were encouraged to write features in any time they got off from the demands of the diary. The rewards were none too attractive, as you have seen. But they were a rather remarkable bunch of chaps, and they churned out some fine stuff from time to time. The members of my generation at Birmingham included some who were to become quite famous. The office which had once nurtured Hannen Swaffer and H. V. Morton was still a good nursery of talent. Among my contemporaries were Don Iddon, of the *Daily Mail*; Norman Shrapnel, of the *Guardian*; Frank Owens, editor of the *Birmingham Mail*; Grahame Stanford, columnist of the *News of the World*; Kenneth Bolton, now an editor in Kenya; Maurice Cheesewright; Ray Hill of the *Daily Mirror*; Reeves Quann; a marvellous writer named Albert Ramsbottom of whom I lost sight; Ivon Adams; and Roland Hurman, now assistant editor of the *Daily Mirror*. The most brilliant local writer, by a mile and a half, was Ivan Roe, who worked for Cater's Agency. Ivan was (doubtless still is) a genuine intellectual. His study of Dostoyevsky, *The Breath of Corruption*, was highly if belatedly praised by Sir Desmond MacCarthy in *The Sunday Times*, and won him the Hutchinson Prize. He wrote many books, yet his great intelligence and industry seemed not to bring him a fraction of the fame and wealth which he deserved. I am out of touch with him now—what am I *not* out of touch with, thank God?—but since I never hear of him, I can assume that you never hear of him either. Yet he was not only the gentlest and most sensitive and in some ways the bravest of us all, but almost infinitely the most erudite and intelligent. I used Ivan's work whenever I could: sometimes he wrote three or four articles a week for me.

And then, of course, I wrote a good deal myself; much of it very bad. I was a dramatic critic and a book reviewer. One of the things I can look back on with some satisfaction is that I initiated the books page on the *Despatch*. I reported motor racing and trials and hill climbs. I wrote innumerable feature articles, leaders, essays and interviews. Where did the energy come from? I know. The answer is very simple. It was not simply youth. It was happiness. I used to get home in the evening bursting with pride and delight in my pages. My poor wife had to go through the several editions with me, page by page, and hear all about it. Poor lass, she took it very well.

During those five sunny years I never seemed to have any money. My pay rose by degrees to £6 15s. a week, on which we married, much envied by old friends; though in fact I never saved a ha'penny and my wedding gear cost me fifty shillings for the suit, half a crown for the hat, and I forget what trifling sum of shillings for the 'suede' shoes. I was still truly feckless and thriftless in practical affairs apart from my beloved pages. Later, after a firm offer of ten guineas from the *Daily Express*, I was given a rise of thirty-three shillings a week, to eight guineas. How wildly rich we felt! Instantly I went in hock for an Austin Seven (we had had to give up motoring in order to get married). I don't think I've really ever felt so rich again.

Even so, the arbiter of so many destinies, the trenchant critic of first nights at the Repertory Theatre, the Prince of Wales, the Alexandra and the Theatre Royal, the familiar of ace motor racers, the reviewer of important books, the dispenser of patronage—this important character rarely seemed to have a whole pound in his pocket. I cannot say that I have often felt very acutely the need to have a pound in my pocket. My feelings about portable money, money-in-pocket, had not changed since my schooldays. I liked to have half-a-crown; given half-a-crown I felt reasonably on top of things, capable of getting home and unlikely to be much put out or embarrassed. Not exactly a man-about-town, no. But in one respect the lack of money did occasionally irk me, for by now I was seriously in thrall to fishing tackle and motor cars, both of which are quite expensive if you take them at all seriously, if you discriminate and construct standards.

Had I had more sense I should have made a serious effort to get into motoring journalism, that highly specialised, esoteric branch of the mystery. Specialisation is doubtless a bad thing for men, but it is a good thing, professionally speaking, for journalists. No beginner or aspirant is likely to find much helpful information in this book, but here is one bit of advice which may be worth actual money, and any small donations, or large ones for that matter, will be gratefully received. Specialise and be serene: that is my advice (professionally speaking) to any boy. One of the distressing things about versatility and general, knockabout, turn-your-hand-to-anything journalism is that one is always having to defer to the opinions of people whom one cannot for a moment (professionally speaking all the time, of course) respect. The specialist has to be respected: he *knows*. The assistant editor may think he knows better than any reporter or sub-editor or photographer, but he knows that he does not know better than the racing tipster, the gardening correspondent, the diplomatic man, the crossword king. There is no such thing as civil service security in journalism, but if it is a certain stability and serenity which you are looking for—specialise. However, I don't really regret that I hadn't enough good sense to specialise, for I should certainly have specialised in motoring, and it is beginning to bore me now, in fact it has bored me for years. Middle age is a funny time, when you learn about your real self at last, if ever you are going to.

I left Birmingham in 1939, shortly after being made an editor, and after the first and last really tremendous row with the old firm, a bust-up which not even dear Ben could paper over. I went to London to work on the *Daily Express*, under the great Christiansen. I might have been said to have 'arrived', in a small way. But I felt that I had lost my way.

Chapter Eleven

The night before the wedding my mother said to my bride-to-be, 'I don't know *what* you'll do with him. He breaks everything he touches.'

Kay privately thought mother might have mentioned her doubts a little earlier, or alternatively kept them to herself. But, being her discreet little self, she swallowed hard and said nothing.

I don't know why Ma suddenly decided to warn Kay off in those intemperate terms. I wasn't all that destructive, really, though it's true I wasn't exactly the man-about-the-house that I have since become. But mother had this genius for the inapposite remark, and I think she enjoyed using it. She enjoyed consternation. She was a non-writing dramatist in real life.

Kay may well have had her doubts. She would be justified. I do not now, and I did not then, see myself as suitable husband material. But I was certain to marry. Like my father before me, I chose a wife who was unlike me in almost every way. Fair where I was dark, short where I was tall, discreet where I was indiscreet, judicious where I was injudicious, temperate where I was intemperate, taciturn where I was voluble, thrifty where I was feckless, reserved where I was eager to confide, practical. ... No, the list is embarrassingly long, I dare not pursue it. The fact is that little Kay accepted the challenge, for such it must have seemed, and at the time of writing our marriage has lasted almost 32 years, which may surprise various cocksure parties willing to predict that no marriage I might make was likely to last 32 months.

Opposites often seem to get on well together, provided they share one basic something in common, something which matters more than the differences. In our case I'm sure that the cohesive factor was that we shared a sense of humour, a sense of fun to some extent, but most of all a saving sense of the often unconscious absurdity of human protestations, including our own. This has saved us when things have gone wrong, and it has also saved us from the more gritty aspects of ambition, including social ambition.

Another saving factor was that she had been brought up among a crowd of boys. A splendid start in life: women's chatter bores her stiff.

We are of an age and we were both born in the same village-town. We met when we were seventeen, at a dance at the Prims.

Nowadays Kay tries to dissuade me from large enterprises, such as taking on a new job, or sailing to Singapore. But I must say that throughout our time together she has loyally supported me in all the hare-brained ventures I have undertaken, the sudden changes of key and tone and direction. She cannot have enjoyed them, but she soldiered on, putting a brave front on it. Several times she has dutifully learned the new idiom, the jargon of the various trades and hobbies and pashes. How bored she must have been. How bored when I used to rush home from the office with the day's editions, sometimes half a dozen of them, and spread them out on the hearthrug and take her on a conducted tour of all the little changes in layout and emphasis, the fine details of the perfectionist dream. When all the time what she really wanted, I think, was just a steady, contented, healthy husband. . . . I'm not sure that writers, newspapermen, or artists should marry. It's too cruel to their wives. Still, we're human, like steadier types. Some of us *are* steadier types, of course: there is a great call in the business for steady men, as ballast for the mercurial goldfish and tumbler pigeons.

Kay was never ambitious, though on the other hand she was never exactly bohemian, to put it mildly. She is one of those self-effacing and adaptable women who take on the protective colouring of their husbands' disguises. She didn't want me to kill myself pressing on, for she had seen something of how the rage for getting-on can get people down and de-humanise them. No-one could be less swanky. On the other hand, she, like me, had known the village in hard times, she knew what ignominious stresses poverty can impose. She may have known them even better than me, for a woman had the job of 'keeping the home together'. I knew the miners and their sons, Kay knew their wives and daughters. If ever there was a natural middle-of-the-roader it was this slender little party with the red-gold hair, wide blue eyes, creamy skin and lovely legs. I've often thought, and indeed said, that she would have been better-off to have married some steady managerial type.

The village wooing was not followed by a village wedding, nice though that would have been. Kay's family moved away, though not all that far, and we were married in 1936, at the advanced age of 23, at St John's Church, Kidderminster. I hadn't saved anything: the tiny capital with which we 'set up home' had been saved almost entirely by Kay. I soon realised that money was safer in her hands than mine; for a long time I let her handle it, such as it was. We have always shared everything absolutely. We have a joint bank account and have made those cross-hands-here-comes-Charlie mutual-aid wills which leave everything to the survivor. Either of us buys anything we really fancy, assuming of course there's enough in the kitty to pay for it. I sedulously give the impression of great generosity, pressing Kay to accept 'gifts' which she doesn't want, and I'm not above mentioning my open-handedness. Actually I have frittered away far more than she has, on my costly hobbies, cars, cameras, fishing rods and reels, boats; and she never mentions my extravagances. Still, when we didn't have it, we didn't spend it. Kay is now a fairly determined non-spender, not because she is in any sense a hoarder, but partly because she detests the cult of obsolescence, the waste and tedium of change-for-change-sake; and partly because she is really most contented when pottering about in her garden. She was no more a gardener than I was, until we moved into our country cottage, somewhat later in the story. There she developed green fingers to an alarming extent.

But the cottage in the country was unimaginably distant on that warm July day when we met—though only just—at the altar. Mother's prediction appeared to be coming true in a rather alarming way. I had sold the latest car in order to scrape together a few coppers towards matrimony, and for the 25-mile drive to Kidderminster I borrowed my cousin Wilfred's new Ford Ten, the first Ford Ten made, before they started calling it the Prefect. It was generous of Wilfred, an inventive mechanical genius who was a connoisseur of fine cars: the Ford was his 'second car'.

My best man Jo and I doddled happily along through New Invention —yes, there's a village of that name, next door to Bloxwich—and Wednesfield and Wolverhampton and out towards the Stewponey and Kinver Edge: and suddenly a gasket blew. It was something of a dilemma: should I get my new wash-leather gloves dirty, or should I take them off and get my hands dirty? Jo and I agreed that it was better to get the gloves dirty and risk outraging the social sense of all present by appearing without any, and so I did, but in vain. You can't cure a blown cylinder-head gasket in ten minutes. We had no alternative but to press on in bottom gear, at five miles an hour, sounding like a very old motorbike. Thank heaven we had started out in ample time—time, we had hoped, to stop off and have a quick one, if not two. Just as well we had the margin in hand, for we arrived at church ignominiously late and noisy, and just had time to slip in guiltily before the bride arrived, looking as nervous as she had every right to look.

Social historians may care to note that our first house (in Great Barr) cost us £1 a week to rent, unfurnished; and at that rate, we had the choice of virtually an entire estate of brand-new semi-detached, very pretty, or so we thought, each with three bedrooms, two living rooms, kitchen and bathroom. We chose a corner house with a colossal great garden plot. Too late, I learned that digging builder's rubble was beyond me. All digging is beyond me: gardening writers pretend otherwise, but it's murder. When a year later we moved into a suburb of Birmingham, to save time wasted in commuting (and to skip the digging) we had a choice of hundreds of perfectly decent semi-detached houses for little more than £1 a week. Ours actually cost us 22s. 6d. a week. You could buy a new house then for £500. True, it might as well have been £5,000. I never even saved the deposit.

One of the pleasanter perks of life in Birmingham was the theatrical first nights, which we attended together. Kay had far more sense of the theatre than I ever had. I could educate her about literature, but she could knock spots off me when it came to interpreting and assessing a play. Every alternate Saturday we attended the first night at the Repertory Theatre, and afterwards had a drink with the cast and management in the Green Room. In those days Birmingham was quite a town for the theatre. In addition to the Rep, which had a glorious reputation (we attended several world premieres there including that of '1066 and All That', the only one I can remember) there was good stuff to be seen at the Theatre Royal, the Prince of Wales, and Derek Salberg's Alexandra Theatre. The little Crescent Theatre struggled gallantly with the avant garde material; and so did I, though to no avail. The Hippodrome and the Empire were still thriving music halls, where we met Gracie Fields and many another star. We spent quite a bit of time with theatre people, in their dressing rooms and digs and in Birmingham's various hotels, which were quite good, you know. We made more or less permanent friends with the late Sir Donald Wolfit; were on friendly terms with such up-and-coming players as Stewart Granger (then known by his real name, James Stewart), Stephen Murray, Elspeth March, Curigwen Lewis, who married Andrew Cruickshank of *Dr Finlay's Casebook*, Brenda Bruce, Donald Eccles, Clement Macallin, Joan Heath, Gwen Nelson, Noel Johnson, the late great Charles Victor, Russell Waters, Renee Ascherson, Jasmine Shushtary, who later changed her stage name to Jasmine Dee, and James Hayter. Actors and actresses fascinate us all: they have got it made, in the sense that they make a profession of what the rest of us have to do as best we can, for free, making up our own lines as we go along. I grew much too fond of some of them, and could not bear to give them bad notices, or even to hint at insufficiencies. This taught me a lesson: much later in life, when I became a television critic, I made it a rule not to fraternise with people about whose work I had to write. If I grew to like them too much as persons, I could not always do my rigorous duty as a critic. If I should happen to dislike them, I was even more stringently inhibited. To Kay, of course, these considerations did not apply: she could enjoy their company without my nagging doubts. We had a lot of fun on the cheap. Most of the players, so glamorous behind the footlights, were about as hard-up as we were. A bottle of whiskey at 12s. 6d. was an event; coffee and beer were more our style. We were all looking at the dawn of life with invincible optimism. Anything seemed possible.

It was at the Rep that we saw a play about poor Jane Carlyle which gave Kay furiously to think about the lot of a writer's wife. Much later in life, she decided that Kitty Muggeridge was just about the ideal wife for a writer or publicist or pundist, and that she admired her most. I think she was right. Though I don't know if Malcolm would have been guilty of what for years Kay regarded as my peak of insensitive behaviour, eccentricity gone mad. Heaven knows it was innocent, in the sense that I had no idea it was abnormal. Kay had a bad dose of 'flu and was confined to bed. I cheered her up by pacing the bedroom reciting great chunks of Macbeth. 'She should have died hereafter' went down particularly well. It was quoted against me for years.

I was a great hand at pacing up and down, reciting. I also did a fair amount of pacing up and down, dictating. Nowadays I sit staring at the paper for hours before I can even make a start on my critical column, and write it all out laboriously, several times. But in those days I was bubbling over. Kay dutifully took it all down in longhand. The compositors became familiar with her neat, scrupulous and regular round hand, which has always seemed so well to reflect her dependable character.

Our marriage has worked out surprisingly well. As I have grown a little steadier and less erratic and more dependable, she has grown more relaxed and carefree. No wonder! I think we have each gained from the other's so different attitude to life. Basically we fancy the same sort of life, at least the domestic and private basis of it. I am a bit more gregarious than Kay, even now, but there is a lot that we can share, including that saving sense of the absurd. She has taught me how to appreciate good music, and I have taught her the difference between good writing and bad. She tries to teach me decorum, and I try to teach her insouciance.

I thought I would introduce my wife here, to put the record straight. She is not responsible for my aberrations though heaven knows she has done her best to minimise their worst effects. She has had a hard row to hoe, all things considered, keeping in touch with my swerves. She has saved me from making even wilder mistakes than those I have irrevocably made, those which my temperament has forced upon me.

I haven't referred to Kay incessantly throughout this story: I thought I would sew it all up, so far as I intend to, here. But she was always there, behind the events which I relate.

She weighs today exactly the same as she weighed when we got married. I weigh two stone more. I'm sure you can read something into that.

Chapter Twelve

I hated London from the start.

I saw the people travelling in the tube trains and I reported back to my wife:

'They are dead and defeated.'

She laughed at me.

But I could not take the hugeness of the city and the harassment of its citizens. I felt it as a great impersonal enmity. I was lost among seven million strangers. It struck me as evil, a place so vast that you could not walk from the centre to the fringe, where the country began. I felt that the green countryside of England had been grossly violated. Everything seemed sordid, cheap, flashy, or pompous and menacing. And the people looking so hunted, evasive, frightened and wan.

No, I did not give a damn that the city was stuffed with art galleries and museums and theatres and palaces and royalty and banks and great glittering shops.

When a waitress in a Lyons Corner House actually said a friendly word I almost wept.

I went into a pub and the barman was remote, neutral, glittering with the chromium-plated barbed wire of his sophisticated self-sufficiency. The doormen at the posh hotels were supercilious. I had lunch at Kettners with Harold Keeble of the *Express*, to celebrate my appointment. The waiters were supercilious and I felt, perhaps rightly, that they did not care whether I stayed or went, loved or hated them. The food may have been good but in my misery I could not taste it. When I had paid my share of the bill I knew that I should have to walk back to Paddington. On the Soho pavement Harold said.

'I'm sure you're going to do very well in London. Don't worry.'

But I did worry. I knew then that I was a provincial, if not a real countryman. I was homesick already for the village ethos. I trudged to Paddington and took the cheap train home and I could have cried.

Of course I was to learn that London is simply a big place full of people. The people are people like any other people. You can make necessary friends and enemies, and you can find neighbours. Born Londoners are among my few dear close friends. Born Londoners at home in their collection of villages. But immigrant Londoners, up from the provinces to make it, bring with them (at least in the professional reaches) the tang of their ambition. Huge aggregations, not communities, of strangers trying to make it. I missed the warm little communities I had known, where you could be at ease with people you had grown up alongside, and, if necessary, hate them happily.

I still find London hostile, meretricious, sordid, impersonal, infinitely gullible, stinking. On the other hand I am not so madly enamoured of Birmingham either and have even gone off Wolverhampton to some extent, which is like repudiating your birthright. I know all the capital cities of Europe and although of course they have different atmospheres they are all to some extent touched by this horrible thing which we go-getting provincials who didn't have the sense or nerve to stay at home bring with us, the taint of the rat race. Brussels is or was a quite habitable metropolis, the most provincial of them all, and Paris is agreeably hedonistic though not exactly, I would say, gay, and so beautiful it hurts, and Prague was once, whatever it may be now, a dream city. But for me, anybody can have the freedom of the city. People say you can live in a capital city anonymously, free from prying and censorious eyes. It is another way of saying that you cannot bear human scrutiny. You can live with perfect freedom in Kidderminster if you have the necessary moral courage. London relieves you of the necessity to show moral courage. It also relieves you of a good percentage of your humanity. I suffocate in cities.

I am going to rattle along at high speed to the war, because everything that happened to me between going to Fleet Street and going to war was sad and second rate, an anti-climax. We innocently took a garden-floor flat in Maida Vale, the prostitutes' quarter then, if not now, and when the sleaziness grew unbearable we rented a nice little house in Bromley, Kent, where the blitz caught us. But I will tell no bomb stories. I went out briefly as a substitute correspondent to France, came back, left the *Express*, worked as features editor of the *Sunday Dispatch*, wrote a column for the *Daily Mail*, and at the height of the blitz joined the Royal Air Force as a flight mechanic.

This, like a number of events in my life, was an accident. I had some notion of joining the Guards as a ranker, but when on the appointed day I turned up at Cheam to clock-in with my contemporaries, the Guards recruiting officer turned me down without a moment's hesitation, on account of I wore glasses, and had no chest development. I was so incensed by his arbitrary lack of interest in me as a physical specimen that I went next door into the Royal Air Force recruiting office, though this had been no part of my plan. But if that was what the Guards man thought of me, stone them all, I wouldn't join any regiment less than the Guards. In this moment of hurt pride and disaffection I stamped into a miserable little pen where sat a miserable little creep of an interviewing officer, one of the dimmest clots it has been my fortune to meet, and my life, like everyone else's, has been full of them.

I rattled off my *curriculum vitae*, which was at least abnormal. But this idiot's ears were shut tight. He was there that day to induct a certain number of souls as flight mechanics, those were his orders and that was all he thought about. Flight mechanics were what they needed at the moment in the R.A.F. I didn't very much care, I must admit—at that moment in the autumn of 1940 one was highly conscious of the clock being about to strike, one went wherever one was supposed to be needed and did whatever one was told. Still, I was faintly surprised that he saw me as mechanic material. I pointed out that I had shown a certain proficiency in reading and writing. Perhaps some simple clerkly job? No, the nit's ears were sealed by orders. They didn't need clerks; they needed mechanics. Well, then, for Christ's sake, I suggested, make me a motor mechanic, eh? At least I have had a certain amount of practice in that line.

All water off a duck's back. I left, enrolled as a Flight Mechanic u/t. That stood for 'under training'. On the appointed day I took train to Blackpool for a month's square bashing (which I actually enjoyed), and before I properly knew what had hit me I was marching in the dark of a winter's evening from Gilestone station in darkest Glamorgan to the penal settlement known far and wide as Saint Bleeding Athan. I stayed at St Athan for the darkest winter of my life. Later I was to know more dangerous and strenuous winters, but none so calculated to chill the soul. Although the Royal Air Force was being expanded and civilianised at a shocking rate, it was still run by the Regular mentality, of course, and the Regular mentality has never gone down too well with the citizen armies which we have had to scrape together from time to time during our long island story.

Not that the technical N.C.O.s who instructed us in the rudiments of fitting were at all bad; simply because they were technicians, they had a certain level of intelligence such as you do not find among the clerkly scum, and the R.A.F. always had its own spirit. But still, the best word

I can find for those days is miserable. Sudden grinding poverty, itchy clothing, service discipline, and above all the enforced propinquity with thousands of other nits . . . and a dark, cold winter full of dreadful news about the war. . . . It was a bad time and there are no funny stories. To while away the tedium I edited and produced and largely wrote a service magazine, but the boredom of aircraft fitting threatened my sanity, never too secure. I hate aircraft now; at the time I was merely bored by them. Unfortunately, though far from good at it, I was not wholly bad, and passed out respectably from the course. This meant an instant return to St Athan for yet another course—a so-called 'conversion course' which turned the Flight Mechanic into a Fitter. Since in this case the flight mechanic had not had one ha'porth of practical experience in the field, it is plain that our country's need for fitters must have been rather urgent. If they would accept me as a skilled fitter, I thought, it must be desperate.

I passed out respectably again, as an airframe fitter. Since I knew precisely nothing about airframes and quite a lot about engines, it argues very well for the intelligence of the higher direction that they made me an airframe fitter instead of an engine fitter, at which I should certainly have been quite happy. I like engines; at least they *go*, they have a positive life and vitality. Airframes, like chassis, are static and boring. So I became an airframe fitter and went on a bit of leave.

I was posted to Hendon for a time, where no-one knew what to do with all the new bods (highly revealing or perhaps ironical R.A.F. slang for people) and life became suddenly rather more bearable, in the sense that there was nothing to do (ever my favourite occupation—I'm not one of these neurotics who have to have something to do) and the sun was shining and there seemed quite a good prospect that Hitler, having attacked Russia, might have his hands full. But of course it was too good to last. I was posted straight back to horrible Glamorgan, to a newly-formed Operational Training Unit on a nasty new airfield at Llandow, which is now a civil airport for South Wales and aren't they just welcome to it?

There followed two of the most dreary and wasted years in my whole life. I cannot begin to find words for the total tedium of working on dejected old Spitfires which never went into action. As I suspected at the time, and amply confirmed later, working on fighters which actually flew against the hated foe could be quite reasonably meaningful; but our pilots were trainees who could just barely fly but had never smelled the enemy. Our Spitfires, naturally, were weary old Mark I machines on which it was no pleasure to labour.

It was during this period that I first came near to losing my taste for democracy and the common man. The men around me were all too common. Of course some of them were all right, some of them were and have remained my friends, some of them were as good as gold. But now I came in contact, inescapably, with the dregs of the system, clods who bore little or no resemblance to my ancient playmates of the Black Country; the sweepings of the cities, attracted into the R.A.F. ground services by the prospect of reasonable security without actual ignominy. There were some lovely lads among them but there were some awful squirts too. The fitters and riggers and so on were not too bad, but the 'general duties' mob were a sad sight—and sound. The degradation of the language was perhaps the most boring aspect of these years. R.A.F. slang was pretty tedious. Almost without realising it, I lost any illusions I might still have had about government of the people by the people and for the people. I didn't greatly care for 'the people', only for people. Abstractions were suddenly suspect. Fortunately I detested the Germans even more. This was one war which had to be fought. It is plain that the war of 1914–18 was a terrible accident, from which we have never recovered; but the war of 1939–45 was a war we could not avoid. The mood throughout was of determined resignation, or shall we say resigned determination? Your own lot was pretty awful, but the other mob was a sight worse. You had to soldier on.

From time to time I was filled with a desire to soldier on to better effect. But I was caught like a vice in the grip of bureaucracy in its foulest form. I tried to get out and get into the army, having realised that danger was infinitely preferable to boredom. Not a hope. I was not even allowed to 're-muster' into some other trade, some other branch of work at which I might make a more rational contribution. Several times, distinguished agencies asked for my release in order that they might employ me on work of national importance which demanded just those few qualities which I happened to possess. The Political Intelligence Department of the Foreign Office wanted me to do propaganda work of a certain sort for which I was rather well suited: I gave them quite a few ideas, which were carried out. But they ran up against the brick wall. The R.A.F. had spent £90 on turning me into a poor imitation of a fitter: they weren't going to waste the nation's money. So there I was, stuck. I rose to corporal, thence to sergeant; not perhaps because I was so brilliant with my hands, for I was not, but probably because I could read the maintenance manuals without spelling out each separate word, could organise the simple duties of a gang, and was enough of an actor to be able to bark out a command peremptorily, with every show of resolution. Also, just possibly, because I wrote the C.O.'s more difficult letters for him, and his speeches; and finally, just conceivably, because I was less trouble as a sergeant than as an air-craftman. As an erk I led several eloquent little revolts against the obtuseness of our immediate superiors; or if I didn't lead them, I was automatically blamed for them, simply because I could out-talk any-body in sight, and sometimes did. Anyway, they made me a sergeant in 1943.

Almost immediately—though not for that reason—life picked up and the war changed for me. I was posted away from the O.T.U., and I'm sure no-one was sorry to see me go, aside from my personal friends, to join one of the new-fangled units which were being set up in the 2nd Tactical Air Force in preparation for the invasion of Fortress Europe. They were modelled on the units of the Desert Air Force, which had been so successful at a time when the British and Common-wealth Forces were not being conspicuously successful, as a general thing. My own little lot was a Repair and Salvage Unit. Our simple mission was to rush off from base when one of our aircraft was reported to have crashed in a given area, strip it down into its major components, load it on to a long lorry, and bear it triumphantly back to base to be sewn together again, as good as new. The more reliable and highly skilled of us were put into the Repair side of the operation, the rest into the Salvage aspect. I dare say it was a reflection on my capacity as a craftsman that I was instantly recognised as Salvage material. How-ever, I did not let that worry me.

It was a change enormously for the better. In one stroke we were made free of the debilitating bullshit of base, the routine and the weariness of living in community, minutely scrutinised by our betters and dying of boredom. My little gang consisted of a corporal engine fitter, two or three rankers, mainly airframe fitters or mechanics, and a G.D. wallah to lend a hand generally and do the cooking. We had a three-ton Bedford lorry, in which we lived and slept when necessary, conveyed our stores of tools, and I had operational charge of a crane and a long articulated lorry. Marvellous! Off we shot, the moment we got the wire, out into the blue, where for a day or two at a time we lived like gypsies in various rustic locations. When things warmed up—and they were getting quite warm in early 1944—we might even go from one prang to another and to another, away from base for days if not weeks on end, our own masters, our only communication with base through despatch riders whom we suborned to deliver the right, or wrong, messages.

In this carefree manner we spent the winter of 1943–44 and the great luminous Spring before D-Day. Our area was in the South East of England. We roamed Kent and Sussex, with occasional forays into Hampshire and even, if memory serves, Surrey, though I can't think what we were doing there. Now we were carefree, slightly piratical, none too scrupulously clean I suppose, but imbued with the feel of action. We were ready for war. And about time, too. And D-Day came.

I backed the Bedford on to a Landing Craft (Tank), the ugly little LCT, on Gosport Hards. The night before we had spent stealthily in a transport laager slightly inland, removing the parts which we needed most from some of the hundreds of parked vehicles, in order to make our Bedford more roadworthy. For it was considerably shot-up. But it was little use asking the M.T. officer for a new one; he simply did not understand the rigours of a Salvage truck's life. We were under the impression, as we got aboard the LCT, that we had craftily procured us a very serviceable Bedford. Events were to prove us credulous.

After heaving and tossing in the Channel for what seemed rather a long time, we went ashore one morning at Sword Beach on the sixth tide. The night had been quite lurid. Individual German aircraft flew over more or less constantly, and all the ships fired at them with every-thing that had a trigger, or so it seemed. Inland, too, the commotion was considerable. I never did get used to flares drifting silently down, illuminating me vividly when I least wished to be noticed. The din was extremely tiresome after a time, though quite exhilarating for the first five or ten minutes. For several years after the victory I felt quite uncomfortable around Bonfire Night.

However, I cannot honestly say that I felt as nervous as I had expected to feel. Indeed it was rather stimulating. Round about the early Spring of 1944 a great peace had descended on my soul, I honestly can't say why. Plainly the crunch was coming, was inevitable and unavoidable, and on the whole, though God knows I don't want to go into hysterical heroics, and have no reason to, one felt that it was some-how fitting that the crunch should come. After all that ghastly bore-dom, it really wouldn't have been anything but anti-climax if we hadn't seen a bit of action against the hated foe.

The hated foe was dug in on our left flank in considerable strength. The paratroops (including Captain Huw Wheldon, M.C., though I didn't know that at the time) had secured a bridgehead over the Orne River and the Caen Canal which was dug to save mariners the trouble of navigating that tortuous estuary. With considerable optimism, our governors had conceived of an airstrip overlooking this sector, up on a plateau near a village called Plumetot. Pioneers were even then scratching it out. It was the most easterly airstrip in the Normandy beachhead. Our orders were to toddle along there as soon as we landed and make ourselves generally useful in the way of keeping the landing strip clear of prangs. At least, that was the general idea.

I drove the Bedford truck off the LCT, down the vertiginous ramp and into five feet of water, in four-wheel-drive and emergency low gear. 'Keep your foot hard down,' screamed the officer who waved us off. I certainly obliged. My foot was so hard down that when I lifted it off the accelerator, on reaching indisputably dry land, the throttle stuck wide open. We had practised this little manoeuvre, during the preceding winter, at the open air swimming bath on Hove front. Each driver drove once down a wooden ramp, round the bath, out again, and smartly back to his unit. Comprehensive training. By dint of playing a tune on the ignition switch I controlled the truck over the first non-stop mile or so inland, urged on by the lurid threats of countless Military Police, threading through ruinous houses and past a few natives who did not seem wild with joy. Then we pulled off into a field where we took the essential part of the waterproofing stuff off our vehicles.

It was at this point that our commanding officer, a Canadian Wing Commander named, if memory serves, Macdonald, did something very good for our morale; or, at any rate, for mine. He trudged from vehicle to vehicle, issuing last orders about the route and destination, and he saw fit to add the interesting threat that any perisher who for any reason whatsoever fell out of line would be court-martialled for cowardice, and/or shot on the spot by himself personally. I did not much fancy this form of exhortation, though having seen the Wing Commander at revolver practice I had little doubt that I could get him with my own gun before he got me, and I should assuredly have tried. He further alienated my meagre affections by reminding me—me personally, the sarge himself, in front of all the men—that the only mishap on the entire way down from Odiham to the present moment had happened to one of my vehicles. As if it were my fault. True, I had in my keeping a flat topped truck on which we had arranged a tasteful display of spare propellers, intended to help us in our servicing operations. We had built them up nicely on interlacing beams of tarry timber, and altogether it was quite a novel little sight. Was it my fault that the oblique blade of an army bulldozer, mounted on a low loader and travelling in the opposite direction, had scythed a tinkling way through all our timbers and brought the propellers crashing on to the road? As

I said to the Wing Commander, fighting back a more instinctive retort, you gotta blame the bleedin' army for that. But he seemed to blame me.

We got under way, which I believe should be written under weigh, being a nautical expression to do with anchors and of some antiquity, and soon we were bowling merrily along, nose to tail, on the high road that leads or led from Bayeux to Caen, or perhaps it was from Arromanches to Caen. I had a chap standing between the cab and the tilt, or body, of the Bedford, with our Bren gun resting on top of the cab, on the lookout for snipers, low flying Nazi aircraft, or even low flying Allied aircraft, on which he was instructed to open fire without a qualm if they fired first. My mate the corporal had his Sten gun poking out of the window, my rifle was handy, and the chaps in the back were positively bristling. For the purpose of this operation we were attached to the R.A.F. Servicing Commando, and several of us have since had few scruples about letting it be known that we served with the Commandos, which is only half a lie. Anyway, the proud sight of the Commando flash all around was heartening if at times a little alarming, too. We now wore khaki battledress, like the army, and felt quite operational.

Tension wound up a bit tighter when a cheerful soldier whom we passed at walking pace while threading our way through some benighted village shouted 'Keep yer 'eads down when you get up there,' indicating the hill we were about to climb. It did indeed seem rather quiet once we were clear of that village. Soldiers were dug into the verges of the road, some with monstrous great pieces of artillery, some with no visible means of support. We fell quiet, too, and a shade thoughtful, and suddenly everybody felt thirsty.

Without a word of warning or even a hiccup, the engine died. It died the death. Howling and roaring, the rest of the convoy snaked round us and on, hurling abuse at us as back-sliders. By driving the truck in low gear on the battery I managed to 'get the bleedin' thing off the pluggin' road', thereby complying with a thoroughly popular request. As we bumped over the tumpy grass verge, which we firmly believed to be sown with mines as thick as docks, I think we all felt the war had come home to us.

But, such is the spirit of the British fighting man, the petrol stove was going full blast before the wheels had properly stopped, and tea was a-brewing. A cursory investigation, helped by the smell, revealed that we had a fractured petrol pipe. There were many spares aboard the Bedford but a petrol pipe was not among them.

I remembered having seen a unit of R.E.M.E., the electrical and mechanical engineers, in a small orchard a mile or so back. There was nothing for it but to shoulder my rifle, the old Short Magazine Lee Enfield, and trudge back along the road. The apparition of this lank figure clad in khaki but adorned with many strange symbols including R.A.F. flashes, and wearing on top a tight little black beret which I had adopted as a delicate tribute to our French allies (actually I bought it in Brighton) caused some consternation and curiosity among the soldiery. I was several times hailed in a familiar and truculent manner, and when eventually I turned in at R.E.M.E.'s orchard the warrant officer in charge was, as he freely admitted, in half a mind to clap me under close arrest. I think that what saved me was my accent, or accents. I gave him Bloxwich pure and undefiled, Brummagem, and Oxford or BBC. No foreigner could have done it; possibly few natives. He seemed appeased, and gave me a nasty cider apple, a petrol pipe, and much sound advice, all of which had the effect of making me wish quite earnestly that I had been born vastly earlier, or later, or practically any other time but when I was born. He put the wind up me, in fact. I trudged back carrying the S.M.L.E. at the ready, not slung. Behind every clump of trees I saw lurking snipers.

By the time we had mended the truck and sorted out various little differences of opinion—I mean by the time I had got a grip on the gang again and rounded up stragglers who fancied a night in the nearest *maison de tolerance*—talk about naïvety—it was high time to get on our way to Plumetot. I was frankly rather worried about the Wing Commander. He was a bit of a lad, and a highly popular figure with us, but not over-inclined to listen to explanations as improbable as ours might sound. We lost our way twice, which is barely credible to anyone who knows the state of that crowded beachhead in early June 1944, and we stopped to fight a private battle with an inquisitive aircraft, and by the time we reached the hamlet of Plumetot it was very dusky. Some slight confusion seemed to be the order of the day. I could not find the Wing Commander anywhere, and took the advice of a fellow sergeant in the Commando whom I found up to his ears in a slit trench tucked in nicely on the westerly (safe) side of a thick hedge.

'Plug the Wing Commander, mate,' he said amiably. 'Let him worry. If you don't find a place to get your head down in the next few minutes, you'll regret it. It turns quite nasty round here at nightfall.'

He spoke with the ineffable superiority of a veteran. Actually he had been there twenty-four hours longer than I had. Next day I was to adopt the same patronising tone to comers later than myself.

But I saw his point of view. He recommended some slit trenches ready dug and recently vacated by the rude soldiery, which were grouped round some very secondhand looking farm buildings. I directed the gang to this haven and we all disappeared from sight with remarkable celerity. Too late, I discovered that my trench had been used as a latrine, or worse, by the considerate soldiery.

It did indeed, as predicted by my fellow sergeant, turn quite nasty. Impudent but hasty enemy aircraft flew over for quite a time, very low, and we added our quota of wasted ammunition to the millions of rounds which were being hurled into the sky. The aircraft flew so very low that the chances of being hit by your own mates seemed higher by far than the chances of being injured by the enemy, who was probably only on reconnaissance, anyway. One thought struck me sharply. Virtually everybody in the bridgehead was shooting at those aircraft, it seemed; every sort of projectile from .303 and 9 mm ammunition, up through 40 mm from the Bofors guns to very large calibre stuff indeed from the big guns—it was positively sizzling round the planes as they made their runs, with tracer lazily going across among the rest ... yet not a solitary hit was registered, at least not within our compass of vision. Strange, I thought. Must be a very wasteful war. Many times during the rest of the war I stood up (or lay down) and pumped a magazine-full of ammunition at aircraft so near you felt you could have touched them with your finger tips. I felt then, and on the whole I feel now, that I simply couldn't have missed *all* the time. Yet I never to my certain knowledge brought one down.

There is no question that if you can manage without a war, you would be well advised to do so. Yet given that you are going to be attacked, there is a distinct consolation in having something in your hands with which to shoot back. Especially if you are being attacked by aeroplanes, nasty noisy things. I made a terrible gaffe one day, not so very long ago, when going down in a crowded lift in Thomson House, where the *Sunday Times* is published. I was talking to Nicholas Carroll, the Diplomatic Correspondent, who is an exceedingly keen shot. He had been complaining in a mild and dignified way, perhaps without really realising the true origin of his complaint, about the difficulty of finding targets to shoot at. Speaking from the heart, as usual, and with that lack of discretion or low cunning which has got me into so much trouble, I remarked that undoubtedly the most interesting target to shoot at was men. A ghastly silence fell on that crowded lift; all the young liberals in Thomson House seemed to have squeezed into it, and the looks they gave me were a treat to see. 'So,' those looks said as plainly as a poster, 'so: just as we thought: fascist reactionary bastard: wants to bring back the lash and the gallows: simply loves shooting people: condemned out of his own mouth.'

Nick seemed quite embarrassed; he diplomatically murmured something about 'provided they are shooting back at you', and I replied 'yes, of course', quite sincerely, but it didn't thaw the atmosphere. The lift was a long time getting to ground floor, then it emptied as if full of plague. I fancy that little incident did something to strengthen a general though quite unfounded belief that Wiggin was a blimpish reactionary. Actually I have a soft heart, and a detestation of war just as wholehearted and well-founded as most. But all truths are relative to one another, unfortunately, and it is a sad and simple fact, confirmed by the experience of all too many, that there is no feeling quite the same as the feeling you get when you aim a gun at somebody who is out to get you and squeeze the trigger. I don't say it isn't a dreadfully *wrong* feeling, but it is also very exciting. To ignore this fact of nature is no help. Peace has to provide a substitute for that feeling, and for several others; perhaps it is precisely because it doesn't, that it is so precarious.

Rattling off rounds against enemy aircraft at dusk was to be the limit of my personal aggression for some time. We were about as useful at Plumetot as the Hambledon Rural District Council, and a great deal less useful than a case of Scotch. It was much too near the enemy's gunners, and much too exposed. We had our artillery all around us and a great deal of it behind us, so you will see we were quite advanced; in fact I've never been so advanced before or since. From the airstrip we were able to watch the whole battle for Caen, which lay smoky and obscure in the hollow below us; beyond the hidden city stood the line of factory chimneys at Colombelles, which diminished every day. It was interesting to watch the tanks trying to work their way through the woods and the small fields, but we were not supposed to be there as interested spectators. Yet that's all we were. Planes did land on our strip, every so often, but the moment they touched down the Germans lobbed over a few 88 millimetre shells, the ones that make such a very unpleasant noise. The planes usually escaped, their pilots making affectionate gestures to us earthlings as they rose. We lost a few vehicles and were plainly out of pocket on the deal.

I believe the strip never became operational. Certainly my gang and I were withdrawn having accomplished precisely nothing. We were not too pleased to leave, for life there had combined interest with leisure. However, the noise level was perhaps too high for good mental health. We slept in holes in the ground in a tiny sunken orchard by the farm, ostensibly secure, but sometimes shelled and even on one occasion mortared. My chaps seemed inclined to take this as a reflection on sarge's perspicacity, but it was a case of 'If you know of a better 'ole, go to it'.

One of the lads expressed a thought which I fancy had been in all our minds when he asked me, as if I should know, 'Where's the bleedin' army, sarge?' I pointed out severely that we were entirely surrounded by up-to-date examples of the cannon maker's art, but of course I knew only too well what he meant: 'Where's the something *infantry?*' Sternly I urged him to consider himself an infantrymen as from now on, reminded him of battle courses and other tonic experiences which he had undergone, and generally strove to whip up morale. If theirs was the same height as mine, I reasoned, it needed whipping up. For after a few days you did begin to feel, or I did, under the external air of nonchalance which all affected, that it was a great pity you hadn't broken your leg when boarding the boat. War can be a tonic experience for a few days, then you begin to miss your sleep.

I took steps to exchange my rifle for a Sten gun, which I later exchanged at a very stiff price for a genuine Thompson sub-machine gun. I had not counted on getting quite so close to the enemy, in person, and prudently argued that something capable of spraying lead was more likely to come in handy than the old World War I rifle, much as I had enjoyed cleaning it and ringing the odd church bell in passing.

Militarily speaking, our experiences in the Normandy beachhead were of small significance, in the context of the general course of the war. But they were not entirely without interest. There was a bit of rather rum fishing in the moat of a château at Ellon, where an important little battle had been fought, and where we made some sort of airstrip. It was hereabouts that the only serious counter-attack with tanks that the Germans launched during the early days of the invasion was finally stopped, after grinding through our forward positions in an unhealthy way. We were sited a little north of the notorious Jerusalem Corner, a '*carrefour de la mort*' if ever there was one, on the road to the ruined little town of Tilly. The family was still in imperturbable residence at the château, and entertained our luckier officers there to musical evenings, as if the evenings were not musical enough. There were, if I remember rightly (I paid no attention) two beautiful young daughters in the family. And there were carp in the moat.

Our disciplinary flight sergeant, Dusty Miller, who was said to be a Glaswegian, though some affected to believe that he had no earthly parentage, liked to fish the moat during the still hour of the evening, when work had stopped and the nocturnal noises had not yet begun. I shared a few vigils with him. He was an explosive yet exceptionally genial chap, capable of generosity and also capable of putting a bold front on disaster. As a disciplinarian he was enjoyably individualistic; if the notion took him, he was as likely to offer to fight the offender as to put him on a charge. We also occasionally fished at dawn, but with no more success despite a lavish assortment of baits all sworn to be irresistible to carp, such as worms of every description, cheese, potatoes, wasp cake, and maggots. *Point touche*, as the old stableman of the château used to say, with a rather sardonic leer. Not a bloody touch, as Dusty learned to translate it.

The old cowman used to come along the moment he saw us at it and lean on the low wall, peering at our anchored floats, which looked as if they never had moved and never would. We gave him cigarettes, as we gave everyone cigarettes. This old b, as Dusty called him, used to chew his, paper and all. A standard size drag would last him the best part of an hour, though of course a Woodbine had a shorter life. When he had finished masticating he would spit out the quid, landing it within an inch of our floats, with an air of deadly solemnity. Dusty was furious with him: he used to swear the old chap did it deliberately, to spoil our fishing. But there was no fishing to spoil.

Whenever it happened Dusty would rave and swear at the old man, calling up all the ghosts of the Gorbals. I remonstrated with the lad, pointing out that these were our natural and gallant allies, to whose succour we had come. No natural allies of *his*, Dusty retorted mysteriously. Plug all frogs, and so on, interminably. The old chap thoroughly enjoyed Dusty's tirade. 'Pardon? Pardon? Ne fait rien'; and he would shrug his bowed shoulders and wink surreptitiously at the assembled erks, all Dusty's natural prey in working hours, who gathered to keep him well supplied with chewing cigarettes, which Dusty stopped giving him early on.

It was rum, fishing in the moat for carp, such a monastic exercise, with a Tiger tank upside down a few yards away, and a fresh grave by it.

At another spot not far from Ellon we spent a few nights in an apple orchard which sloped away in one corner to a rather filthy pond. I wished to try for a tench in that scummy pond, but we were rather busy at the time and it was always dark when we got back to our tent. My lorry had taken a direct hit near Caen and I was temporarily attached to the Repair department, which I liked much less than Salvage, while they found another truck and gang and gear for me. However, I whiled away the odd leisure hour in producing a highly scurrilous unit magazine or newssheet, which contained so many libels it makes *Private Eye* look like the parish magazine. There is really no joy in journalism to compare with writing what you know to be libels.

Having failed to catch a tench by day, I thought I would try a night line. I duly tossed it in, baited with a bit of American canned cheese, and slept with the end of the line wrapped round my hand. *Point touche.* Next night we dreamed up an elaboration of this technique. There was a chap in our tent of whom we could not with the best will in the world be whole-heartedly fond, a rather miserable and calculating character whom we will call Elmer. Elmer's temper was uncertain. This night Elmer happened to have dropped off to sleep quickly, and he slept like a pig, as one or two observers observed. We tossed the baited hook into the pond, trailed the line back up the bank and through the open flap of the tent, laid it lightly across Elmer's naked throat, and put a stone on the free end. We turned in quietly, trusting that a fish of character might take a pull at the line.

Sure enough, in the middle of the night there was a yell from Elmer, so powerful that a nervous sentry forty yards away dropped his Sten gun, which aroused the next sentry along the lane, who told the sergeant, who sent a patrol down the lane to investigate. Not that we knew about all this, at the time. Somebody flashed a torch on Elmer. He was sitting bolt upright on his groundsheet, in a considerable state of nerves. I nipped out with a muted torch and found a big rat in the ditch, entangled with the line. The rat must have been responsible, for there was no fish on the hook. Elmer was in a shocking temper when he discovered what had happened, and his language brought complaints from tents far and wide. The duty officer came pounding along with his revolver out, a terrifying sight to anyone who had seen him at revolver practice, and there was even some vague intemperate talk of a court-martial. But we never did catch a tench.

I said a few pages back that after a day or two ashore one began to regret having come at all. That was true, but morale was and very likely still is a very unpredictable and changeable thing, and after a time one really did become almost wholly acclimatised to the absurdity of the situation in which one found oneself. The nastiest part was at the very end, when deliverance was so near that one thought what a pity it would be to be bumped off *now*, and became unduly, even censurably, cautious, or alternatively wildly reckless just to show how little one was affected by such extraneous factors. My own turning point came, I think, on a rainy day at one of our airstrips when I thrice came uncomfortably near to actual pain and loss, and thrice survived. Thereafter I felt quite certain that my cause was good and I was likely to survive (though at a much later stage I was suffused with certainty that my number was up. But one lived, if not exactly for the day, at any rate for the day off).

During our time in Normandy I was twice taken up for flights in a little Auster spotting aircraft, as used by the artillery to look down on enemy positions and direct the fire of our guns. We serviced several of these nice little things, from time to time. I liked them better than most because they were high-wing monoplanes, which meant that in normal flying attitudes the wing was above you and you got a splendid view of everything below. Of course, if you were upside-down you lost that advantage. There was a custom in the Royal Air Force of making the NCO in charge of an overhaul or repair or inspection sign a dreadful document called Form 700. There are chaps who to this day wake in the night sweating at the thought of Forms 700 which they signed a generation back. When you put your signature to this piece of paper you were making a binding declaration that the aircraft was airworthy. Speaking personally, I never had an aircraft through my hands of which I was convinced that it was fit to fly, but of course when you'd done all that you could do, there was nothing for it but to banish your natural doubts and sign on the line. If you were lucky that was the end of it, but if the aircraft failed to return you found yourself hoping that some-one would turn in a convincing eye-witness account of how it was destroyed by enemy action, and if it returned in trouble, I mean mechanical trouble, you had some uncomfortable moments.

Just to push the standards of maintenance higher, certain officers had the agreeable little habit of inviting the fitter concerned to go up for a trial flip. It was an invitation difficult to turn down. In our Spitfire days we were comforted by the thought that our aircraft would only carry one, though at the O.T.U. they kept some two-seater Miles Master and Magister trainers, constructed it seemed mainly of thin wood and cloth, in which I have made several uneasy flights after overhauls. You could see the wingtips flexing up and down alarmingly. One's attitude to this treat was conditioned, perhaps, by a sight we saw very early on in our careers as fitters. A chap who had serviced a Beaufighter went up in it on the test flight and the wings fell off. It was a dreadful business for those concerned but I'm sure it had a wholly salutary effect on the craftsmanship of all the spectators.

As I said, I was twice taken up in an Auster over the battlefield of Normandy. Not that I bummed or begged for the trip, but when it was offered I thought it would be unbecoming to plead pressure of work.

The first time, we took a small calibre shell through the starboard wing. The second occasion was on this climactic day I was talking about. We were dozing along quite happily when there was a funny sort of small abrupt unaccountable noise. I noticed that a hole had appeared between my feet, and a corresponding hole in the roof above. That was a bullet. I made bold to mention this to the pilot and was pleased to notice that he smartly turned for home, if you could call it home, instead of laughing it off heroically. I duly gummed patches on the fabric.

Scarcely had we settled back to the busy routine of the day than a rare enemy fighter buzzed us, very low indeed. This was becoming a very infrequent event in daylight. He did not let fly at me personally, nor indeed at anyone else so far as I know, but our wide-awake gunners were extraordinarily quick on the draw. Bofors and small cannon and machine guns opened up in tremendous style, and as I was meditatively strolling across the strip at the time I seemed to be at the exact point where several streams of tracer converged. I lay down, which seemed the most reasonable thing to do, and had been prone for some seconds, rather long ones, when a shaking of the dirt beneath me warned me that two of our Typhoons, ever in readiness, were roaring down the runway in my direction. Never mind the weather, they were going to get up and chase that impudent perisher. I rose and ran. It was my distinct impression, on which Marshall Hall himself would not have shaken me, never mind Edgar Lustgarten, that one of the wing tips brushed the small of my back. Later the pilot put in a quite bitter complaint to the C.O. about dozy so-and-so's ambling about on the runway.

That evening I was relaxing in my slit trench, in which of course one slept, cleaning the Sten gun and preparing for a recuperative doze. How it happened I never understood, but suddenly the horrible tinny thing went off with a chatter that seemed inordinately noisy in the pup tent. I had it in my lap at the time. The bullets cut a deep and ragged hole in the end of the trench, between my feet.

Totting up the score, I concluded that Fate was definitely on my side. If I had survived a day so crowded with near misses, I must be lucky. Thereafter for quite some time I moved as one armoured by destiny.

In the fulness of time, the army having done all the dirty work, as usual, we moved out of the bridgehead in stately procession. I was still without a truck of my own, but was nominated to head the mile-long convoy as driver of the sanitary van. It was not perhaps a very glamorous assignment, but as the M.T. officer, who accompanied me, shrewdly pointed out, if *he* didn't mind riding the stink wagon, why should a mere sergeant, and a bloody difficult sergeant to boot? I saw the justice and transcendent democracy of the man's line of thought. Any drive was better than being a mere passenger.

So there we were, doddling happily along at the head of a mile-long convoy of nominally non-combatant vehicles full of decidedly non-combatant troops. The weather was grand and as we made our dreamy way through Normandy we were greeted by the liberated populace with every evidence of affection and gratitude. They accepted our cigarettes and chocolates, thrown out with a lordly gesture that concealed acute misgivings, just as they accepted similar tributes from more valorous soldiers. After all, they were not to know that the Commer van we drove contained nothing more lethal than a cargo of stinking crap buckets and lids.

We were under the impression that the war was as good as over, and perhaps it might have been had Montgomery had his way and driven North and East in one terrific thrust with all the available Allied power. But the diplomatic Eisenhower had *his* way, instead, and everything slowed down so that we could all move nicely up to the Rhine in line abreast, like Trooping the Colour. So we got stuck with the winter war. Arnhem was fought and lost, everybody was highly brassed-off, we bogged down for a miserable winter in Holland and elsewhere, and only the Russians profited.

Not that mature considerations of high strategy and national policy weighed strongly with us at the time. That was hindsight speaking. At the time we were simply a bit tetchy because we were sex-starved, bored, and growing older. It really was a boring winter. My lot were operating in South Brabant mainly, with excursions here and there. The Brabanters were a dour lot, indistinguishable from the Germans in some of the less interesting respects, very much under the thumb of their priests, and far from willing to let out their daughters. The chaps had got on well with the Flemish people in Belgium, and also, indeed, with the Walloons. But the Flemings appeared to speak almost the same language as our North Country element; it was easy to make oneself understood, there were quite strong similarities with home, in architecture, landscape, manners and customs; beer was the staple drink, and as a bonus, there seemed to be a bit more promiscuity. Though whether that was a true reflection of the populace, or something due to the war and/or liberation, I would not care to say. I remember calling at a rather drab little café at a tiny town a few miles from Diest, looking for certain stragglers (I found them, yes). It was quite a lot like a North Country pub of the more severe urban sort. Everybody had prudently taken his bicycle inside, which was a bizarre touch, but otherwise you might almost have been back home. A fairly nice looking young girl who helped at the bar had just lit a cigarette which one of my lads had given to her. She took a deep drag and then, holding the cigarette delicately like a conductor's baton, she announced to no-one in particular, to show her new-found command of English:

'Smokking und fokking, ver gut.'

I had quite a job getting the lads out of there and back to work.

But the Brabanters, not very gregarious, deeply religious, and highly suspicious, offered no fraternisation to speak of, though I dare say there were occasional pockets of non-resistance to be found. In our peripatetic way, we got around the country, staying the odd night in barns and outhouses, often sleeping in the lorry itself, seizing any opportunity to get merry on various strange drinks (but such opportunities were far from frequent). Just once we were invited in, when dismantling a pranged aircraft in a lonely, frost-bitten marsh. We spent the evening in the kitchen with the peasant-farmer and his family, around the stove, singing because we could not communicate by talk. Farmer's family were obviously used to ending the strenuous day by singing a few songs, which they did unselfconsciously and sweetly. Our lads were not to be outdone, and sang several pleasant choruses. We were shamed by the poverty of the Dutch: everywhere it showed, the result of four years of cruel occupation. They were right down on subsistence level in the towns; even these farming folk, naturally a little better-off so far as food went, were barely keeping going. The chaps respected the Dutch, really, for being puritanical and standoffish about frat, and helped them when they could with small gifts. But there's no doubt about it, the Dutch were less welcoming, as a general thing, than the Belgians. However, we took to this utterly plain-living, hard-working, pious family, and helped them with their chores to some extent. After the sing-song, when we had written our letters home and brewed our various nightcaps, we went up the ladder through the trapdoor and swept aside a mound of golden corn in the barn, and slept there happily, among the corn and onions and apples. There were few such happy nights in 1944–5.

Every soldier who fought in that campaign will recall certain proper names with appropriate emotions: S'Hertogenbosch, Gennep, Roermond, Venlo, Nijmegen, Grave, Volkel. . . . Thank God I am at last beginning to forget them. We were up with the army most of the time, of course, picking up our melancholy loads. In the autumn it was quite unpleasant: the Germans, great fighters always, put up a stout show, they seemed miraculously recovered after the disaster of Normandy, and there were some eerie journeys up and down that narrow corridor from Eindhoven to Nijmegen. We had airfields, of a sort, at Grave and Volkel, which I shall always remember with unease. Sometimes, in the early stages, the Germans seemed too close and too free; tanks roamed near the verges, sticks of actual mortar bombs dropped close behind and close ahead (once when I was sitting on the tailboard of a truck crammed with ammunition) and wrecked and burned-out vehicles littered the ditches. But the situation was 'stabilised', as the communiqués say, meaning that the poor infantry heroically pushed the Germans back. There was a period almost of stalemate, in a dismal way, and then in the New Year our chaps began to clear the country between Maas and Rhine, a terrible battle of forest- and street-fighting, the worst kind there is, and finally we passed through the apocalyptic ruins of Xanten and rushed across the Rhine at Wesel and streamed across the North German plain in the cold Spring weather.

It was terrible to be in an occupied country for the first time. One felt no exultation. Now, suddenly, we were not among allies more or less pleased to see us; the sullen populace, proud fighting people brought low, glared at us with a hatred that could not be concealed. I do not say that this attitude invariably persisted very long, but the first shock of entering Germany proper, the inhabited country beyond the Rhine, was icy. One wanted it over and done with, now, as soon as might be. Quite soon, some of our chaps, living among the Germans, came to recognise a kinship which they had never felt with the French. I do not offer this as an opinion, nor with either approval or disapproval, but as a fact of reporting, quite incontrovertible. This happened quite soon (to those to whom it *did* happen) after the victory of 8 May 1945. We had reached the Elbe and recoiled, pushed on to the Baltic and pushed off again, and were caught by victory laagered in the appalling dreariness of Lüneberg Heath. Later we went up into Schleswig-Holstein, where there were several Germanic towns including Kiel which sent a chill through my thin blood. But, as I say, some of the lads got quite to like the Germans: they found them scrupulously clean, diligent, hard-working, tough, durable, and several other things which have always appealed to some of the English more than others.

Although I considered the Germans the wreckers of Europe, which they were, and had no conscious wish to fraternise, yet I had my own moment of uncertainty and bewilderment, and it came about in a curious manner.

The Steinhuder Meer is a great big beautiful lake about ten miles from Hanover. On its shores were a nice collection of chalets and bungalows, with private jetties and landing stages. I fancy it was a sort of summer vacation resort, at any rate in peace time, for the good Party members of Hanover. When we took over the airfield at Wünsdorf the war was still going quite strong, in a racketty sort of way, and we walked down to the lake along a path through dark woods with our eyes peeled. There was no sign whatever of the army, which was swanning cheerfully all over the Reich, and current talk of Werewolves and all that sort of stuff was beguiling but not comforting. So we went armed. In fact we trudged down that dusky and tortuous woodland ride feeling absurdly adventurous. But there it was: odd shots did tend to ring out, odd innocents to fall. It wasn't dangerous, that would be pitching it much too high, but it was odd. You were keenly aware that civilisation was in ruins.

The moment I saw the water I was itching to fish it. I hadn't really fished for far too long. It looked so enticing a sheet, sheening in the late evening sun, with the dark woods coming down and the cheerful little chalets fringing the shore. I simply couldn't resist it. My friends pushed off to investigate some sort of *gasthaus* which we discovered nearby, and I pushed through a little garden and found an old German sitting in a wicker chair, on his private landing stage, placidly fishing. For a moment I thought better of the enemy. He got up at once, and after a long moment of perplexity, and possibly fear, I guess he saw my eyes on the rod and divined that I was more interested in fishing than in rapine, loot, or vengeance. Anyway, he made a gesture to offer me his rod. Perhaps one fisherman can detect another without words.

I shook my head. He stood there uncertainly for a few moments, obviously not caring to sit down again in the presence of the conqueror; neither of us quite knew where we went from there, for the conqueror was precisely as ill at ease as the conquered. His line was still in the water, and to avoid looking at him I looked at it, and suddenly the float bobbed in that characteristically perchy manner and went under. I pointed, and called out 'Look! A bite!' which was perhaps a bit silly, and he struck and began to play what was obviously a good fish. I guessed that it was something rather out of the ordinary, for the old chap was showing unmistakable signs of excitement, and his rod was bent beautifully. He was plainly a practised hand at this game, though, and he soon had the fish under control. He looked round for his landing net. It was leaning up against the wall of his chalet, out of his reach. He looked at the net and he looked doubtfully at me, standing there in my stained old battledress with a gun under my arm, and he looked at his bent rod. He was in a state. Well, I walked over and picked up the net and sank it in the water. He brought the fish over it and I duly ladled it out.

It was a lovely perch, a good two pounds, I guess. The old German made no effort to take the fish, so I unhooked it and stood there weighing it in my hands the way you do. You could see he was all eagerness to get his hands on it, but he wouldn't make a move. I realised I was grinning and saying 'Jolly good show.' I made a gesture to knock it on the head, and he nodded vigorously. So I killed it. I then handed it to him. He seemed unwilling to take it, and kept indicating that I could have it if I wanted it. So I firmly put it in his hands. His old face lit up.

He turned and called over the fence to his next-door neighbour. The fences were high and opaque and ran right down to the water; they liked their privacy. Another old German peeped over the fence and his eyes nearly popped out when he saw the big perch. He looked furtively at me and muttered something. 'My' old boche jabbered away at him, very excited and as pleased as Punch, and in a moment it was a sort of party. The two old wives came timidly out; they had been hiding themselves away. They all jabbered away, congratulating the old boy, and they smiled at me slyly but obviously in a more or less friendly way. I dare say he had been telling them how I helped him to land his big perch, and they were pleasantly surprised, that was quite obvious. Finally they all shuffled off again, the old chap baited up again and made his cast and laid his rod down. He made an urgent gesture which I understood to mean 'Please wait a moment' and he rushed into his little doll's house. He was out again in a moment, with a roach pole and a stool. He placed the stool and motioned me to sit on it, and put the pole in my hands. Then he stood anxiously waiting to see if I would. Well, I thought, this is a damn funny war. I sat down, and within a few minutes we were both fishing placidly away, like any old man and young man on the edge of any lake anywhere in the world. A few appropriate remarks were doubtless indicated, but thank heaven we had this language barrier between us, such a boon, so we had to manage without all the bromides. We just sat there silently fishing, smoking my tobacco, and the sun went swimming down below the rim of the water, and bats began to fly. It was absolutely peaceful.

I knew the old man wouldn't be the first to show a willingness to pack it in, so I got up and indicated thanks, and he got up too. I gathered without much difficulty that he was trying to tell me that I should be welcome to use his tackle and stool and landing stage, any time. Suddenly a burst of small-arms fire rattled out, sounding very loud and close across the water. He looked haggard and old again in a moment. He looked at me miserably and questioningly. I guessed—at least, I hoped—that it was just some of the chaps cutting loose in the woods: there was a lot of loose shooting in those trigger-happy days—and I tried to pass this on. Not very successfully; he still looked miserable. I picked up his big perch and put it in his hands and his tension seemed to relax a bit.

It was a ruminant walk back to the airstrip and my truck. When I arrived the lads told me that there had been a bit of shooting and some-body had been killed. There was always a bit of shooting, and someone was always getting killed, as we pushed through the wide spaces of Germany, miles and miles behind the army. A corporal was giving his opinion of the Germans, and warning his erks what he would personally do to anyone he caught fraternising. We had a couple of guests for the night; ex-prisoners of war on their way home after several years behind barbed-wire. They had something to contribute to the discussion. I kept quiet about my bit of fishing. Finally we broke it up, and in the silence and darkness I lay looking at the stars and wondering what they would have said if they had known how I had spent my evening. I could not feel wholly guilty, yet I was not easy in my mind.

But I was never easy in my mind during those few nights we spent between a frontier and a frontier.

There are many strange experiences which befall bedless men who stay awake all night under an open sky. Nothing is stranger than night, and it is stranger because more wholly itself when you meet it under the sky. In a house it is strange enough, whether you are lying sleepless under the roof counting the hours and pondering a problem, as all men do from time to time, whoever they may be, in the course of a life. It is strange, even, when you sit in a lighted room downstairs, with the night (as you might think) banished from your hearth by firelight and lamplight and voices; even then it is strange, and creeps in to touch you with its cold hand. But it is strangest by far, utterly and fantastically strange, when you meet it defenceless out of doors.

It must come to every man to find himself walking along a road long after midnight, far from towns. To some it does not happen very often in a lifetime: these are the prudent and saving sort of men, who know at first night that night is profitless to them, unless perchance it be spent counting and calculating or up to no good in one way or another. But to another sort of man it seems to happen quite often in a life's course, and although he too may make no sort of profit from it that can be put up in a strong-room or buried in a vault for his sons to squander, yet there is no loss in it for him, for he meets the rooted springs of human fear face to face and knows them for what they are. He feels around him in the immense void of night the palpable forces of fear, and having withstood them, as boldly as he may, he meets the morning and understands the mystery and miracle of sunrise.

The fearful essences of night appal my godless soul. There is neither mercy nor charity nor justice in the night. One walking in a lonely glade through a forest, or one on a high mountain, or one in a valley by a watercourse, he feels these things. The absences of night are terrible. It is drained of virtue. This a man feels like cold, which is the absence of heat.

But there are positive things, also to be felt intensely in the vacuum of night, flitting and fluttering and sidling in, and whispering, and at length peopling the void with presences. These a man knows in his heart to be evil essences. The certainty is in his blood. They are the dispossessed: shady remnants of forces driven out of daytime by the conquering will and ingenuity of mankind.

Shepherds and sentries know this to be true; but sentries less commonly than shepherds; and sentries are relieved and demobilised. Shepherds on the high hills know it well: these are apart from other men.

Even on the sea there is sometimes an intimation of these unruly presences, though not so often as on land, for water spirits though fierce and large are not so palpable as the presences that haunt contour and thicket. Mostly perhaps it is men who sail small craft silently through the night with a bubbling wake who feel most keenly the things of which I speak; and oftener, perhaps, in coastal waters near to the spur of hill and promontory than on the great plain of ocean. As inland men wakeful in the night are easier in the plains than on the hills.

I was walking the fringe of the wood at 2 a.m., thinking of werewolves and trolls and the dead faces of German soldiers lying sightless under the sun in attitudes of despair. The great dark forests of Teutonia enshroud countless ghosts. I was thinking of the long-ago impossible aspiration of the Holy Roman Empire, and how it was very nearly the salvation of mankind, and I wondered if it might be so again, when the fever had passed away. I thought of Charlemagne and of Attila and of the deeps of the Teutoburger Forest and the acid horrors, not far behind us, of the Reichwald. Over the whole brooded not merely melancholy, which is manageable and saving, but active horror and malignance. I had a chill and doubtless a slight fever, and I was sick

183

from lack of sleep and from seeing too many sad sights. And perhaps it was these elements of heightened perception and feverish unreality, the compost bed of dreams, which created the personage that now approached me through the trees. Of that I cannot ever speak with certainty. What I saw was as real to me then as the mists of the forest.

I raised my gun but knew that no shot would halt this invader, knew it as soundly as I knew simple arithmetic and the conjugation of *amare*. It was transparent: it was light walking. It was a man who wore a helmet, and a breastplate or cuirass, and he carried a short broad sword. I knew that I saw face to face a Roman legionary, lost in eternity. He passed by me a few paces distant, marching at the tread of the legions, which was twenty-four miles in eight hours, neither more nor less, which looks easy and is indeed easy for the first half of the first day. He vanished down the ride or glade that led to the mere.

I felt a transfiguring horror at this sight, and a fulness of pity too for the Roman who never left the German forests, and I felt a terrible clutching fear, amounting to certitude, that I too should never leave those dark woods. This was the third time that the certitude had come upon me. Once in the night near Nijmegen in the depths of winter I felt a foreknowledge of doom, and again lying one black calm night near the Maas or Meuse, a curiously quiet night with only a few big guns thumping across the river from time to time, and no danger. Now it came again very positive. I had no further doubts about the business. I was very sad, for we knew that the war was almost over, and already Germany was defeated. Habit is stronger than fear, and having wakened my relief I went to sleep on the ground, and next day ate hearty and travelled far.

Three times during my last few weeks in the R.A.F. I was involved in motor accidents, all spectacular, all while I was merely a passenger. I began to wonder if it were my fate to be knocked off not 'gloriously' by the enemy, but ignominiously by some idiot at the wheel. But the day came, after five and a quarter years of unheroic toil and boredom, when I collected my chalk-stripe demob suit and cardboard trilby and paper mac at Cardington, and for the last time rode out past a guard-room sitting up on the tail-gate of a Bedford truck, singing 'Bless 'em all' with utter sincerity and fervour.

I was rising 28 when the war engulfed me; just turned 33 when it released me. Undoubtedly I came out coarser than I went in; five years in the ranks had completed my education in the realities of human intercourse and the unrealities of speculative abstractions concerning human behaviour. I think my manners were worsened, and my natural in-genuousness had turned towards scepticism. I had had confirmed several theoretical notions. I had seen for myself, what I had always tended to suspect, that the brave and willing, salt of a society, are just as likely to be rewarded with death and degradation as with honour and profit. It was very clear that selflessness was its own reward. It had to be. It was clear that some are naturally bossy, some naturally subservient. I had not yet quite learned that in this cockeyed and infinitely gullible world, you are taken at your own valuation, and the chief gift you need to 'get on' is arrogant conceit and over-weening self-satisfaction. But I was beginning to learn.

Not that theoretical knowledge ever helps you to change your natural way of looking at things. We are all slaves of our own tempera-ments. We can only be what we are.

Though courage had not been required of me, I had seen brave men at close quarters. It was as I thought. Courage, like grace, is elective. It is a beautiful quality to possess. And so (I still believed) is tenderness. I was still a hero-worshipper; but there were several sorts of hero.

I had seen all I wanted to see. I had seen men at their best and at their worst. I will not say that the native romanticism had been beaten out of me, but I had had enough of belonging to any community larger than two.

All I wanted now was to set up a little home, where I could be private.

Chapter Thirteen

The cold city indifferently received its returning veterans. Bleak and dirty, weary and graceless, London in December 1945 was no place in which to build the new life. But London it had to be. Unlike 1918, unlike that frenzy, this was a cold, numbed, cynical, dusty, degraded, worn-out, weary old capital that had seen its better days and knew it. Knew in its parched and sleazy old soul that the good times were gone, if ever they existed, never to return.

There was no hysteria of thankfulness and deliverance.

When we got the news that the war was over we were camped on Lüneburg Heath, in a desolation. I had just returned from an expedition to the Elbe, where, in enormous caverns carved deep into sandstone cliffs on the east bank, millions of bottles of wine were stored. There were British, American and Russian soldiers milling around, ransacking the caves. We carried away hundreds of bottles of immature, vinegary stuff in our truck. I got back to Lüneburg Heath to find the victory a fact; we had expected it hourly for two days. The wine was shared out and drunk with a sort of brittle and feverish insistence that there was something to celebrate. So there was, of course: victory. Nazism was defeated. But the enthusiasm, even there, even then, seemed factitious. One had the sense of duty done, but not of liberation and horizon. The Germans had been beaten, yet *again*, but no-one was in the euphoric mood of 1918. This was getting to be a habit. No wild romantic dreams (that I heard of) of setting up as chicken farmer with your gratuity, or renting the old stone shack at 1s. 6d. a week, in Devon or some such place, to write in a nirvana of timeless enthusiasm. No new Jerusalems. The result of the 1945 general election might have been deduced, though it wasn't. OK, mate, you made it, you survived, it's all organised, get back to your miserable boring job again after the long wearisome interruption, only this time, we're the bosses, they can't stuff us around any more. No enthusiasm even for the people's democracy. Just back to work, a bit better off, in terms of weekly pay, than you were before. What a wild utopia, bureaucracy in our time, nationalise the mines, nationalise the railways, start the Welfare State, one moron one vote and Jack's not only just as good as his master but just as arrogant, and lazier. The flower was in the seed.

London, December, 1945: the great anti-climax. I should have packed up then, should have shot out to British Columbia, Vancouver Island, with the friends I had made in the First Canadian Army. There were familial reasons why we didn't. We were dutiful.

I became features editor of the London *Evening Standard*. The Editor was Herbert Gunn, who succeeded Michael Foot. Gunn had been Managing Editor of the *Daily Express* in my day; had been promoted a few doors up Shoe Lane. He wrote to me while I was still in Germany, offering me the job. I had always got on well with him, and although the *Evening Standard* had always seemed to me an uncongenial and unexciting paper, naturally I accepted his offer. It reached me while I was washing my spare shirt in a petrol can, in a wet field just on the wrong side of the Rhine, at a sinister little place called Dam. They were as stiff as plywood, those shirts. I spread the shirt out on a hedgerow to dry, but it came on to rain. We got a movement order and I carried that wet shirt around for quite a while. Who cared? Here was somebody talking turkey about jobs and peace time. Yes, I said, yes, you bet I'll be features editor of the *Evening Standard*. I'd have accepted almost any suggestion. There was still a bit of war to be got through and the Germans were always capable of nasty surprises, right up to the end.

But it wasn't like I remembered. Is it ever? Chaps came back from the war, one by one, and then it brightened up; but the bulk of the staff I found there had been there some time, for one reason or another, and I got the impression, rightly or wrongly, that they didn't particularly want their cosy wartime routine interrupted overmuch. I never knew a newspaper office with less camaraderie and esprit de corps and all that stuff, until I left to join the *Daily Graphic*. There was one exception, a very nice chap named David Williams, the permanent deputy editor. He was a sailor. Everyone got on well with Dave. I don't know if he was ever offered the editorship, but even if he was, he had enough sense to refuse it. He stayed deputy to a whole succession of editors and everybody was real fond of him. He was clean-cut, tolerant, imperturbable, with a strong jaw and twinkling eyes. He knew his stuff.

I don't say they didn't *all* know their stuff, but they weren't somehow just like the fire-eaters I'd known on the *Daily Express*, nor yet like the 'golden lads and lasses' I remembered from Birmingham. There were some who gave themselves airs as young intellectuals *and* men-about-town, both, but those who gave themselves airs, gave me heartburn. 'This is the boulevardier's paper,' one of them loftily informed me, when I arrived and tried to make friends. Stuff me, I thought, if that's a fact, it's got a funny features editor. That may have been the general view, for all I know. It seemed a stuffy little paper to me, and I couldn't see why anyone on it should be complacent. Not that I was exactly bursting with great schemes for revitalising it. Having tasted the communal air and found it both supercilious and stuffy, I immediately more or less lost interest. I can only work well with sympathetic people. Friends.

Bert Gunn was duly bidden to take me along to see Lord Beaverbrook. I had never met the great man, though he had sent me two messages of congratulation when I wrote leader-page articles for the *Daily Express* of which he approved. But that was a long time before. We drove to Arlington House, where the old man had his flat. Bert said he could do with a drink, but we were too late to stop off for one. I didn't feel any need of a drink just then, but a few minutes later I wished we had found the time. We were ushered in by the dark faceless man and there was the legend himself, standing up at his lectern, reading some bumf or other. Gunn introduced me. The old man shook hands and stood back and looked at me very hard, and his first words were:

'Well, Mr Wiggin, what ideas do *you* have to make this paper great and good?'

I thought for a moment and realised that this was a time for total candour, if ever there was one.

'I haven't got an idea in my head,' I said.

Lord Beaverbrook was not easily thrown out of his stride, but you could see this perplexed him. I don't say he didn't ever have other people around him who were short of ideas, but I doubt if many of them came clean about it. It was true that at the moment I hadn't got an idea in my head. I had had one or two a minute before, and I caught up on one or two a little later. But the shock of the confrontation with that tremendous character, the douche of his opening words, cleaned me right out. However, I didn't like to see him standing there, so unhappy and incredulous, so I said:

'I had an idea yesterday, and I dare say I may have another tomorrow. I do get them from time to time.'

You could see it wasn't enough ideas. Lord Beaverbrook dismissed me then, in a manner of speaking. He turned to Bert and spoke to him quite severely, about various editorial matters which bored me even to hear other people discussing them. I began to float away into the daydream—rocks, torrents, fish, the stone hut in the glade by the waterfall; just the usual imagery. I could see it was the end. I'd never manage to get interested in all this crap they were maundering about. I wondered if I'd have enough to pay the fare to the shack. It suddenly struck me I hadn't even *got* the shack, of course, and my poor wife waiting back home to hear all about my first momentous meeting with the great man. For Christ's sake, Wiggin, snap out of it, try to *look* interested, anyway. I shut off the escapist imagery and came back to the meeting in time to hear Bert telling the old man *his* various plans for making the paper great and good. Among them were one or two ideas I'd put up myself. Bert attributed them to me; very decently, or perhaps in order to show that he hadn't been a complete idiot in setting me on. Unfortunately they happened to be ideas which Lord Beaverbrook did not greatly care for. He might have cared for them some other time, but that evening he did not care for them. He brooded a bit and suddenly he said:

'You promote your men too fast, Mr Gunn. That's the trouble with you.'

This is marvellous, I thought; I'm finished before I even started. Never mind, what the hell. I hadn't come through a long war in order to worry about what bloody civilians thought about me. Or about anything else, for that matter. The old man couldn't have devised a better shock therapy. Suddenly I felt a treat, calm and happy and gay. Gunn was defending himself quite stoutly. He reminded Lord Beaverbrook that he had known me long before, that I had done this and that and so on, that it wasn't at all a case of taking a fancy to a new face and promoting him injudiciously. He made quite a fair job of it. The old man still looked dubious, but not quite so dubious as before. By now I was walking on air. Having suddenly realised that I didn't give a damn, one way or the other, my mind cleared, and I contributed several sharpish ideas in a terse take-it-or-leave-it style. It just about saved the day, I think, and we left without actual outburst. I thought all was well now, and even if it wasn't, what of it? But Bert was gloomy.

Next morning Bert was looking for me sharp and early. We began the day's work at some godawful hour like 8 a.m. When I saw his face I knew he was not radiantly happy about something, and I thought I knew what. It had been agreed between us that I was to contribute a new and brilliant and highly idiosyncratic column, once a week, in addition to my chores as features editor. We were going to call it Wiggin's Wednesday, since that was the day it was scheduled to appear and we couldn't think of anything else to call it. The first column was quite a nice bit of knitting. The day before, Tuesday, Bert had greatly admired it. Or at least, he had expressed warm satisfaction, which was near enough the same thing. Now he came up to me and said he wasn't happy about the *title*. I knew what part of the title he wasn't happy about.

'Let's just call it *Wednesday*,' Bert said.

' "Mr Gunn, you promote your men too fast," ' I said.

He gave me a dirty look.

I wrote the personal column for about five weeks, swimming against the tide, and jacked it in. Instead I started to write an angling column which I signed John Lea. It went down very well. Specialisation again, you see. You can't go wrong if you're the one who knows. And one thing I did know something about was fishing. I was mad on it. It was just about the only activity which reconciled me to life in peace-time London. I got the hell out of the place on every spare day I could carve out of the demanding schedule of work, travelled miles by bus and train and Green Line coach, fishing the Thames, the Mole, the Wey, the Adur and the Arun, various lakes and ponds and gravel pits and reservoirs, and quietly graduating to the great game fishing of the West and Wales.

This was a period of swimming against a tide. As an executive on the boulevardier's newspaper I did not experience anything like the pre-war joys of making up pretty, dramatic and jolly pages. I found that I had only a limited interest in the politics of the day. I did my best, of course, but it was joyless work. I wasn't really interested in editing features any more. I wasn't really interested in public life, public affairs: any interest I dutifully showed, as a journalist, was forced and feigned and factitious. I was deeply interested in various individuals; but aggregates of individuals—societies or simply society—were infinitely uninteresting. It's all you can do to learn about one person in all that person's infinite quiddity and variety; you can never know anything worth knowing about a group, outside the bare abstractions and generalised formulations which pass as knowledge. I gave up trying. To me, a person is a person, an infinity in himself. And herself.

But I did my duty, the thing began to shape all right. I had bad days and good days. I could cope. If you have enough professional experience and expertise, you can cope. But it isn't living. One day dear old Horace Thoroughgood retired, and I saw a ray of hope. Horace wrote a brief half-column or corner about the goings-on in the London magistrates' courts; had been doing it for years. His career provided any amount of food for thought. When he joined the *Evening Standard* his appointment was the Page One lead story, in the first edition at any rate. Arnold Bennett was literary critic of the paper at the time, and he trumpeted his discovery of the young Horace Thoroughgood. So well did he do his stuff with Lord Beaverbrook that, as I say, they announced Horace's appointment to the staff as the front page lead. Great guns! When I first knew Horace he was a sweet old chap who had long out-lived any illusions which that dramatic declaration may have fostered. He was a Hazlitt-lover, like Michael Foot, who edited the paper just before my time. He was also one of the sweetest and gentlest and best-informed men I ever met in journalism, and of course he hadn't a notion of how to push himself, so gradually he had declined—I don't like the word, I am merely trying to tell you the bare facts—he had subsided, shall we say, into this quiet dusty corner of the courts sketch. Now he was going to take his ease. Papers are always really delighted when their old men retire, for it is a young man's game without a doubt and the young men coming up, full of new and bright ideas, see the old men as dusty reactionary impediments to the brave new world they are about to create. I understand this and shall not be unduly surprised or hurt when my time comes. What the young lions don't always remember is that the distaste may be mutual.

When I heard that Horace was leaving, I put it to Bert Gunn that I would very much like to retire from my executive position and write a courts column. He saw that I was hankering to get back to being a writer, that I had lost the first fine careless rapture of being a features editor, and to be fair he knew that a happy newspaperman is more likely to be competent than an unhappy one, other things being equal. The rival *Evening News* carried that celebrated column by James A. Jones, Courts Day By Day, which was a big selling point. Bert said all right, if I was set on it, I could have a go—provided I found him a replacement features editor and also provided it was clearly understood that I had to get on terms, as a public attraction, with the *Evening News* column. I didn't know about *that*, but I found the replacement features editor, right to hand, in short order. He was Charles Curran, the Tory lawyer-politician who became M.P. for where was it? Charles really does believe in the actual reality of public affairs and all that rubbish. He is and he was a strong active worker never happier than when half-hidden by a load of bumf, a vigorous man with a grey crew-cut and a mouthful of huge strong teeth and a powerful jaw and a great big Irish smile and a very acute mind. He had a strong carrying voice the sound of which did not disconcert him unduly, and a wonderful facility for arguing the hindleg off a brass pot. Whenever Charles explained some contentious point I found myself in total agreement with him. He had great force and logic. Like Enoch Powell, he was one of nature's intellectual Tories, which is a different thing from being one of nature's emotional Tories, i.e., a safety-firster. I put him up for the coming vacancy with great eloquence, and he got it. He was a first-rate features editor. He didn't waste his energy brooding over bits of design and typography, he really thought in terms of contentious topical issues, he was right on the ball in every way.

So there I was again, off the chain, a writer of sorts. I began writing an enlarged column called My Court Casebook, and to fill in I wrote short idiosyncratic weekly essays which I signed Joseph Fry, and of course I wrote John Lea's angling column weekly. This was the start of the good life all over again. I suddenly got very happy with the *Evening Standard*. Of course the chaps were not really the bunch of stiffs I have indicated, not all of them, anyway: it's just that to the new-comer fresh from itchy Air Force blue some of them seemed a bit standoffish and not quite my type. Which is another way of saying I was not quite their type. There were some lovely lads on the *Evening Standard* about then. The sports desk was peopled by the salt of the earth, as so often it is; Pat Murphy was there, about to leave to become sports editor of *The Sunday Times*. There was a lovely chap in charge of pictures, whose name eludes me, and two cheerful lawyers, Arnold Maplesden and Hugh Hickling. I love a cheerful lawyer. The only thing you can do with a newspaper lawyer is fight him every inch of the way. They are there to suppress every last ha'porth of personality and interest in your writing, if they can, and you have to jolly them along remorselessly. When you have a cheerful lawyer you can fight the good fight without rancour. It becomes a daily exercise more healthful than Indian clubs. In time you can educate a cheerful lawyer into taking a broader view of life than his training inculcates. Old Mapes used to be a champion amateur boxer and sometimes he set about me if I was par-ticularly unco-operative. He was so much my senior that I felt I had to let him bore in to close quarters instead of stabbing him off with my left. He could still hit quite hard.

I was happy in my work. I went to court every morning, to sit with the regular court reporters who were there to get hard news, in the little pens assigned to the Fourth Estate. Oh these hard benches, my bony bum is flattened by too much sitting on them. They were a tolerant bunch of chaps; they tolerated me, this 'amateur' without shorthand, who idled through the hard news stories when they were scribbling away, and feverishly scribbled down every word of the little oddments which were not worth their while. It was a tolerant working arrangement. I went on a sort of rota to Bow Street, Marlborough Street, West London, South London (an old house at Balham, actually) and sometimes to Old Street on the eastern or City side of the city. This was great, getting to work about ten in the morning, when the chaps in Shoe Lane had already been sweating it out for two hours. After court, a bite of lunch, sometimes with a criminal or a probation officer, then to the office to hand in a story and correct and cut the one already in proof, then home to write a column out of the morning's doings. Sometimes I was rich in stories and wrote three at a time; sometimes we were desperately scraping the bottom of the barrel, constructing comedies out of very discouraging scraps of dialogue by penitent drunks, taciturn coppers, resigned beaks. But when the stories were there, it was a great life, the stories were *real*, it was a challenge to give them form and life and style. I suppose I did the best work of my working life in these days.

Sometimes in tube trains I saw people reading my column. It was a funny feeling. I watched to see if they would smile, or burst into tears. Usually I watched in vain; for the tears, at any rate. But at least they generally read right on to the end.

My attitude to London changed. I felt part of it, in a way I never felt part of it while working in an office. I was free and footloose among the people of the capital, a sort of hobo, yes, an eavesdropper on the comedy and tragedy of low life. I knew the probation officers well, and a few of the police, though I did not ever become a familiar of the police. I was conned from time to time by various interested parties; one or two old lags, and young lags, for that matter, got past my fragile guard and touched me for tea and sympathy, and various other commodities. I was enchanted though not bemused to find myself in touch, for the first time, with the smoky and flame-lit obscurity of the world of crime. And not only the world of crime, but the rich stew of life on a certain ill-organised unintellectual level, a squalid level, which resulted in petty misdemeanour, as of course it does. Though all the obvious stories were naturally snapped up and used as hard news, and I was left to construct the best I could out of the unconsidered leavings, I never resented this nor wished to become a 'real' crime or court reporter. I enjoyed the necessity of making a story where 'normality' saw no story. The requirements were a sense of humour, a sense of pity, and a sense of style. If I may say so, it called for a touch of insight.

My relationships with the office, the city, and the citizens had now changed radically for the better. I was even getting on good terms with Lord Beaverbrook. That great man ignored or overlooked the unpromising start of our relationship in a wonderfully generous way. He supported and encouraged me like a true friend. Sometimes while I was still features editor he would ring me up and utter words of vibrant encouragement and advice; advice which, alas, I could not always follow. But it was when I began to write My Court Casebook that he really warmed to me. Several times I received the royal summons and trailed off down to his vast gloomy country house at Cherkeley, near Leatherhead. There was a ritual about this engagment. I never quite got used to being met at the station and popped into the back seat of the disgusting old Austin by the silent chauffeur. I wanted to sit up front and talk to the man. I had the same feeling, always, about taxis. But these discreet servants of the rich know better than to talk to the boss's guests. In this unnatural segregation we arrived at the great house, an equally silent flunkey ushered me in, an equally taciturn butler waited on us. I wasn't trained in the routine of the rich and never felt at ease. The rich are trained early in the art of pretending that the servant simply isn't there. I cannot do this. If a person is there in the same room, you've got to include him in as a human being. He might be a right bastard, very well, but he's human, and to freeze him out, to carry on as if he were simply not present, was something I could never learn. Right up to the end of my dining-out life, I kept on committing this solecism of trying to include the flunkeys in the conversation. It could be disastrous. *They* are sometimes as embarrassed as the rich stuff on whom they wait. *They* sometimes resent it. They sometimes *want* their segregation, its own special sort of peace and quiet, the distinctive and impassable class fence (often invisible to me) that ensures privacy. I realise that sometimes my natural spontaneous good manners, rooted in humanity, were a real nuisance to them.

The few meals I had with Lord Beaverbrook are memorable to me still. Especially two. Once at dinner he suddenly asked me if I thought I could write the Beachcomber column. I knew he meant the William Hickey column, knew it was a slip of the tongue. No man living could ever double on the Beachcomber column. Talk about *lèse majesté*. But the old man was in spate, and I never did quite manage to correct him. I even left the house without having corrected the slip. I carried on as if he had indeed said 'Hickey', and it turned out all right. That *was* what he meant. But with his Lordship, you never knew for sure. He was unpredictable. I did a few dummy runs as Hickey, but of course it was the very last job I was cut out for, and the idea was quietly dropped. I don't know why editors think you want to write a gossip column when plainly it is the last thing you are capable of. I was even invited to write the Atticus column in *The Sunday Times*, I think it was just before Ian Fleming took it on and after Sacheverell Sitwell had given it up. As delicately as possible, I pointed out that I rarely even read the perishing column, much less aspired to write it.

Once we were having lunch out on the terrace at Cherkeley, just Lord Beaverbrook and me. We had cold boiled ham, very decent chips, nearly as good as Jack Smith's, and asparagus. I had a glass of lager, and his Lordship had a whisky. I had brought down the midday edition of the *Evening Standard*, as in duty bound—that was always the visitor's job—and the old gentleman read my current column with a ferocious frown of concentration. He laid the folded paper aside and took a moody looking sip of whisky. I feared a lashing.

'You have a genius as a writer,' Lord Beaverbrook said.

You can hardly expect me not to put that in my memoirs, can you? But it stopped the conversation stone dead. When anyone praises me I freeze.

He went on to tell me how I should employ my genius, but deeply as I respected him as a great man, one of the outstanding characters of our age, I could not quite follow him there. He suggested, among other things, that I should fearlessly attack the magistrates when I caught them in error. Who did he think I was—John Gordon? I realised yet again that as a writer you have to jog along as best you can, nobody ever (or hardly ever) realises what sort of writer you really are; including yourself, often enough. When you do something well they want you immediately to do something entirely different; it's all a wild gamble and great editors are scarce. Ideally it's one writer one editor. But that is not very practicable.

We were strolling in the grounds of Cherkeley after luncheon one day when Lord Beaverbrook pointed dramatically with his stick to a spot on the cornice or pediment or whatever it is, where a little bit was chipped out. I should never have noticed it.

'My house is falling down,' he said, like Irving announcing the fall of a dynasty.

How do you react to a remark like that? If I knew the answer to that question I might be sitting with the carpet up to my ankles in a mink-lined room, dictating memos about millions. I'm afraid I laughed. I could see it wasn't the right response, but went on recklessly sewing my own shroud.

'You ought to see mine,' I said.

Not that I had a house. We were living then in a flat made available to us by our good friends the Bartletts, Alistair and Eileen, with whom we had 'lived out' of camp in various Welsh farmhouses and so on, during the darkest days of the war. Friendships rooted in such suffering are unusually tenacious. The Bartletts had, they still have, a big Victorian house in Herne Hill and we were literally in on the ground floor, in nice spacious rooms and a friendly atmosphere. But it wasn't very much like Cherkeley.

Lord Beaverbrook forgave me that gaffe, as he forgave me much. To the end of his life, long after I had left the old firm, he remained interested, friendly, warm and helpful. He was capable, they all said, of autocratic anger: but though God knows I must have provoked him direly, if innocently, to me he was the most generous genius. He didn't give me money, but hope. He forgave me my trespasses and he encouraged me to believe that I was a writer. He was infinitely kind when he might have been quite understandably out of patience. Right to the end, there was always a job to go back to on his firm. When I finally declined the last offer, well, I suppose it was the last, he wrote me a sweet letter saying how sorry he was that we were not to work together again. I could have cried. I met him only once after that, at the great dinner which Lord Thomson of Fleet gave, at the Dorchester, to celebrate Lord Beaverbrook's eighty-fifth birthday. It was his last public appearance; he had only a very short time left to live, a matter of days. He made the speech of a lifetime, a simply marvellous speech. I got near him only for a moment—all Fleet Street had gathered to honour him—and I just murmured congratulations.

'God bless you, Maurice,' he said.

People say and write this and that about the old man. I don't myself think I was ever really a dyed-in-the-wool Expressman, in the sense that I never cared enough about the politics, never for a moment shared the official optimism, and only intermittently believed in the let's-make-more-money-and-get-more-things-and-then-we'll-all-be-so-much-happier line. It seemed to me naïve, and I couldn't help noticing that people with the most things weren't necessarily nicer, let alone happier, than people with rather few. The *Express* was the paper for the rising bourgeoisie, for people who actually believed in 'getting-on'. With its great vitality and its incessant glamorisation and flattery of the getting-on petty bourgeois way of life, it grew and prospered mightily, until, after the war, when that image seemed suddenly rather irrelevant, it was outstripped by the *Mirror* with its incessant glamorisation and flattery of the working class, who were on their way fast to becoming the petty bourgeoisie. But even if I was not an Expressman at heart, I was real fond of Lord Beaverbrook, I really was, in so far as you can be fond of a millionaire, and you can. He was real kind and nice to me and I adored him for his tolerance. For we had nothing in common. He must have realised, several times, that I wasn't wholly in the mainstream of Express-think. But he accepted me as a harmless eccentric with a touch of word-love and a gift of occasionally, unpredictably, saying something in a way that got through. He never said of me, as he said of Godfrey Winn, 'he shakes hands with the heart of humanity'. If he had I should have laughed in his face. I got the notion that he knew that, too. He was the great scaly old eagle that brooded over the nest and all its droppings, and I was just one of the little birds that flew waywardly around chirping an occasional tweet-tweet. He knew I came out of the wrong egg. What I loved him for, more than I loved any other employer, was his gift of allowing that there could be other eggs, other birds, and they could fly free. The cage door stood open and you could fly away if you were so foolish. And you could fly back.

I could look Lord Beaverbrook right in the eye, and see there another sort of creature altogether, and respect its otherness, and not feel flustered or put down or intimidated, and go right on being my own sort of creature, happily and freely.

There were other lords, other employers. I never got a good look in their eyes because their eyes were always veiled. They were politer, more remote; affable but not really with me, not humanly in touch. I never claim to have known any other employer as a creature, a fellow man. They were all quite all right with me, in the ordinary sense; I've no grumbles. On the rare occasions when I see him, Lord Thomson of Fleet calls me Maurice. But my other lords were figures. Lord Beaverbrook was a man in my life. His eyes reached right out and searched you, as a man. I can stand that. Of course, the fact is he was a journalist himself, he was a writer, a man of words. He actually knew what he was talking about when he talked about journalism. When you were talking about words with Lord Beaverbrook you really were talking about words, words meant something to both of you, you were in that lovely sense chewing the fat over your joint obsession with a fellow addict. I suppose this had something to do with it. But the main thing is he was a man, a non-Establishment man who remembered small beginnings and knew that writers begin young and poor and reckless and extraordinary and loving and remorseful. And that they suffer.

He had some funny little ways. Who does not? He used an old-fashioned Dictaphone machine which stood by his armchair. He was forever snatching it up and dictating memos to his followers. 'Mr Gunn, there were three mistakes in the leader today ...' 'Mr Wiggin, why don't you get off your backside and find out the truth about ...' His secretary, or I suppose it was probably secretaries, used to type out these exhortations on sheets of the very cheapest newsprint copy-paper, the sort we used to scribble and type our stories on. Each memo would be a line or two or six, and when a page was typed the secretary would put a ruler down and tear off each little slip, a slightly ragged and infinitely cheap-looking slip of the very cheapest, pinkish-yellowish bumf. And these would be duly distributed to the recipients. I loved this. It was so cheap and casual and informal, such a nice change from elaborate fancy bumf such as circulates these days and elsewhere.

One day in the office some discussion came up about Lord Beaverbrook's intentions on some matter or other. Needless to say I can't remember what it was all about.

'Well', said Bert Gunn, 'it's soon settled. Show me the memo.'

'I chucked it away,' I said.

There were looks all round, a stiffening.

'Chucked it away?' said Bert.

'I always chuck 'em away. I get the message then I chuck 'em away. Why not?'

Bert struggled for words.

'Never, never, never. Never under any circumstances whatsoever do you chuck away a memo from Lord Beaverbrook. You keep them. Always.'

'Well, they ain't the tablets of Moses.'

'To you, they are.'

But I went on chucking them away. Never does to hoard paper. If you've got to the point where you can't remember the general drift of a matter, and have to get legal and put it down on paper and save it in a file against a future quarrel, you're adrift. My dear wife hoards the basic minimum of legal paper. I have to admit this. Thanks to her, we can usually find the car registration book and insurance policy and so on. Left to myself I honestly wouldn't bother. I freely admit this is hedging—*she* does it, and saves my bacon. But she agrees with me that over and above absolute basic necessity, it's very mistaken to hoard paper. Even the books get cleared out now and again. About two years is enough to tell you, of a book, if you are going to read it again and again. The rest go, armfuls and carfuls, to lucky lucky them. The house still stays full of books. We collect books and records, in a vague unplanned way, but precious little else.

Though I suppose I've collected quite a few jobs, in my time. The period during which I wrote My Court Casebook was ineffably happy, in a way; work happy, at any rate; but of course nothing quite lasts as it begins, and the day came when discontent began to grow. I still had the itch to change. I did quite a few pieces of reporting aside from the courts—covered the Silver Wedding (or was it the Jubilee?) of King George the Sixth and Queen Elizabeth in St Paul's; covered the wedding of Princess Elizabeth and the Duke of Edinburgh from a rooftop in Whitehall; met the first shipload of West Indian immigrants at Tilbury one drizzling dawn and accompanied them to their first English homes, in deep shelters on Clapham Common. And a lot of funny-peculiar stories. I was discovered to be a fair hand at breathing some imaginative personal life into such a wild riot of hard news as a junk sale. Covered Tommy Handley's funeral. Covered chess tournaments and horse shows, all sorts of dross like that, the sort of 'descriptive story' that depends entirely on the writer. It began to feel a bit foot-loose and racketty in the wrong way, I suppose, though I was reasonably content. But I was beginning to cook up stories that weren't really there. Then suddenly I received an invitation to join Kemsley News-papers as an executive, and for various reasons which I cannot now recall, accepted. This was the last but one of the pendulum swings between executive work and writing, which have marked my working life.

They wanted a bright features editor for the *Daily Graphic*. They really did. This was incomparably the worst newspaper I have ever been associated with in any capacity whatsoever. It was a stinker. Why did I move? Change has always smelled sweet. The grass is greener on the other side of the hedge. I had about reached the limit of what I could do as a writer on the *Evening Standard*; or thought I had. I had done the courts almost daily for two and a quarter years, which was quite enough. The other sorts of writing on which I was employed had that funny feeling of pointlessness. Of course it wasn't any more pointless than any other activity; but I didn't feel it was getting anywhere. I suppose the fact is I was beginning to grow middle-aged and settly. My private life was stabilising as never before, and I suppose I almost subconsciously wanted my work to match my life. Anyway, I signed on. In the long term it was a good decision; in the short term it seemed almost disastrous.

I'd forgotten what a slog it was to be features editor on a morning paper; the strange hours, the long hours, the unnatural hours. In addition I found myself working with a very rum set of characters, to a very rum brief. Lord Kemsley ran the *Daily Graphic* on a shoestring and it was hedged around by all sorts of absurd prohibitions. It could not possibly succeed. I should have known it. I *did* know it, I guess, in my secret heart, but change was always exciting and you never could tell, a gamble might always come off. With the last remnants of my youthful energy I chucked myself head-first into trying to making the *Graphic* bright and sharp. Absolutely hopeless from the start. I enjoyed fiddling around with the layout, as usual, but even that soon palled. The top editorial men on the *Graphic* at that time were beyond question the least congenial I have worked with. The paper reflected them very accurately.

However, before we got the message 'fly, all is discovered', I had been promoted assistant editor and also, just to make sure I didn't find time hang too heavy, made production editor of the *Sunday Graphic* as well. For a dreadful year or so I had a responsibility for a paper every day of the week. I began to grow an ulcer, not wholly surprising in the circumstances, and the doctor with whom I went fly fishing on the Berkshire Kennet said I'd better change my way of life, or else. I was nothing loth. I told them that I'd have to give up executive work and revert to being a writer. I must say they took this very handsomely. I began to write a column weekly for the *Daily Graphic*, a column weekly for the *Sunday Graphic*, and of course my angling column for *The Sunday Times*, which was the joy and consolation of my little life. Pat Murphy, who had left the *Evening Standard* to become Sports Editor of *The Sunday Times*, remembering John Lea, set me on writing this. It began as a tiny little piece tucked away on the back page, but as the paper began to expand again after its wartime austerity, the little corner grew a bit, with the paper. It became a nice visible little half-column inside the paper, and later it even became a nice little essay on any subject I cared to write about, not simply fishing.

The Editor of *The Sunday Times* was then W. W. Hadley, known to us all as Pop. He was the first of four Editors of *The Sunday Times* for whom I have worked. (I think I saw nine editors of the *Sunday Graphic* come and go.) Pop was well over eighty when he retired. He went to live in a little bungalow at Bramshott Chase, near Hindhead, and I visited him there quite a few times, during the period when I was fishing for trout at Waggoners Wells nearby (Richard Dimbleby's home) with a philosophical old farmer named Tom Jones. In fact I got to know him rather better after he had retired than while he was Editor, but it still wasn't what you would call an intimate association. The only person I have got to know really rather well, of all my bosses and leaders, is Leonard Russell, the Associate Editor, who knows me far too well. With all the rest I have maintained a pleasant cordiality, shattered occasionally by moments of mutual dubiety when I have written something staggeringly unacceptable. But the great rows have been few and far between. They may have all from time to time had their doubts about my entire suitability for office; I shouldn't wonder; but they have been astonishingly tolerant, I must say, of a toiler who has never even bothered to wonder what the line is at any given moment, much less toe it.

Yet, on second thoughts, I did at first try to follow some sort of special line. Not a line of opinion editorially laid down, of course, but a stylistic line. When H. V. Hodson finally confirmed my appointment as critic, after I had done a couple of trial pieces, he saw fit to say, 'Now remember, Maurice—you're writing for *The Sunday Times* now. Write *carefully*.' This rather brought me up short. For several months I did write carefully, I mean laboriously; at the back of my mind some sort of dim picture of what '*Sunday Times* style' might be. Of course it was not at all good for *my* style. It became pompous and strangulated. But nature will out, and eventually I relaxed. I have never quite relaxed, in the sense that I worry continually about the rightness and justice of my opinions; but so far as their expression goes, I think I managed quite soon to shake off that vague cloud of worrying about conformity to '*Sunday Times* style', whatever that may have been.

H. V. Hodson was a tall handsome man (well, he still is) who had been a Fellow of All Souls. At one time we had three men on the paper who had all been Brackenbury Scholars of Balliol: Hodson, Cyril Connolly, and William Rees-Mogg. Undoubtedly it would be some sort of record, for what it's worth. Although we were as unlike as well could be, or perhaps because of that, we maintained this good un-intimate cordial tone. Harry was indulgent to me, as all my editors have been. I never met him outside the office. He wore formal clothes including a black Homburg or bowler and was really very much an academical; he was a member of the Athenaeum. He could be quite jolly, though. He was the last Editor I worked for who was older than me. He has gone back to the academic world now, as Provost of Ditchley. I went down there once to address a gathering of international television producers, or do I mean an international gathering of television producers? Well, they all spoke English, anyway. It was an Intertel convention assembled by John Macmillan, the chief programme executive of Rediffusion. A portentous collection of amiable Canadian and American and Australian producers assembled round a huge table and I stood up and droned on for what seemed hours. I very much detest this sort of thing but for once greed got me down. They offered some enormous fee in dollars; I think it worked out at about £75. The offer was conveyed to me by an old fishing friend called Brian Begg, who was then public relations man at Rediffusion. 'Easy money, Maurice,' said Brian with a sinister chuckle. He was my top favourite PRO, probably because he never confused public relations with private relations, never tried to bamboozle me, and was himself strongly in favour of the pursuits I too found so much more interesting than work, such as boats, water, fish, motors, and one or two other things. He became a friend. I fell for this easy money line, and said yes, all right; then it struck me that to earn such a fee I really must try to turn out something interesting and relevant. In the event, of course, I worked like a pig for a week on that address, about six thousand golden words, and lost more sleep and weight than the money was worth. It was the last time I ever accepted an invitation to address anybody, anywhere. Or even to listen to anybody else's address. Then we had a fish lunch served by the Ditchley butler, and Harry Hodson in a typically graceful speech mentioned his 'old friend Maurice Wiggin, the countryman', which struck me as an incomplete description, as, I'm sure, is mine of him, and that was our last quasi-official contact.

Harry's successor as Editor of *The Sunday Times* was C. D. Hamilton, who was actually several years younger than me but more or less of the same generation and incontrovertibly an 'elder brother' in my private mythology. Though new to the actual Editorship, Denis had long been Editorial Director of the entire Group and the most powerful figure among us. I am sure he regarded me as a whimsical fellow. Perhaps I am, though that isn't how I look at it, of course. Denis was patient and kind to one who must have tried him sorely. We had only one big bust-up, when I persisted in taking what he regarded as an unduly blimpish, square and reactionary view of a certain development in contemporary culture. I think we were both wrong; or both right; anyway, I stuck it out, and we agreed to differ. Strangely enough, he is actually squarer than I am, in a way. He takes very seriously activities which I regard as a complete waste of time, such as administration and organisation, he is a great family man and a devoted, ceaseless worker, and the honourable values he stands for are to my mind absolutely unquestionable though that does not stop the with-it intelligentsia, bad cess to them, questioning them morbidly.

Denis and I were both in Normandy at the same time, but whereas I became a sergeant at 30 he became a Brigadier at 26. It is to his credit that he has never held this against me. As I say, he is an elder brother to me, always was, despite being five or six years younger. I think I have been a disappointment to him but he has not been a disappointment to me. I look up to him as an embodiment of precisely those qualities of character and willpower which I lack. His view of the nature of success does not entirely square with mine. When I see him (he is now Editor-in-Chief of *The Times* and *The Sunday Times*) bustling in and out with briefcases bulging with bumf, I think 'There but for the grace of God'. Still and all, in a firm as big as ours we surely do need somebody at the top who takes the business more seriously than I do. I can always approach him in a brotherly way and he has been very tolerant of my foibles and generous to a degree, though sometimes you can see he is fighting back a soldierly remark about 'idle on parade'. On the rare occasions when he actually finds me in the office he tends to remark on the rarity of the occasion, but as I tell him, I'm paid to turn in a piece of writing, not a body, and it is my intention to appear in person ever more rarely as the years roll by.

The present Editor of *The Sunday Times*, my fourth, is Harold Evans, whom we all call Harry. He is 39, which brings me right bang up against it. Now I really am getting on for a generation older than my boss. It's a funny feeling. Harold used to work for my old group, but he tells me that they are less parsimonious than they used to be in my day. He was editor of a provincial morning paper, as I was; and though I was even younger when appointed editor, he lasted better.

I like to see him whizzing through the office like a flame; literally at the double, in his shirt sleeves. He has galvanised the old firm. He is the complete working newspaperman, and when I see him bringing his galvanic perfectionism to bear on every detail of the paper, I am irresistibly reminded of those far-off days when I, too, really loved the craft of newspaper production better than almost anything else. Harold Evans is infinitely tougher than I ever was, and he has that genuine feeling about news and public affairs and all that tosh, whereas I was only really and truly concerned with the drama of the layout and headlines: nevertheless, making these allowances and *mutatis mutandis*, I do see a likeness, it does me good to see the old enthusiasm permeating every cranny of the paper, the restless perfectionism, the personal touch, the insatiable inquisitiveness and above all the zest and the contagion of his zeal. I think he has come at the right moment. The old world is dying and the old *Sunday Times*—the one I joined—is changing to meet the demands of the new. Needless to say much of it is meaningless to me—I am so incurious, compared with my boss, that I can't even read all we print, I'm simply past wanting to know—but I do know that this is the way to do it, this is the face to present to the future. Dear old mandarins telling their beads in their ivory towers may disagree, but there it is. Most important of all, I fancy, is the liberalism which Harold brings to the paper as it forges on like a bloody great juggernaut into the unimaginable future. I think we are approaching a crunch where the innate crusted conservatism of half the population will meet the innate liberalism of the other half head-on, and it's nice to be on the decent side. Though personally I'm on both.

However, I've run ahead of my story, breaking one of my rules. Why not? If you can't break your own ...

Nothing that happened in London or in journalism had anything like the effect on our lives of something we did privately, soon after I joined Kemsley Newspapers. We moved to a cottage in the country. Yes, the classic gambit. So far as we were concerned it was *the* climactic decision, and we knew it: no lure, no threat, no magnet, no power on earth would ever draw us back. We had been living for about three years in a relatively rather posh flat in Hampstead—Hampstead proper, I mean, the uplands near the Heath, not the dejected swamp around the Finchley Road and Swiss Cottage, not West Hampstead or Camden Town. It was quite nice, the air was good, the rooms of the converted Victorian house were large and airy and if you like town life you might like it as well as anything. But to us it was just another dump in the city and every day for years we read the small ads in *The Times* and *The Sunday Times* and what we were looking for was a cottage in the country. I seem to remember J. B. Priestley sneering at the cottage-in-the-country myth, or image: doubtless it *is* better for a writer to live among his fellow men, in pullulating propinquity. But either you like rustic living best or you like town living best, and we liked rusticity. So we went on looking.

One day we spotted a small ad in *The Times*: 'Elizabethan cottage. To let unfurnished.' Of course we had no money: it *had* to be 'to let unfurnished'. I got £1,000 a year when I was demobbed, and it had risen by degrees to £1,750, but we never saved. It cost £20 to have a little party at Hampstead. And we had quite a lot. I was back on motors, too, my God I was. We had had to build up our stock of household goods, including furniture, after the war, at post-war prices. We were pretty near broke in the sense of not having any capital. But still full of beans. We went down to East Clandon and saw this dear old timbered heap, and fell for it in a genuine way, fell in love with it. It wasn't particularly pretty, as half-timbered rustic cottages go, but there was a genuineness in its undoctored roughness and simplicity. We went into Guildford to have an interview with the estate agent, who chilled us with the remark that there were literally hundreds of people after it. (Actually there were 256 applications.) He told us a bit about the owner, Harry Stuart Goodhart-Rendel, of Hatchlands, the bachelor squire of East Clandon, and asked if we were willing to be interviewed by the old man. It sounded a bit feudal, but just *how* feudal, we were yet to learn. We went back to Hampstead to wait as patiently as we could.

One morning when we could wait no longer I telephoned the estate agent. 'Oh,' he said, 'I was just going to write to you. The cottage is yours.'

I went and told my wife and she burst into tears of relief.

In one sense this was a real turning point. 'Of course I shall have to come back to London at least once a month,' my wife said. She has been back exactly once. And that was eighteen years ago.

You can certainly live without London. About two thousand million people do.

It depends what sort of life you want to live.

Life in East Clandon was quite peculiar, in a way, but to us it was delightful. There were probably other villages run on similar lines, but there couldn't have been all that many, and I shouldn't think there are any left now, especially within thirty miles of London. The squire, Harry Stuart Goodhart-Rendel, really still was the squire. He held the estate in trust and he administered it on lines which could have changed little from Victorian days. Some of the cottages were let at sums like 1s. 6d. and half-a-crown a week, some paid no rent at all. He didn't want things changed. Ours was the first cottage in the village which he had, reluctantly, decided to 'modernise' (in a very mild degree) and let unfurnished to some outsider. He was very nervous of getting some cocktail-swilling types in who would use it as a weekend brothel or bar. He wanted someone who would actually live in the village as a villager. That is why we got it. Anyone less like a gin-sodden madam with henna'd hair and a penchant for parties than my wife you could hardly imagine. The old man may have made his mistakes (he was very innocent in some ways and was remorselessly conned by practically everybody in sight) but he could hardly fail to see that we were intent on settling-in and putting down roots and growing lichen. So there we were, practically laughing-and-crying with joy and surprise and relief. The rent was only £150 a year, plus rates—half our London rent—and though it went up later to £250, it remained pretty dirt cheap, all things considered. We began to dig in.

Professionally there was just one more swing of the old pendulum before stability set in. After I had lived there through a very wet winter, writing my three weekly pieces, Denis Hamilton offered me the assistant editorship of a strange luxurious travel and holiday magazine called *Go*, which Lord Kemsley had just bought, and which Leonard Russell was editing. I didn't see how I could very well turn down a kindly-meant offer, so for the best part of a year I became a commuter. This was nasty. I had no feeling for a glossy travel-and-holiday magazine, of course, and although Leonard Russell became and remained my best friend in the organisation, I don't think I was really a great deal of use to him, though perhaps I wasn't entirely useless, either. But it was a bit of a bore, and the routine travelling a very great waste of life, and when one day in the summer of 1951 Maurice Gorham, the radio critic of *The Sunday Times*, suddenly left to become a big shot on Radio Eireann, and they offered me his job plus the new job of television critic, I felt that my ship had come in, and jumped aboard.

Just how it happened is another example of the charming fortuitousness of life. I was strolling down one of the darker and narrower corridors of the old Kemsley House, chatting with the late Ian Fleming about fishing, in which he was getting interested, when I saw the Editor and Managing Editor of *The Sunday Times*, respectively Harry Hodson and Valentine Heywood, locked in close conversation, and looking worried. This would not have meant too much to me; they were both serious and responsible executives who had that gift of looking serious and responsible, which is the same as worried. But when they saw me, their eyes lit up. 'Ah, Maurice,' Harry said. 'Just the man! How would you like to be radio and television critic of *The Sunday Times*?'

I said I would like it very much.

I had always thought how nice it must be to be a critic on *The Sunday Times*. This went right back to my earliest days in journalism, when I used to read James Agate, Ernest Newman, Sir Desmond MacCarthy and Dilys Powell every Sunday morning. I even read them aloud. The other journalists whom I read were J. L. Garvin in *The Observer* and John Gordon in the *Sunday Express* and Robert Lynd in the *News Chronicle* and Spike Hughes in the *Daily Herald* and Henry Williamson whenever I came across him. I have thought for a long time that a journalist should not read too much journalism. He should read the best there is, he should read good books. He should be soaked in the best writing there is to be found. Or alternatively he should read nothing at all. But that is an impossibility for me. Without something to read I am lost.

No doubt they would have offered me the job anyway, but I like to think that meeting them by chance in the corridor gave the inevitable event a nice little push. It's more elegant; it fortifies my theory that propinquity is the great matchmaker and everything important is either preordained or accidental. It is a theory which cannot be defended very successfully as a logical proposition, perhaps, but it gives life a certain touch of style and makes it more interesting.

Of course I was not wholly without experience. I had done a great deal of reviewing and critical writing of one sort and another, though by nature I am far more a reporter, an observer, a narrator, than an analytical critic. I had reviewed thousands of books, and had had some years as a dramatic critic, first in Birmingham and later on the *Evening Standard* when I stood in or deputised for Sir Beverley Baxter, who was then the regular man. This was before Ken Tynan and Milton Shulman had been heard of. I had no great feeling for the theatre, though. As you must have noticed, I was sold solid on make-believe, my whole life in one sense has been make-believe: all our dreams, aspirations and ideals are make-believe. Without make-believe most lives are unlivable. But I would not like to have to defend the proposition that it is more innocent and harmless than scepticism or cynicism or realism. In the theatre I was too often conscious that this was just a bit of communal self-deception and that a more interesting world lay outside the theatre; more dramatic, not less, more exciting, because open-ended, for real, unscripted and infinite. Of course I had moments of laughter and even moments of absorption, caught up in the drama on the stage. But on the whole I could live more excitingly outside the theatre than in it, and did.

I loved the cinema, and rarely left, blinking in the afternoon sun or skipping lightly into the spangled velvet night, without feeling a different person, a gone coon, translated into some other fellow, some taller hero. The cinema was marvellous for the daydream. The theatre rarely had the same effect. Why was this? I fell for novels and short stories quite readily, and powerful poems were meat and drink to the daydream, and even newspapers ministered to it strongly for quite a few years, all through boyhood and right into manhood, even when I knew how they were produced. I was absolutely a sold soul, in thrall to the magic-tragic flux of the actual world and its penumbrous hanging dreams, the mists of the motley. But the formal theatre in its formality left me relatively cold: the actors too near and too plainly acting, perhaps, the proscenium arch too literal, the intervals thoroughly destructive? I cannot say. It was so.

But television was another thing again. Up till then I had seen nothing on television but the boxing, at a friend's home in Hampstead. Of course it was not so good as real boxing, sitting at the ringside among coarse betting men, spattered sometimes with real blood, hearing the gasps and grunts and seeing the bruises grow and reading the fight in the fighters' eyes. Television boxing was a wan shadow of that. But it was all right, even though the BBC showed nothing but amateur boxing, in the forties. On the first night of commercial television in 1956 the main event was a professional fight, at middleweight, which is perhaps the perfect weight, fought with great energy and courage and ferocity. I always thought it was the shrewdest stroke they played. It was a way of saying 'Come this side, pal, we've got the blood and guts of real life, we don't palm off imitations. We know your coarse brutal tastes and we minister to them.'

But if I hadn't seen any television, to speak of, neither had anyone else, to speak of. That was what it was all about. Television was just starting, really, just beginning to get under way. So we decided to take some notice of it, and the job fell to me. It was still so uncertain a thing, the plaything of a minority, with the BBC putting out only about two hours television per night and Thursday a repeat of Sunday, that we didn't go raving mad about it, and to make weight I was radio critic as well. In fact I was Radio and Television Critic: it was some years before I became Television and Radio Critic, and I did not drop radio altogether until the imminent coming of the second channel, the commercial one.

Even so, the editor assumed that I should carry this important chore as a paid extra, something I'd do at home in the evening, in my spare time. It was that important. And he figured I would jump at the extra money. Not so. I did not give a hoot about the money. It was the life that interested me. I made it clear that in my view it was almost a full-time job (of course, I continued to write my weekly 'angling' piece, now enlarged into a country essay, and my weekly column for the *Sunday Graphic*). But to Leonard's and everybody's surprise, I refused to carry on as assistant editor of *Go*. I left the executive desk for the last time. The week in which Randolph Turpin beat Sugar Ray Robinson for the middle weight championship of the world (live on radio, filmed to be shown *next* night on television) I finally said goodbye to the executive dream. In June 1951 I finally began to earn my bread wholly and solely as a writer, living away, in a shack in the country, a non-commuter, a non-runner in the race for big money and big ulcers.

Chapter Fourteen

I have written getting on for a million words about television, for *The Sunday Times*. You will not expect any more here. At least, you need not. Television I take seriously, it is a great big ever-growing mirror and ray-lamp of life. I watch it for about forty hours a week and I spend about two days writing my piece about it and I rarely stop worrying about it, one way and another. And that is enough. It has no place here except as a big fact which makes other facts possible and understandable which might otherwise be impossible and incomprehensible. So far as this book goes, television is a job like going to the shop or knocking doors selling something or being away for months on the boat. I am not going to write one word about television as television though so many of my waking hours are spent thinking of the words and what they shall convey. But that's another part of the forest. Times out of mind I have been asked to write a 'big, important' book about television and times out of mind I have refused without a backward glance and got on with living. The bit you see in *The Sunday Times*, assuming of course that you do see it, that 1,200 or 1,300 word slab is just the tip of the iceberg, what shows above water, and down below it out of sight is an infinity of complex cross-thoughts and wondering and aching, yes, aching, and anger and remorse and wild hopes and regrets and longings. I surely do work at being a television critic. I never write a paragraph or even a sentence without searching the old soul and I am never satisfied with how it comes out. And that is all I am going to say about the activity that earns me a substantial portion of what I have to spend on getting on with living, which is the interesting subject. I will just put it straight about my routine, which is a legitimate interest, and then thereafter there will be nothing about television if I can help it, not because I am sick of it but because I can only stand just so much.

Naturally being a television critic is strange and unusual and not everybody would really like it though everybody is sure he could do it standing on his head, and in fact everybody could and several do, though I may say in passing that being a television critic for one week or even two is not the same experience as being a television critic year in year out. I am in a position to say this having just completed seventeen years at it. 'Just do it for a year,' said Harry Hodson when he signed me on. 'A year will be as much as you can stand. More would drive you mad.' Possibly it did, how can I say?

Your social life is completely dominated and changed by this job. You have no evening freedom. You have to settle your mind to this right at the start. From teatime to bedtime you are on your own, or at least you and your domestic circle are locked together in silence, slaves of the box. Most people who are capable of writing about it simply cannot stand this. It happened to suit us right down to the ground. We had had all the parties anybody could want. What do they amount to? This is a booze-soaked civilisation. Of course I always loved booze, but you can't go on for ever, you have to beat the bottle or give in. Without my wife I should almost certainly have given in. I love drink —it's so wonderful to feel irresponsibility creeping over you, to feel insouciance coming up like a dream that floats you away from your problems like a grounded boat rising on the tide. But what's the use of that? Sooner or later, at some point, you have to decide to be yourself or be merely a hapless figment of the cosmic imagination. I beat the bottle and that's one thing I don't regret. I was never an alcoholic or anything approaching one (they all say that) but when I had a drink I liked another, and there was one phase of four or five years during which, very gradually, the 'couple of drinks' became three or four or five or six and by lunch time I was having to hold myself on a tight rein, and after lunch, about four in the afternoon, I didn't feel too good. I never drank after lunch. Well, only twice. Just twice in all those years I have seen television when more or less under the influence, but I never wrote about what I so saw. Apart from those two occasions I have always seen it sober and written about it sober. That may explain a lot of things. Since I cut out the morning aperitif I have been better and better-off, healthier, and of course I have been me, the real one, however horrible, not the false figure created by alcohol. I am now virtually a teetotaller though on Friday mornings when I go into the office I may possibly have a pint of stout with the managing editor, and again I may not. But a pint of stout a week is the limit. It's hardly worth having, though after an hour in London I need it. The simple fact is that drink poisons me. It doesn't poison everybody but it poisons me. Drink is the great hoax on our civilisation. When you stay sober at a party and listen you see it all. The voices grow shrill and even sillier than they start off. It's a very terrible thing to stay sober at a party. The only answer is to stay away.

Staying away from parties was the easiest bit of self-denial I ever had to practise. Come teatime we would settle down snug behind drawn curtains, rain maybe splatting on the old crooked casements, the fire in the inglenook, the yellow lamp alight, the fat cat on the hearth, and who wanted parties? There were always books and music and old friends even before television came to provide not merely an excuse but an actual reason for shutting ourselves away. This tranquil private patch between tea and bed was good. The day had been full. Sometimes the night was full, too—I loved to walk in the woods after midnight. But between tea and midnight-ish we had it to ourselves, very snug and cosy. One or two of a small company of very old, trained friends might be with us, but they were disciplined from the start, to silence. When I'm taking it in I'm taking it in.

Of course this routine would drive most people mad. Seven nights a week, forty-eight weeks of the year, devoted to the box. No dinner parties, no evenings out. Yes, and no goddam meetings, speeches, committees, or any other of the multiple tortures people dream up to inflict on themselves and one another, either. I revelled in it. The perfect, cast-iron excuse for shutting the door. Needless to say, it was only workable because the days were so full, so fascinating. I balanced the glory of the day against the peculiarity of the evening. The one thing kept the other thing possible, and going, and perhaps balanced.

Instantly we reverted to the old northern custom of high tea. It suits my stomach and my social sense very well. Of course I was brought up on it. I am a dab hand at cooking a high tea. I love it, too. In the holidays we have a few sumptuous dinners, when we feel like it, but somehow it doesn't suit any more. Lunch is the big meal—midday dinner. And a nap after it, if we're home. I don't want to be in anybody else's house in the evening. If I spend only four or five hours a day in my own home, they have to be the evening hours.

This centrality of the fireside was very congenial. Life began to revolve around it. The new pattern was quickly established. I reserved my sober attention and anguished responsibility for that particular part of life, television/*Sunday Times*, and lavished, squandered the rest of my restless energies in living the real life, or what I took to be the real life—the life that is incontrovertible and impossible to counterfeit, the life of outdoors, the life of the woods and fields and stream and sea. I lived my life and I wrote about it. It was a great life in many ways. I learned a bit about the making of a garden but never became much of a gardener. I was always for getting away, to the waterside and the woods, the hills and the overmastering sea.

When the tide turns the seaweed turns too, and streams out over rocks and reefs and the ribs of ruined ships, pointing long undulant fingers towards the river mouth, where fresh water meets the tide.

Sea trout roaming the scrabble of rock and weed taste the thin water in which they were bred, and are excited by memories of home. Smolts of another generation are daring the turbulence of the bar: they are tasting salt water for the first time and they too feel the excitement of adventure. The two generations, seagoing and homeward bound, caught in their compulsions, meet and pass in the mingled water beyond the bar.

And farther out, where the dark stain of the spate river begins to spread and mix and disappear in the ocean, spiny silver bass with big mouths and hearts lie in wait for the adventuring smolts.

Then a man roaming the sea's margin in a sound little boat, armed with a light rod and a small selection of streamer flies in several sizes, may come to the cream of a summer's sport. Casting among the streaming weed we caught sea trout, fat and gleaming from several months of rich feeding in the sea. By the end of May the bigger sea trout, veteran spawners wise from several journeys, have made up their minds and crossed the bar. If it is going to be a dry summer, they will know. Their mysterious foreknowledge tells them to run for it while there is yet water to carry them up the weirs and passes and the thin streaming stickles and the angular falls. But the young school fish, pupils of Time who are learning the ways of their world in the only academy that is open to them, the only school worth attending, they will still be gathering and playing together; preparing, until well on in June, for the great communal dash up-river to the ancestral spawning grounds. With the boldness of numbers then they all run together, making a festival of the rite; running by night, if need be, up water scarcely deep enough to cover their dorsal fins. Many the night I spent tip-toeing along knee-high in Western streams, casting a dark fly for the dark shadows. Many a day, quiet on a quiet sea, casting a feathery tandem or squirrel-tail tube fly amongst a school of maidens and bachelors feeding and frolicking among the streaming weed.

And if one missed, as miss one might, the main gatherings, there were always the stragglers, the rebels, the individualists and the dopes who travel alone. The animal kingdom too has its anarchs and individualists. And there were always the bass, the hunters of the hunters, edging ever closer inshore as summer waxed and the water warmed up and the migratory fish turned towards their ancestral home. The bass that grow bolder as night falls.

Once we were afloat from dawn to dark, a whole day on the brilliant lovely water, that changed as the hours changed, as the sea floor changed, as the wind changed and the clouds changed; from sheer ultramarine through violet and slate grey and a sort of tender diffused gold; through inky murky cliffside cavern-colour to cactus green and pine green and the slender shimmering grey-green colour of sage; through from the sheen of a hamster's coat at loving time to deep indigo and tender dove's-breast and woodsmoke-blue; and once at least, as a squall crooned off the cliffs, to the bronze-green changeling colour of a walnut tree's leaves in nut time.

As the colours of the sea changed and the light wind shifted and rose and died and rose again, as the clouds chased and chaffered over the great bowl of the sky and the sea birds screamed and idled, planed and loitered and fell like stones around the façade of cliff, so our mood changed constantly and we felt differently from hour to hour about fish and fishing, and were indeed different persons with incompatible ambitions and diverse dreams; yet all the time and through the ineffable hours, timeless yet racing by, there persisted unbroken the deep dreaming trance of joy, the unspeakable joy of belonging to this infinite heaven of earth and water and sun and appetite. Sensual somnambulists lost in a dream of eternity, lovers and hunters, destroyers and participators, we roamed the ocean's edge in all the lights that the day brought down, and like chameleons felt the change as the light changed, and the sea's floor, fathoms beneath our keel.

Destiny drove us, it drives all, out from the river mouth and over the tumbling deadly bar, the keel-catcher, breaker of ships and reputations. But we drew nothing, we were an eggshell, a walnut's moiety spinning on eddies and caught in the weaving currents of the tide. We passed the bar laughing at the morning and singing a sea song such as fishermen chant.

We cruised about the foot of a cliff and we edged along parallel with a shingly shore and a shore that was sandy but stippled with crops of black rock and hairy with weed. We went out to sea and heaved on the ocean for a noontide spell, so far out that to watchers on the cliff top we were a speck sitting on the waves like a fishing bird, and to watchers at water level, in the estuary, invisible. In the late afternoon we crept along the very edge of that long sandy bar that thrusts out to sea abominably, from a mariner's or a navigator's point of view, though to returning fish it is not abominable but as exciting as a banking on a track which guides them home. Altogether we thoroughly adventured and prospected all around the sea-course of that little river, for we knew very well the way it wrinkled and squirmed far out into the ocean, still indubitably a river, and loth to lose its identity in the mastering sea.

A constant slow journeying in and out from the sea's edge to a position which you can only (from a dinghy's point of view) call oceanic—that is a very wonderful and satisfying way of spending a day, and there is perhaps no part of it which you would rate higher than another, in terms of emotional and imaginative and sensory satisfaction. There is something in the feel of distance, when you are so far out (and you so small) that even the large cliff is receding to the dimension of a wall, which gives you a not-unpleasant notion of departure and immensity and the extreme loneliness of the sea. Then there is the indescribable minute pleasure of a small-scale scrutiny, as it were in fine focus, of the very margin and bafflement and extremity of the sea, where it fails to conquer the land, the hated land, the sea's enemy.

And there is always the changing aspect of the land, as seen from the changing sea. You see without feeling, in a calm detachment, the hours making their mark on all earthbound creatures and institutions and organization. You observe breakfast time, office time, shop time and siesta time, and from another life, a life lived long ago when you too were landbound, you remember what it felt like and how the convention of the hour shaped your feeling and your response. But out on the sea, though ever-changing, you are indifferent to the organisational human changes of the shorebound. The deep and cumulative depression of afternoon is almost powerless to brush your spirit with its grey rat's pelt; you are liberated from ennui. You have the sea's rhythm in your blood instead of the clock's, and you count yourself lucky in the change. Then at sundown you feel the presences which daylight keeps at bay beginning to steal in on you across the sea, and as the light weakens they creep nearer, and you shiver and prepare to meet the ghostly presences of night, the essences no doubt of innumerable unremembered yet unforgettable acts and omissions. On the great plain of ocean there is nothing to bar or hinder them; they enter the soul and possess you in the inner recesses of your thought and feeling. And you head for home.

It was not all fishing, that heavenly day of deepest dream and action, death and love. There were moments when we edged right close in to the cliff face and studied the minute world of the tide-line; moments when, held carefully an oar's length off black basalt rocks, we peered down, lost, into the crystal pools and basins and the miniature cataracts and caverns, absorbed in the endless fluctuating life of the marginal territory, the area uneasily spanned by two tides, neither land nor sea.

The life of the tide's edge is most mysterious, abundant, and insatiable. You are far indeed from the jolly and sparkling world of tackle shops, the world of toys and gadgets. You are alone then in the fervent and unlegislated world of primitives and predators; caught up out of your habitual life of secondhand, immersed in a flux of creation, so beautifully poised and self-supporting, the interlocking necessary layer upon layer of life ascending from the minutest helpless organisms up to the complicated, strong, almost-thinking migratory fish, which have found room in their organisation for joy and for play.

Small wonder if sometimes the rod rests on the gunwale, unheeded, while you rise and fall on the unresting tide in a trance of wonder.

Ah, but the homecoming! Those were the moments—setting out and coming home. This is the central marvel and jewel and magic of the life: no matter how glorious the day, afloat or in the woods or wherever you might spend it, there was no anti-climax in coming home. In through the kitchen door, fish piled in the sink, off with the salty old outer clothes and down with a cup of tea, first, then everything in its place or hugger-mugger after. Aye, it was a kitchen to come home to. Old squire had made a masterpiece there, he must have known I was coming. It used to be a mere lean-to shed at the back. The steep wavy old roof of the cottage swirled down and down, and where it used to be supported on the outer back edge by pillars, it was now walled in: so the old back wall of the cottage was now an inner wall, the inner wall of the kitchen. There it was, all curvy lovely beams that used to be the ribs of ships. You could see it so clearly; the shipwrights' marks still on them, and in between botched up with rubble and daub and cowhair wattle and odd bricks. A wonderful wall to sit up by, at the table, with the old back-door frame (now leading to the living room) all bashed and battered by centuries of weather and peasantry. Snug now, with a stove and a sink and a cooker fed by calor gas. I loved that room: saw it on first waking and last waking, ate there, read there, tied flies under the lamp, received the confidences of friends, cleaned and gutted fish, learned to cook. And all around it the new latticed windows and beyond it the trees and birds and the creatures without homes.

This last squire of East Clandon, Harry Stuart Goodhart-Rendel, was the only man I ever heard of who was both Slade Professor of

Fine Art *and* the author of an infantry training manual for the Brigade of Guards. He was a Grenadier. He was also a convert to Roman Catholicism. John Betjeman came down to visit him; they were friends. He wandered into the cowman's cottage one Sunday morning asking for a loan of a socket to power his electric razor: couldn't find one at the great house, Hatchlands. Squire used to give a children's party at Hatchlands for the children and the tenantry: faithfully stuck around until it was over, then, with his asthma, disappeared to the south of France. We attended all these parties, with a hired conjurer and gifts from the tree handed round by the butler. Where else was that going on? When we went to lunch at the big house there was champagne, for just the three of us in the great dining room, as often as not, and lovely food, and squire talked ceaselessly about art and architecture, music and poetry. He was an aesthete and a Guardee both. The Guards sent a band down one day every summer, to march and counter-march and play on the lawns of the big house, and the tenantry and their children attended and were fed appropriate food and drink. He was full of loving-kindness towards his tenants. They did not always love him back. He was an aesthete, and a religious aesthete at that; the local farmers and the sporting gentry and the bucolic food-killers among the peasantry could not understand him at all, could not divine what it was that made him eschew field sports, which to them were the *raison d'être* of the country gentleman's life. He walked through the village daily when he was in England, with his dogs racing ahead of him, and his stick and old hat: he did not look very unlike another Grenadier, Harold Macmillan; though his moustache curled up instead of drooping. He would shout with a tremendous parade-ground voice, 'Dogs! Dogs!' but the dogs knew better than to obey. Sometimes he came in and listened to something we had found for the gramophone; but he was a very hard man to please in that way. His taste was too severe for this age.

I was his only non-native tenant for a long while, then there was one other. It is different now. One day he came and sat by the ingle and told us what he feared would happen when he died, and every word came true. Now the village is full of invaders, there are very few of our old mates left, people have bought up the cottages and houses and the big house is an educational institution, there is an approved school down the lane, vast modernisation and tarting-up has been done, and cocktail and coffee parties are the order of the day. Vast prices have been realised, vast profits made; where rents are still paid they are paid in pounds where they used to be shillings. The time came when I inherited a few thousand pounds and offered to buy our cottage. They quoted me a figure which would have made squire spin in his grave, though to be sure they knew what they were doing and I dare say it was the market value. But I saw which way things were going and went away.

But we had ten years or a dozen that were among the richest in our lives. I think I was writing better, and I know I was living better. I was as brown as a berry and as thin as a lath.

I must have written two million words in that cottage, in my little study with the wood fire and the walls covered with fishing rods and books, where one day a horse put its head in through the window and one day a bull ambled by, going down the narrow path with my wife behind it crying calmly 'Get along.' I wasn't making much money but on the other hand I was making enough, and if I hadn't squandered so much of it on motors I might have had a bit in the bank.

I have told the whole true story, quite fantastic, of my long love-affair with motors, in *My Life On Wheels*, published by John Baker and still in print, I'm glad to say. So I can't go all over it again. Sometimes when I re-read a page or two of that awfully candid book I get an attack of despair. How could anyone be so crazy? Yet a cousin of my wife's had so many cars he stopped counting after a hundred; I have had only thirty-six. So there are others with the same weakness. The truth is I have a taint of perfectionism in me and although practically any car is interesting for the first few miles, while you learn its little ways, no car that I have owned has come up to expectations after the first few thousand miles—some of them after the first few score. Theoretically I hate machines and everything they have done to human life (not to mention animal life) and I certainly hate the men in white coats, the scientists and vivisectionists and all those ghastly diggers who want to change the face of life instantly and irrevocably; yet, being of my generation, I love the feel of the motor, can't get it out of my blood, love the delight of driving fast and well, elegantly, gracefully, beautifully, the thing an extension of my mortal powers, very much an enhancement of my physical powers, hurtling along the straight at high speed and swinging, swinging, dizzily round the lovely curves. I said earlier that even if I had specialised in motoring journalism it would have been boring me now, and perhaps it would, but I only meant that reviewing and testing dreary family cars and listening to the chatter of salesmen would have bored me. The population on the road is a terrible bore. But the sport, the non-utilitarian holy escapism of fast thorough-bred cars, that's a wholly different matter and still makes the blood sing a bit. Of course it's just about all over and done with: the multitude is on the road and the road is just another part of the city, where you can't get away from the requirements of living together, crushed and cramped. The roads are slums. We have to have all these laws and regulations, signs and breathalysers and restrictions: once the crowd is in on anything, it's finished for the fun. Chaste respectable dodderers, got to be legislated for, cradle to grave. I'm glad I knew the open road when it was actually open, and motoring an occupation of enthusiasts.

There is one escape from the congestion of the roads, for those to whom movement is essential, and that is the sea. Though always in love with water, I was born practically in the centre of the island, just about as far from the sea as one can get. Sailing was not in the family, and when I was young very few midlanders thought of it as a pastime. I spent many years in and on and by the water, fishing, and in the last few years of that occupation I grew increasingly interested in sea fishing, but it never struck me that sailing was the perfect answer to life's crush until I was too old to make a real go of it. I was in my fifties when I bought my first boat, a racing dinghy suitable (had I known it) for a teenager. I had a cheerful season with *Rosie*, learning what was meant by all the delightful jargon: 'sheets' meaning ropes, clew cringle, tack, luff, leech, Samson post, belay, transom, elbows, bilges, close-hauled, free, on the quarter, gaff, crosstrees, shrouds, and the wonderful names of the sails. The people were all enthusiasts, though even so, on sheltered waters the yobbos are muscling in and the old chivalry and comradeship is dying out. But generally it is still a very fine way of doing nothing gloriously, and once you get away from the shoreline you can have all the privacy and solitude and elbowroom you want, you surely can. I realised in that season that wet-arse sailing is well-named and that my old behind was getting a bit past being dunked continually in the salt, and I sold my little racer and bought a three-ton sloop known as a Mistress, which was thought appropriate. It was what is known in the jargon as a JOG boat, meaning up to the requirements of the Junior Offshore Group. It had a little cabin for two and a deck to walk or scramble around, and a proper cockpit where you could sit with your hand on the tiller feeling absolutely great and good. It rode the waves buoyantly and heeled over tenderly to the breeze and zipped through the salt in great style. My eyes were opened to the dreamworld of the sailing man, whose rigours are entirely self-inflicted and mainly solitary and whose rewards are beyond price. If I had a particular regret about my life, it would be that I did not discover this escape route until I was a bit too old, say forty years too old. If I had known about it sooner I might well have taken to the ocean as a way of life. There is a vested interest in pretending otherwise, but in fact sailing is very much easier than I thought it would be, though it is not altogether easy not to be frightened, and as a nonmathematical guesser I find navigation beyond me and get lost all too easily. But there it is: the sea has not been shrunk, and never mind what happens on the land, nobody is going to crowd or seriously pollute or in any substantial way mess up the sea. I think if I were a good deal younger I would make my aim to acquire a real good sailing boat, a stiff, tough six or eight tonner, something like a Hillyard, which is really about as big as one man can handle comfortably, and that would be my home. The sad nut cases can't very well blow up or pollute or contaminate *all* the world, only most of it, and I would take my chance out on the ocean, hoping to find an island refuge where fruit grew and fish swam and fresh water was still drinkable. Even if it were unfindable, better to go down to fate at your own helm, lonely and defiant on the lonely sea, than be crushed miserably in the choking debris of the ruined city-land.

But I must say I did not brood very brokenly over the possible fate of civilisation, during these halcyon years at the cottage. I *did* brood over it, of course, as everyone must, but it became quite clear that (a) the atomic bomb had in a rum way provided a balance of terror which was substantially indistinguishable from the usual uneasy peace, and (b) I was utterly helpless as an individual to change the nature of man or the management of his world. Now, all these years later, it begins to look as if total annihilation is the only risk men will not take; as if the insatiable evil and beastliness and plain nasty quarrelsomeness of men is erupting in 'conventional' war with 'conventional' weapons just as though the atomic deterrent did not exist. In which case we are back to square one with the added possibility that the big bomb might yet be blown in some moment of panic or wounded pride. But through those rustic years the balance seemed fairly secure to me, as indeed it proved, and my nerve was equal at that time to the contemplation of brink-manship. From Berlin and Korea through Suez to Cuba, I had a fairly decided feeling that the atomic holocaust would not be let loose, and (though with more or less profound feelings of disgust and helplessness occasionally becoming uncomfortable) I managed to pursue the aims of the good private life, which are not incompatible with a good public life. Indeed, a good public life is the sum of innumerable good private lives, not the other way round. I have no doubt that if every man and woman lived only to make one other person happy, it would be relatively speaking a paradise. Whereas with 'everybody' intent on managing the lives of everybody else, private lives are ruined on an enormous scale, for no good cause, and public life stays exactly as it was, rotten and wretched and fractious and futile, a mess of interferences and restrictions, prohibitions and exhortations and diminishment and ever-growing nervous hysteria and pollution.

There were moments, increasingly frequent as the years rolled past, when I came to doubt the very fundamentals of the ethic on which I had been raised. True, the old *argumentum ad hominem* stayed with me stickily. Philosophers despise it, but it is difficult to avoid, I find. The essence of this heresy, if heresy it be, is this: when you have looked at the argument, look at the man who puts it forward. Often you find that you cannot trust the man, or approve of him; in which case the argument which he advocates becomes suspect to you. I understand why this course is despised by rigorous logicians: a man may be every sort of villain or even a complete phoney in his acts, and still have an utterly logical, unanswerably logical, mind and argument. Contrariwise, a man may be utterly attractive, honest, charming, good to his wife and his dog, and still be utterly at sea in his reasoning. Yes, the *argumentum ad hominem* is philosophically dubious, to say the least. But one needs to be something more, or less, than human, not to have resort to it from time to time. I had resort again and again, faced with the irreconcilable discrepancies between lovely, loyal, decent, openhearted friends and their reactionary intellectual stances, between obvious phoneys and their irrefutably logical and liberal theories. All through these blithe years I had friends with whom I fished, contented as a tick in a sheep, whose intellectual worlds I simply could not enter. And I read with increasing passion and admiration the works of some writers whose lives and codes were infinitely removed from mine, yet whose intellectual attitudes I could not fault. This was not exactly a dichotomy, being outside myself; it was a touch of bewilderment which is not yet entirely resolved. But it sometimes seems on the way to being resolved, and resolving it is the task (or one of them) of my remaining years.

Though, to be sure, life is not conspicuously logical, and sometimes I wonder if the intellectual satisfactions are all that important. You can talk yourself into and out of almost anything. But if you lose your genitals, or your digestive juices, there is no substitute. I have spent most of my life among words and ideas, trying to find meanings; but life is undoubtedly physical, that is the absolute key and entrance fee to living. I don't mean anything so crude and simple as that 'health is everything'—some of life's keenest satisfactions involve spoiling your health, some of the healthiest specimens are the biggest bores—but I do mean that the physical life is the indispensable foundation: sex in its season, food, drink, the sensations of warmth and coolness, the sun on your back, the breeze in your face, darkness and light, rest, speed, all the treasures of eye and skin, the tactile heavens and hells. The emotional life, notions of style and dignity and panache, of hate and love and loyalty and tenderness; the ethical life, notions of due and duty and equity; the intellectual life, notions of interpretation and possibility—these are all the infinite heavenly top-structure of the basic physical foundation.

Where does music come from? What exactly is poetry?

While I could, I reached out eagerly for the life in the sun and rain and wind. I am less hardy now than I used to be. Once, sitting like a statue in a little boat on the Arun, spinning for pike on a desperate winter's day, I felt suddenly, irrevocably, colder than I had ever felt before. That is a dank and dangerous valley, a valley of miasma and phlegms. I rowed ashore and ran about beating my arms, but it was too late. The irreversible iron had entered in, my left lung has never been the same since the pleurisy which followed, I was slightly but permanently maimed in that moment. One recognises these moments as they come. Now I have to 'take care', just a little, and cannot enjoy and withstand the bitter cold as I used to do. It is merely a slight significant reduction in the rate of burning life's kindling. There is still the sun when it shines, and the soft warm rain, and the hearth. But for many a year there was the hardy and insouciant outdoor life. I tried to commemorate it as it came.

During these halcyon years I wrote my books about fishing and so on, I wrote my articles about the natural creation and the rustic life we were living, altogether I wrote a tremendous amount which sprang straight out of daily life. I have re-read most of it while I have been engaged in writing this book, and I realise that I can neither reprint it nor re-write it. I cannot reprint it because although, like everything else, it was 'true at the time of writing', the man who wrote it is dead: I would not write it just the same way now. I cannot re-write it because it was the best I could do, it came straight out of intimate experience, and any other way of putting it now would be a falsification. All those words, some of them lovely, whipped away by the wind. . . . It seems a waste, but that's journalism, you catch life on the wing, it means something at the time, but it won't live.

Still, it was not only a living, it was a way of life. I have no regrets on that score. Work and life blended harmoniously, it was a marvellously integrated existence. I rarely wore a collar and tie, I met my deadlines and then I was free, I concentrated hard on what I had to do and relaxed completely when I had popped the envelope in the post box by Miss Burling's little shop, where she sold stamps and groceries and sweets and papers and tobacco and griped continuously about her rotten lot and the shortcomings of everybody else. There was nothing in the least romantic or rose-embowered about this particular village shop. Miss B, now dead, was a grimy old soul who never in my hearing had a good word to say for any living soul, and she kept the place like a pigsty. Mice ran around among the butter, her hands were black, her heart was heavy. I was quite fond of her, and she welcomed me as an audience. I do not know what it is in my face which inspires life's bores to unload, but on innumerable occasions total strangers have confided in me their most intimate secrets, secrets I did not especially wish to share. Of course they always ask my advice, but they do not really want it, have no slightest intention of following it (thank heaven) but merely want an audience for their woes.

But Miss B's confidences were merely one flavour in a life of many flavours, most of them minty, water-scented. My life came to fruition during those lovely lively years in the old cottage, when we were neither young nor old, rich nor poor. No wonder I wrote about it with such zest. Nothing that has happened since is worth recording.

Chapter Fifteen

I have a fascinating and many-sided friend named Reg Hall, a sort of tycoon in the photographic equipment business; I helped personally to lay the foundation of his fortune by buying better cameras than I knew how to handle. Reg explains his swift contradictions (he claims to be schizophrenic) in the delightful phrase, 'I should have been twins'. I obtained his permission to use that phrase as my title, but reflection showed that in my case it should be triplets. There are these three men in my head, battling for possession: the one who knows quite well how lonely we all are and how unmanageable and chaotic and terrifying the world is, how strong the force of evil; and the one who wishes well, the one who loves and lives to love and probably falsifies the account, from time to time, in favour of love's transient power to modify and improve on chaos; and finally the romantic one who responds to vigour and style and panache and the splendour of open-hearted men.

Journalism is a tidy trade, for all that it feeds on drama. You have a little space and a little time, you contrive a beginning and a middle and an end, it has to be tidy. In the sense that life is rarely tidy and never ends, that change is continuous and every account is an abstraction infinitely simpler than what it purports to describe, this must lead to a certain sort of falsification, innocent or less innocent. Reading again what remains of the dry husks of my journalism, great yellowing crumply mounds of cuttings, themselves only a fragment of what might have been hoarded, perhaps ten million words, I detect this wish to isolate, to round-off, to compose. Sentimentality, romanticism, and optimism may be disabling diseases, for the artist, in the end. It was not exactly that I wished to please, though I did, too often for good art: but sometimes I wished to please and reassure myself, as well as the unimaginable reader, and I was too indulgent. My weakness was optimism, if it be a weakness; my crime against art was courtesy, if it be a crime. Sometimes I had this feeling that comes over you at times of enchantment, this romantic feeling that by a little manipulation and selection you can, no, not falsify, but actually *modify* experience, to suit that intuitive part of you which cries out, 'God should have done this better. God should have managed more neatly.' I think that is the element which I can smell out now, when I re-read my prose stories. Sometimes I suppressed the Manichee in me, the knowledge of evil, which should have shone through my writing like a stone. I was sometimes too reluctant to pass on my intuitions of malevolence. The three men in my head, a jostling tribune or troika, pulled me on a stumbling course. Seeking to amuse and reassure, I wrote for my living as my nature made me write, and my living was shaped by many contradictory concepts and divided loyalties and of course by the mixed strands of my character, the alternating sensuality and intellectualising, the fears and hopes, the feckless affections and petty hatreds, the deep, fleeting, unsuspected sadness, and the lovely, dangerous, irresistible laughter. I have a notion that a sense of humour may be bred out of the human race by the pressure of survival: it has little value for survival. My sense of humour has kept me intermittently entertained, but it has probably cost me quite dear, for if humour has any real roots in your nature it invariably makes you laugh when you need most to be deadly serious; prudentially speaking. Since I could never take myself or my fate too seriously, it followed quite naturally that my fate and I were not taken any too seriously by the arbiters of my professional destiny, I mean the 'short-haired mad executives', as Auden called them, and the public whom they more or less accurately represent. Not that I have any grumbles on that score. From time to time I have been caught up in postures indistinguishable from theirs. I am so sickened by false claptrap and phoney attitudes that I attack them and in so doing sometimes seem to be defending attitudes with which I have no sympathy. For I am more revolutionary than the progressives whom I attack, from time to time; I want to modify God and man.

When I inherited my bit of money, it was not enough to make a radical difference to our lives, it did not by any means hoist us up into a different 'socio-economic stratum', as the cant phrase goes, nor change our way of living at all. It simply meant that we could now buy a habitation of our own. It made us owners of our own home. It makes a difference. It was a coincidence that the pattern began to change about this time. My mother died in the summer of 1960 and my father died of a broken heart, there was no other reason, before the year ended. They were both 79. My mother grew increasingly placid and dreamy towards the end of her life. She was told by some medium that she would die suddenly, in the afternoon, with her family around her. One Saturday afternoon she was in the old family Rover, with my father driving and my elder sister in the back seat, on the way to have their ritual Saturday high tea with my younger sister and her little brood. Half-way between the two homes, which were only a mile or two apart, she had a heart attack and died. She had had one or two premonitory small attacks, and she had been a diabetic for some years, though neither disease caused her in any way to abate her joy in living. She approached the end with an ever-deepening conviction that death was but a portal through which she had to pass to rejoin her loved ones who had gone before, and to await in glory the loved ones who would follow. She had total faith. She enjoyed her life to the very end and she enjoyed her certainty that the end was but a beginning.

I suspect that my father's faith had long been eroded by secret doubts; I think he had no such certitude in his heart. He was lost, as I should be lost, without the companion whose wishes were more important than his own; so much so that in time he came to have no wishes but hers. When she had gone there were no wishes left in his life. There was nothing to live for.

Looking at the face of my dead father I saw myself. I said goodbye then in my heart to the old life, altogether. I saw myself lying there. I heard the whirring clockwork as the wheels whiz round, very loud. Driving back numbly through the night I acknowledged to myself that it was too late. Everything undone would stay undone.

We had not been really 'close', in the old sense, for many years. All the time my parents were alive I had made the regular journey up along the spine of England, the lovely old road, Guildford, Henley, Dorchester, Oxford, Woodstock, sharp left off the Stratford road opposite The Quiet Woman, twice burned down; then Chipping Norton, so cold and windy, Moreton-in-Marsh, Broadway, Evesham, Pershore, Worcester, Kidderminster, Wolverhampton, home. I don't know how many hundred times I took that road, in all my various cars. We 'kept in touch'. But the lives were diverging, as lives do, it was affectionate and filial but somehow we had less and less to say, their lives changed and our lives changed, new friends appeared in the old home whom we knew not, the family past was receding and the future became unmentionable.

When the agent of old squire's successors asked me such a stiff price for the ancient cottage which we had been renting for a dozen years, we looked elsewhere. We found an isolated little house in Sussex at the end of a long rutted track, with its back to the woods. The names of

the woods were music: Songhurst Furze, Hope Rough, Beggar's
Copse. I felt that they were symbolic names. A tiny trickling tributary
of the Arun flowed along one boundary of the odd-shaped acre. There
was an orchard. From the upstairs windows you could see the crown of
Chanctonbury Ring. All around through a wide arc there was not a
roof or chimney visible; in just one small sector you could see the
nearest habitations, a mile away. It was full of peace.

My father had left me little money but a block of ordinary shares in
the family firm, worth several thousand pounds. I sold them. Many expressed astonishment when they heard. Alan Whicker came to visit us,
a man with a keen eye to the value of an equity. 'Why did you *let* him?'
he asked my wife, aghast. She only laughed. Like me, she does not give
a hoot about equities and accountancy, interest and saving and the
spoils of usury. We might have kept the shares, watched them fluctuate
and grow in value—yes, they grew—and gone on paying rent, which
the interest might have covered. Or we could sell the lot, wash our
hands of them and their history, and put the cash down for a bit of a
place which we could call our own. There was no battle in our minds;
to people of our temperament there was only one course open. We
bought the cottage for cash and there was a bit left over which we put
into the building society, the nearest thing to not having to give it a
thought, and there it remains, my wife's tiny nest-egg, the 'bit behind
you' that my parents always spoke of so approvingly, but which I
never saved though I suppose I could have done. So in the end we
became capitalists, usurers, by accident. Though God knows the
interest barely keeps pace with the fall in value of money.

What would have happened if we had had children? I suppose I
should simply have done without my indulgences, the merry motors,
the lovely fishing rods and cameras; and perhaps worked or at least
worried even harder, taken my 'career' seriously, sweated and saved.
I really don't know. How could I know? We never had any. I do not
regret that. Children are all right, but having been one myself, I do not
glamourise them. And family connections are false connections, arbitrary and artificial. You choose your friends but your relations are
chosen for you. Ours was a happy family and that circumstance shaped
life to a considerable degree, as you will have seen, but it was an accident, albeit a happy one. I know lots of unhappy families, don't we all?
My luck held.

Life in the isolated old cottage was all right, in some ways fine, but it
really *was* isolated, things could become a bit tricky at times, such as
the great freeze of 1962/1963. Then BBC2 came along and we couldn't

get it, even with a forty-foot aerial in the garden. And my wife's father died and her aged mama came to live with us, and hated the isolation, was sad in the silence, being a highly gregarious old sport who had lived her life in towns. For this reason and that, then, we moved again, this time to a ranchy little bungalow in a thicket, on the fringe of a village-town which we sometimes call 'the Bloxwich of the South'. It resembles Bloxwich only in its dimensions and in the way the main street straggles along, but sometimes we do get a feeling that, *mutatis mutandis*, we have come home. Our road is the last; beyond us it is the country again. Trees surround us. We have an acre of our own. Yet there are the amenities of town life, in a mild way; shops available a mile away, a doctor in our own road, a cottage hospital, a bus at the end of the road, various little things which tend to console you for what you are missing. It took us a long time to get used to having neighbours on either side, and longer still to get used to modernity; but you get used to anything, the road is a dead one that leads nowhere, so it is quiet, often as quiet as the cottage in the woods. Of course we missed the period charm and style of the antique cottages we had lived in so long, missed the inglenook and the old lattices and the oak beams and curious latches and all that characterful and charming stuff, which we enjoyed so much. But everything is compromise, as I did not realise when I wrote my first article for the Birmingham *Evening Despatch*. This seems quite a good compromise. We looked after ma-in-law as best we could for five years and when she died, passing away in mid-sentence in her chair by the fire, on a talkative day when she felt happy and comparatively well, we wondered if we should break again and return to the woods. But we had left it a bit too late. We are not young enough to face the rigours of *real* rustic life any more, rising 56 and spoiled by mod cons. I fancy we are settled here. It's a strange thought.

Our life now is irreducibly simple, and it suits us well. We share nearly everything. We can do the chores of the bungalow in no time, we are not house-proud and we whistle around as we feel like it, putting things to rights but not bothering over-much. It's very easy. We have seen a lot of how old people live and manage, and decline, we have first-hand knowledge of what age means, its cruel limitations and its indignities. Although not usually prone to looking far ahead we cannot quite ignore, at 55–56, the fact that we too shall quite soon be old. It does not intrude greatly on our thoughts, we don't worry about it, but knowing it is so, we make our modestly prudential dispositions. We are virtually interchangeable in the house-work line. I can cook quite reasonably well, and although bad at tidying-up, hopelessly untidy in fact, I have absorbed some rudimentary notion of how things go and am not thrown clear out of kilter by minor misfortunes such as little illnesses. I am a bad nurse in the sense that my wife's pains anger me far more than my own, I grow furious at Fate when she suffers; but I am a fairly good nurse in the sense that I can cope, more or less, do what is needed, though with a black face, growling at God, talking back to Him, chuntering, very far from a ray of sunshine. Each of us separately can manage this little place quite comfortably, together we find it a doddle. So I dare say we shall stay. I wouldn't guarantee it, I wouldn't underwrite *anything*, the whole essence of life is its unpredictability: but though the sea coast beckons still, sheer inertia, the balancing of desires and needs, will quite likely secure us here, limpets on our last rock. It is a base from which to make forays into the physical world which we still intermittently find beautiful and exciting; a base to come back to.

As my thoughts grow ever more adventurous, as the radicalism I was born with suffuses my mind and spirit, so that I almost hope to live to see the breaking of the dams and the Christ-tide of love and acceptance sweeping over this hate-filled world, the Tao-tide of tolerance coming in, so my material life becomes less adventurous, more conservative if you like, my habits grow settled and my routine hardens into habit.

We are completely impervious to the neurotic gimmickry of the colour magazine mentality and its sedulous following of fashion. It is a matter of some indifference to us whether we are in fashion or out of it. Of course all culture is a matter of fashion, I realise that, but if you stand still long enough the whirligig will come round again and catch you up. Our place is full of bits and pieces of all periods and none, they mingle and harmonise quite happily, each has its use and its claim on our affection, we don't go round totting up their cash value and we don't buy anything to show off to other people. We are really very snug, and quite possibly smug, God forbid. But I think it is true, I hope it is true, that we are both reasonably well-equipped to face whatever may betide. We accept our present snugness gratefully, we know that our luck has held, but if things were to change for the worse, we think we could face it manfully. We enjoy what we have, zestfully; we spend, when we find we have something to spend, cheerfully; but we think we could manage contentedly in reduced circumstances, and doubtless they *will* be reduced, quite drastically, one day fairly soon. It doesn't prey on us, or weigh on us. We have friends who live full and interesting lives on much smaller resources than are at our command, we know how it is done, and when the day comes, we think we shall manage, if need be, with bread and books. Bread and books—all you need, though not always all you want. We are so plain in our tastes, these days, that a meal of bread-and-butter quite often strikes us as a delightful luxury. If it comes down to bread-and-butter and tea, no more motors, no more clothes, well, we've a good stock of records, a vast stock of books, a good local lending library, the garden, and the countryside at our doorstep. Doubtless it will take some adjustment, but we have often had to adjust, we are experts at it, we have lived on every sort of income from about thirty bob a week when I joined the R.A.F. to well over three thousand a year in the most affluent times. I might have made twice as much, I think, had I cared to try. But making money would have eaten into the time for living. The thing is not to get so used to a high 'standard of living' that you dare not contemplate its reduction. We know quite a few who have become so habituated to living on many thousands of pounds a year, and/or lavish expense accounts, that the prospect of losing their jobs, or simply the prospect of retirement on a reduced income and without the expenses, is simply unnerving. They live in dread, because they have lived to show-off, lived to impress. I have enjoyed my little spending splurges as much as anyone, I've frittered away a fair amount, and I may say I've given a fair bit away, one way and another. But I've never come to count on prosperity, it has always been temporary in my mind. I may of course stay lucky and go on enjoying my modest prosperity to the end of my days. It's quite possible. On the other hand, I've queued up in the Post Office to draw old ma-in-law's Old Age Pension many and many a time, and when it comes to queuing up to draw my own, I shall feel quite at home.

I think the best thing about my life as it has gone on is this, that I've gone on growing more and more classless and carefree of all social and racial and particular divisive distinctions, feeling more and more as my mother felt, that every living soul is a soul like you, with equal rights on your courtesy. I don't say I always live up to it. Of course I'm quite pernicketty, as you must have noticed; I have a sharp temper, and I have standards in this and that, I am tolerant of human weaknesses but intolerant of sloppy work and sloppy thinking, though God knows my own is sloppy enough at times. I am vividly aware of natural inequalities, I can hate quite heartily, I'm not such an idiot as to believe or pretend that people are equal—except in this one fundamental way, equal in the sight of ... heaven? Strange how difficult it is to define this one concept of basic equality: yet it is clear enough in my heart and blood, if not in my mind. I'm not clubbable, I would run a mile to avoid a bore, I can be real nasty-tempered and 'sarky' at times: yet

I assert the equality of human souls and try to live it. I've been sneering and bitter about 'the mob', 'the crowd'—and doubtless shall be again, and with reason. We don't want mob rule, the apotheosis of mediocrity. Yet I suspect and fear mightily the specious notion of 'élite' formations: they bring nothing but death and misery. We may each strive for élite quality in our private ways; we may not assert it socially. To me there are fascinating and sometimes embarrassing differences in manners, I.Q.s, customs, characteristics—but no differences in soul-potential, or social value. To me it makes no odds whatever if a man is black, white, brown, pink, yellow or grey, if he is an Old Etonian or a New Zealander, a labourer or a managing director. Poor bugger, he's as human as I am.

So here I am, a grey-haired thin man in a little bungalow among the trees, waiting for the warm weather. Grey so soon? Is this all there is?

Yes, it is all there is.

It's the end of the book. I must fight against the rhetoric now. Dad, you would make a great little old peroration now, wouldn't you? You'd have the tears running down their cheeks. I must fight against it. I am so like you in so many ways, I acknowledge my parenthood, all you gave me, including the Celtic rhetoric, the dangerous gift.

I've been at it a long time, sitting here in a haze of smoke and memories, some too painful to be borne. It will soon be done now, and then I can clear the mess away and get into the workshop and start cleaning my tools and pretending to be practical again. The odd jobs around the place have multiplied while I have been immolated with my memories, a prisoner of the past. I dare say it wouldn't really worry me if the grass grew knee-high round the house and every gutter dripped, but keeping the wilderness at bay is a form of therapy, I suppose, and my wife has the female creativity of the snug nest. I certainly shan't go mad at it. I enjoy a bit of hugger-mugger, and need to be led into the paths of order.

Looking back over what I have put down, I am appalled at the irresponsibility it reveals. But the candour pleases me almost as much as it frightens me. Even so, it is by no means a truly candid book. There is much concealed. Some secrets are incommunicable. I daresay that in one sense I have made myself out to be more irresponsible than I am. In a simple practical way I am highly responsible: I have been a highly responsible toiler ever since I came down from Oxford, with few lapses—probably too few. Editors trust me, and my wife trusts me. Manuscripts are delivered bang on time, the right length; I am known to be dependable. I owe no man money. I regret every injury I have done to every living thing, and every one I have still to do.

I acknowledge the disproportion in my story, the foreshortening, the acceleration of time in the later parts. That is how time and memory work, as one grows older. What is most distant is most near.

Not enough jokes. Life is full of them.

I think my wife would say that though full of faults, I rate her happiness high and do what I can, sometimes mistakenly, to procure it. I am at ease with old friends. Yes, in many ways I am a sober citizen now, perhaps a very dull one, a square who believes almost passionately in honouring obligations. Oh yes, that's so. But it is what goes on in my mind that surprises me, now that I have had a good long look at it. The bits that I have put down, and the bits that I have dredged up and mulled over and suppressed ... Can this be me? I don't know.